8.2.06

ASPECTS OF ISLAM

ASPECTS OF
ISLAM

Ron Geaves

DARTON·LONGMAN+TODD

First published in 2005 by
Darton, Longman and Todd Ltd
1 Spencer Court
140–142 Wandsworth High Street
London SW18 4JJ

ISBN 0–232–52535–8

A catalogue record for this book is available from the British Library.

Designed by Sandie Boccacci
Phototypeset in 10/13.5pt Palatino
by Intype Libra Ltd
Printed and bound in Great Britain by
The Cromwell Press, Trowbridge, Wiltshire

CONTENTS

I have been teaching Islam to undergraduate and postgraduate students in several institutions over the last ten years. During that time I have published two monographs and several articles that have explored some key issues in contemporary Muslim communities in the West. My perspective on teaching Islam has always been committed to both a horizontal and vertical approach, exploring the history but only in the context of it forming a background to understanding what is happening in the present. But my main aim has been to enter inside the faith tradition and discover what Muslims believe with regard to Islam and how they feel about their religious beliefs, practices and events taking place around them, both in the Muslim and non-Muslim world. Consequently, the strength of this work has been the horizontal approach to the research, based on detailed fieldwork and knowledge of living Muslim communities, especially those in diaspora, which form significant minorities in the Western world.

During the course of teaching Islam I have made a practice of offering students the possibility of undertaking seminars and presentations, and topics covered in the book's chapters are based upon the most popular choices made by students, and, also, on their oral feedback about which topics excited them most during the course of their modules on Islam. In addition to gathering information from undergraduates, the book is indebted to information from extensive Muslim contacts concerning the main areas of controversy both within Muslim communities and also those which originate from perceived outsider stereotypes of Islam.

I believe that a book of this kind is timely in view of the events since 11 September 2001 (from herein, termed 9/11). I have noted the interest with which students are asking questions concerned with 'real' issues as opposed to theological or historical topics. Thus the subject matter of each chapter is gleaned from these informal attempts by students to develop their understanding of contemporary Islam. The book will also attempt to explore the diversity of Islam by presenting a series of dichotomies or differences in belief and practice that will assist readers in moving away from the idea that Islam is a homogeneous entity. It is hoped that the contents will contribute to the pool of knowledge demanded by the interest in Islam and the Muslim world generated by contemporary world events. Therefore, this book will differ from many of its competitors in that it will attempt to explore many of the issues and debates current amongst today's Muslims rather than take a chronological approach to the faith tradition, and, in so doing, its main focus will be on religious issues rather than the approaches of social or political science, both of which contribute to the study of Islam. Some of the subjects covered are not dealt with in detail by any one single text. Other topics are covered in great depth by a number of books but are not summarised in one text. Thus the book should provide a useful undergraduate key text but will also be of interest to anyone who wishes to become informed about contemporary events in our world and to understand the conflicts within the Muslim world.

It is hoped that this book will provide readers with a deeper knowledge of contemporary Islam through an exploration of a number of Muslim religious concerns, and that the understanding of these can be utilised as background knowledge to assist the comprehension of events taking place in particular Muslim societies or communities.

CHAPTER 1

Introduction

Since the events of 9/11 and the subsequent invasions of Afghanistan and Iraq, there is hardly a day that goes by without media coverage of Muslims, usually associated with suspected 'terrorist' activities, their apparent hatred of the West or actual outrages involving the deaths of innocent civilians, both Muslim and non-Muslim, in various parts of the world. However, the positive impact of this very one-sided media coverage is an intense curiosity concerning the beliefs and practices of Muslims, something acknowledged by Muslims themselves. On the downside, there has been an increase in racism and acts of aggression towards Muslims in the West, to such an extent that the word 'Islamophobia' has been coined to join with 'anti-Semitism', to describe respective religious and ethnic discriminatory or hateful behaviour and attitudes.

After a decade of close contact with Muslims in Britain and else-where in the Muslim world, I find myself horrified by the opening of a Pandora's box whose contents are over-simplification, overwhelming ignorance, and blatant racism directed at a religious community. This is combined with a fear of the 'other', which at the beginning of the twenty-first century, it is to be hoped that any thinking member of the human race would view with great distrust and suspicion, especially as we are all familiar with the historic consequences of anti-Semitism that so blighted the twentieth century.

A recent poll in 2004 revealed that only one in ten of the 'white' population of Britain had any contact with members of the migrant communities in spite of several decades of their presence in the country or the official government policy of integration. I was proud to number myself in the ten per cent of the population, not only in contact with, but counting many significant friends within the South

Asian communities, in particular, many Muslims. Since I began my studies over a decade ago, a mosque is now no more unfamiliar territory than my local church, and the places in our inner cities where Muslims are concentrated are not merely visited in order to eat exotic food or to drive through on route to somewhere else. However, since the tragic events of 9/11, I have come to realise how beleaguered and misunderstood many of my Muslim friends, acquaintances and informants feel. Branded with the mark of 'terrorism' and condemned as followers of a bloodthirsty and primitive religion, seen as at odds with the modern world increasingly invested with the value-judgement of 'civilised', they wonder how they can convince the citizens of their newly adopted nations that Islam is a religion of peace.

On Monday 9 August 2004, the *Guardian* provided an article entitled 'Muslims put faith in written word to fight prejudice' (Dodd, 2004:8). It was revealing both in its content and its visual image. Three Muslim girls sat with each other on the floor of the mosque surrounded by boxes of books. Two wore traditional Muslim dress with their heads and bodies modestly covered. Their companion had her long hair loose and was dressed Western style, but their intention was the same. They were involved in a project to distribute £1million worth of books, DVDs and videos to be sent to over 300 public libraries in Britain. Their aim was not to convert or proselytise but to educate the public about their faith and try to offset the negative image of Islam increasingly portrayed in the media since the events of 9/11.

Ironically, the mosque acting as a distribution centre was only two hundred yards away from the more notorious Finsbury Park mosque used by Abu Hamza and his supporters to spread vitriolic hatred for the West and its institutions. Yet here were young Muslim volunteers motivated with the desire to integrate and forge links with the other communities around them. The contrast between the activities in the two mosques begs the question, 'which is the real reflection of Islam or the more typical portrayal of the Muslims who now increasingly live alongside us?' Do we really need to feel afraid of al-Qa'eda sympathisers in our midst? Are the claims made within Oriana Fallaci's book *Oriana Fallaci interviews Oriana Fallaci*, published in Italy, that 'Europe is becoming Eurarabia' substantiated or do they merely echo the fears of all populations throughout history when confronted by new arrivals representing the unfamiliar in colour, religion, customs or values? Certainly the book struck a chord in Italy, selling half-a-million copies within hours.

Britain is not exempt from this new racist rhetoric directed at religion. The summer of 2004 has seen a number of highly inflammatory articles appear in respectable newspapers such as *The Times* and the *Sunday Telegraph*. In the former, respectable Muslim academic institutions, known for their moderate views on integration, were accused of links with extremism (O'Neill, 2004), and in the second, under the protection of a pseudonym, Islam was vilified and Muslims were accused of being 'foreigners who have forced themselves upon us' (Cummins, 2004). In comparison with the circulation of these national newspapers and their ability to form British opinion, the work of the young Muslims in the Finsbury Park mosque would seem to be a drop in the ocean.

The paranoia is not only found amongst the journalists of right-wing newspapers and their readers. Young Muslims on the streets often feel victimised, interpreting media coverage of Muslims as an indication of the West's war on Islam. Conspiracy theories are prevalent not only amongst the young but are even held by some of the community's elders and leaders. The high profile arrests of Muslims utilising recent anti-terrorism laws does not help. The facts of 562 arrests but only 14 convictions fuel Muslim conspiracy theorists that it is all part and parcel of a cohesive plan to target Islam, rather than a war on terrorism (Panja, 2004:17).

The arrests are far from the only grievance. The *Guardian* article mentioned above recounts disturbing stories of Muslim women in traditional dress being spat at in the street or abused when walking with their children. Mujib Miah, the organiser of the book distribution project, wants to present Muslims as the same as other people with similar aspirations rather than an enemy in our midst. He states: 'Muslims want to be presented as normal people trying to live and make their way in a sometimes hostile world' (Dodd, 2004:8). Perhaps of more significance was the fact that the books used on the project to defend Islam were not the 'insider' literature produced by the mosques, published with the intention to convince of Islam's religious truths or encourage the faithful to continue in their worship, but rather the works of Western academics, such as John Esposito, who tries to deal with the causes of terrorism in a neutral and informative manner, or other academic works written on gender equality in Islam. I would hope that the organisers of the project would feel that this, my own small effort to inform about Islam could be included in their selection of volumes.

Arguably, the most contentious issue that faces Muslims and bewilders those looking on from the outside, is the activities of the so-called 'suicide bombers'. Although it is easy to withdraw to adjectives such as 'evil', 'pathological', 'terrorist' or 'fanatic', such terms do not allow us to understand the motivations behind such acts of violence. Yet, uncomfortably perhaps, Suba Chandran reminds us that the profile of the 'suicide bomber' is usually young, educated and from higher economic and social backgrounds. He states they are typically 'neither fanatics nor mentally deranged' (Chandran, 2003:133).

How can we explain educated young men and, increasingly, women choosing to end their own lives, along with the lives of other innocent victims? Chandran reminds us of the classical study of suicide carried out by the nineteenth-century sociologist, Emile Durkheim (1856–1919). Although vintage, Durkheim's classification of the motivations for suicide into 'egoistic', 'anomic' and 'altruistic' remains relevant. In 'egoistic' suicide, individuals take their own life because they have failed to integrate with the values and belief systems of their society or family. However, young Muslims in Palestine, who choose to kill themselves while resisting Israeli occupation of their lands, are celebrated as martyrs by the wider society and even their own families.

Durkheim's second category of 'anomic' refers to the breakdown of society, leading to a degree of insecurity and frustration which is unsustainable, where the powerless individual takes his or her own life. Although there may well exist such conditions in parts of the Muslim world, ravaged by war or poverty, rarely do we hear of such suicides. This may be partly to do with the teachings of Islam, which do not countenance such an option as a solution.

Thus we are left with the uncomfortable dawning of understanding that the 'suicide bombers' perceive their own actions as 'altruistic', an ultimate sacrifice on the part of the individual for the greater good of society. If it is true that the 'suicide bomber' believes that his or her society is under such economic, social, cultural or political domination by an external or internal enemy, whether the belief is justified or not, that they are ready to self-sacrifice for the sake of freedom from perceived or actual oppression, then we need to be aware of their motives. It becomes imperative for us to understand the links which exist between historic events in the Muslim world, the belief systems of Islam and relations with the non-Muslim world in order to discover why Muslims feel as they do.

It is necessary for us to answer the following questions. What is Islam? What do Muslims believe? Why does the Muslim world appear to be in such conflict? These are crucial questions as we enter the twenty-first century with a self-proclaimed war against terrorism led by the US and British governments which is predominantly targeted at various factions within the Muslim world. It is not only the Western world that has to re-evaluate itself in the aftermath of 9/11, but also the Muslim nations. However, the transformations taking place in the Muslim world did not begin in 2001, but were already gathering pace throughout the twentieth century; these conflicts and the changes which generated them need to be understood before any theory can be put forward to explain the events of 9/11 or to understand why the Muslim world seems to be in such ferment.

Islam is probably the only one of the world's major faith traditions to be known by the name that it has given itself, rather than being originally identified and labelled by outsiders. Islam means peace; a peace which arises from being in harmony with the will of God – a God who is best expressed through Islam's central doctrines of unity and uniqueness – yet Muslims everywhere find their world torn by conflicts which shatter the ideal of peace. There is a lack of unity between themselves, within their religion, amongst Muslim nations and with the rest of the non-Muslim world, which undermines the sense of social cohesion that should ideally arise as a consequence of God's unity, manifested through revelation to human society.

Thus any attempt to understand the contemporary sense of crisis within and without the Muslim world will need to be aware of the inner struggles that are taking place and their causes, both in the world that we live in today and their political and religious roots in Muslim history. It can be argued that these conflicts arise out of the nature of the revelation itself, which asserts Muslims to be the final people of God, entrusted with the fullest articulation of God's historical unfolding of his relationship with human beings. In effect, a revelation that completes and renews the earlier revelations to Jews and Christians, bringing them both to renewal and fulfilment.

An explanation needs to be provided on terminology. Throughout I have used the terms 'traditional' and 'orthodox', often in juxtaposition. It is problematic to assert 'orthodoxy' within Islam as there is no central authority, such as the Papacy in Roman Catholicism, that can issue dictates that determine correct doctrine or practice. In Islam, those that assert themselves to be orthodox claim to have an authoritative understanding of the Qur'an and the Hadith, usually framed within a discourse of literalism. However, there is not a Muslim movement, even those considered to be unorthodox, who would not claim to be in line with the primary sources of Islam. Orthodoxy has to be understood as self-proclaimed and usually refers to nineteenth- and twentieth-century revivalist movements.

Tradition is sometimes referred to in the sense of time-honoured but unconscious allegiance to cultural or religious practices often associated with rural areas as part of a natural order of things. However, in the context of contemporary Muslim debates, 'traditional' is rarely used in this way. On the contrary it refers to a conscious process that frames time-honoured practices within an articulation of what determines orthodoxy. Sufi movements, in particular, argue that their practices are legitimised because they were permitted by tradition and were acknowledged by the four schools of Islamic law. Thus, I have used the terms in the way that Muslims themselves utilise them. 'Orthodox' describes those Muslims who go direct to Qur'an and *Sunna*, whereas 'traditional' indicates the majority who acknowledge the body of work interpreting Qur'an and *Sunna*, developed by the *ulema* throughout the centuries and which incorporates local customs.

Each chapter in this book attempts to shed light on areas of significance in understanding Muslim perceptions of the West, or the background to a variety of conflicts and schisms that continue to undermine the Muslim ideal of unity. In addition, they try to show the diversity of opinion, practice and belief that one would expect to find in a religion that is over fourteen centuries old and consists of over a billion people worldwide stretching from the USA to China. Showing the divisions that exist within a community of God that longs for unity, is not done to disparage it; on the contrary the motivation is to demonstrate that such conflicts are creative and a sign of health, in spite of the extreme forms that some solutions take. Above all, we need to counteract the overwhelming simplicities that seem to dominate popular discourse, in which it is assumed that all Muslims are the same. This essentialist view is dangerous and needs to be challenged, as do parallel views of the West found within some Muslim circles.

The following chapters will either focus on providing a greater awareness of the religious variety found amongst Muslims and the ongoing conflicts that such divisions can create within a religion that upholds the ideal of unity as a primary concern, or will engage with areas of controversy and misunderstanding by outsiders, such as the issues of women, *jihad*, fundamentalism and Islamic legal codes.

Chapter 2 will focus on the crucial and contentious issue of how the Western media (both popular and academic) represents Islam and will demonstrate that such representations need to be assessed in the context of the history of Orientalism. Thus the chapter will hopefully direct us to a deeper awareness of how our individual and group perceptions of Muslims are a result of stereotyping and misconception arising from historic conflicts between European and Muslim cultures. The process is not one way, but rather a two-way process in which Muslim perceptions of the West are equally distorted.

Chapter 3 will explore the central doctrine of God's unity and oneness through an exploration of religious architectural forms within both mosque and shrine networks found throughout the Muslim world. The main conclusion will be that mosque and shrine respectively provide alternative spiritual resources for those who seek contact with either transcendence or immanence. The irony is that the uncompromising ideal of *tawhid*, central to understanding Islam, has been sundered into its two component aspects: namely, the unity and the uniqueness of God which were never intended to be separated. For those who predominantly perceive Allah as unique, an overwhelming transcendence, the mosque supplies the place of surrender, worship and performance of the obligatory prayer rituals. The shrine, on the other hand, is literally the final resting-place of those who sought God's unity. By focusing on both mosques and shrines, the chapter will highlight the tensions between immanence and transcendence that exist within divergent forms of Islam – thus readers will be introduced to concepts of both traditional and orthodox views of *tawhid* and how the architecture of mosque and shrine outwardly manifest divergent interpretations of Islam that cater to the human need to either worship a distant transcendent deity or become intimate with a loving being whose domain is the human heart. At the same time, readers will be able to explore the close relationship between sacred space, architecture and perceptions of divinity that exist within Islam.

The content of Chapter 4 will highlight the tensions that can exist between the processes of law-making, involving politics, economics, and response to social change, with the claim that Islamic law (*shar-i'a*) is the inviolate and final law of God rather than the product of human reason. This chapter will allow readers to assess the processes of Muslim law creation and to assess the views of Western and Muslim academics regarding its historic development. Here differences of opinion are not so much between divergent Muslim communities, but between Muslims and Western academic scholars who have written on Islamic law as a cultural construct. Although the subject matter will focus on the processes of Muslim law construction and the various authorities that determine legitimacy (Qur'an, Hadith, *ijma, qiyas, ijtihad*), there is also the intention to challenge stereotypical and uninformed views of Islamic law, which are usually based on a limited understanding of *shari'a* as being only Muslim criminal law.

Having earlier introduced the idea of divergent views concerning God's unity, Chapter 5 will explore the Muslim concept of *umma*, the Muslim understanding of community as an expression of Allah's oneness. Those factors in Islam that promote a sense of a unified community will be contrasted with the lived reality of a fragmented or diverse series of worldviews that exist within the larger framework of the totality of all Muslims. This dynamic relationship between the ideal of a sacred community and the lived reality of the Islamic community, will be explored to show how it moulds and shapes action to transform Muslim society in the contemporary world.

Yet there are tensions which undermine unity and Chapters 6, 7 and 8 will introduce some of the various factions or competing views of Islam. Chapter 6, rather than dwelling on the historical causes of the divide between Sunni and Shi'a, the two main Muslim factions, will instead focus on the differing attitudes to martyrdom in the two traditions and how these attitudes arise out of doctrinal interpretations originating from historical circumstances. In the process of exploring martyrdom, in itself a controversial topic which demands understanding in the contemporary political environment, the chapter will also show how the two main divisions of Islam have diverged politically and religiously as each experienced a diametrically opposite response to the theology of 'Manifest Success' found in the Qur'an.

Chapters 7 and 8 will further develop the themes explored in Chapter 3. Difference will continue to be explored by locating Sufism within Islam, and assessing the claims of contemporary Sufis to represent traditional Islam, at the same time, considering the implications of the label 'traditional' for those who self-consciously utilise it as a marker of legitimacy. The contrary view of Muslim revivalist or reform movements, such as the Wahhabis and Salafis, who criticise Sufis, will also be considered. Thus the themes of transcendence and immanence, unity and uniqueness, picked up in Chapter 3, will be further explored to facilitate understanding of the tensions that exist between a variety of nineteenth- and twentieth-century revivalist movements and those who lay claim to traditional Islam, especially in its relationship to manifestations of Sufism.

Chapter 8 will consider the last and final Prophet, Muhammad, the historical founder of Islam. It will demonstrate how traditional Muslims, Sufis, and the new orthodoxies, differ considerably in their view of the Prophet. Debates over the role of the Prophet, his relationship to Allah, and his historic existence as opposed to his cosmic role in salvation history, dominate contemporary discourses between various factions competing to be the voice of authentic Islam. As with the founds of most historic religions, tensions exist between the Muhammad of history and the Muhammad of popular piety.

Chapter 9 introduces the second controversial issue to be covered, that of *jihad*, and argues that it is often narrowly understood as religious warfare. The content of the chapter will explore the controversies surrounding *jihad* and examine the idea of religious warfare in Islam, its origins and justification. The various views concerning *jihad* amongst diverse Muslim movements will be assessed along with consideration of the wider Muslim understanding of *jihad* as personal and communal effort to promote Islam (*da'wa*) or to defend its beliefs and values. In addition, the ideal of the greater *jihad*, as primarily manifested in the spiritual disciplines of the Sufis, to overcome the frailties or imperfections of human nature, will be placed into the context of the struggle to realise Islam.

Chapter 10 will examine the penultimate contentious issue to be explored in this book, that is, the apparent creation of Muslim fundamentalism in the contemporary period and will introduce various movements that are labelled as such. In this chapter there will be a theoretical concern as to whether it is useful to label Muslim movements as 'fundamentalist', and to what degree Muslim 'fundamentalism' is unique to the tradition or part of a universal religious response to globalisation and secularisation.

Chapter 11 will ask the question whether Muslim women are the victims of patriarchy or of an oppressive and discriminatory religion.

It will examine a number of issues that are considered problematic in the West, particularly Muslim dress, marriage customs and gender segregation. It is here that I need to insert an apology. At a recent book launch of Humayun Ansari's *The Infidel Within: Muslims in Britain since 1800*, held at the House of Lords in Britain under the auspices of Lord Ahmed of Rotherham, the author of that work was criticised by a representative of Jamait al-Nissa Women's Group based in North London. Her complaint centred upon the organisation of the book, which allocated a single separate chapter to women's issues. She correctly pointed out that many books on Muslims were organised in a similar fashion, thus relegating women to a marginal position rather than their reality, which encompasses the whole of Muslim life and represents half the population. I am guilty of the same offence; in mitigation I would argue that women share in and contribute to, many of the features explored in the other chapters, and it is deference to their unique significance in contemporary events that insists upon a distinct chapter. However, I acknowledge that the limitations of being a non-Muslim male do not easily allow any other organisation of content. The book demanded by Hamayun Ansari's critic needs to be written by a Muslim woman and is beyond the scope of this author.

However, the chapter will provide an overview of the situation of Muslim women, examining Western stereotypes and the various challenges to them provided by women from within Islam. The main content of the chapter will be on the unique claim made by some Muslim women that they will be able to liberate themselves from patriarchal domination only through the application of correct understanding of the Qur'an and Hadith as opposed to the secular feminism of the West.

In each of the major topics examined in the contents, I have tried to see the world from the view of Muslims themselves, following the famous dictum of Ninian Smart to 'walk in the other man's moccasins' (Smart, 2000). It is not always possible, as any religion the size of Islam will contain a cupboard full of shoes and not all will fit comfortably. Some fit my feet more than others, and discerning readers will recognise my particular affinities. Where the shoes do not fit, I have tried not to dwell on my discomfort, but rather to try to further understanding of why some people find them comfortable, or perhaps consider it worthwhile to walk in discomfort. I guess what I am saying is that my approach approximates to a phenomenological one but the reader needs to maintain caution with my form of empathy. I cannot claim neutrality on issues that I feel strongly about nor do I consider a dispassionate 'objective' stance to be desirable or even possible when studying my fellow human beings.

CHAPTER 2

The Western Media:
a misrepresentation or a factual
account?

The following chapter will elaborate on how the Western media, (both popular and academic) represent Islam and will provide an historical framework as a background tool to explore such representations of Islam in the West. The intention is to open readers up to a deeper awareness of how our individual and group perceptions of Muslims are often a result of stereotyping and misconception which has its roots in historic conflicts between European and Muslim cultures. There is an historic focus because it is necessary to introduce Western attitudes to the Orient in general, or Orientalism as it is known, showing the different stages through which it has passed to the present day. It is, however, essential to view this as a two-way process and introduce Muslim perceptions of the West and ask whether they can be perceived as a form of 'Occidentalism' that mirrors the formation of Orientalism.

Introduction

The West and Muslims have known each other for many centuries now, but often on antagonistic terms, in spite of the contributions they have made to each other's cultures. At first, it was both Eastern and Western Christianity which felt the impact of the success of Islam, both as a military threat and through the attraction of its austere but rigorous monotheism, also manifested in successful mystical traditions. Later, it was Europe itself that felt threatened as the Muslim empires came up to its heartland, pushing back the frontiers of its Christian heritage in Spain and the Balkans. In turn, Muslims felt the impact of the Crusades in the Holy Land, which they had occupied in the seventh century, but far more significantly, the turn of the tide and the colonisation of their territory by the emergent European powers from the eighteenth century onwards. This problematic relationship began in the era of colonisation and remains to the twentieth-first century with Muslim reactions to post-colonial domination and fears of global capitalism and secularisation, whilst the West created new stereotypes consisting of oppressed women and 'suicide-terrorists'.

In addition, the post-colonial era has witnessed the new arrival of Muslims in the West itself, arriving through both economic and political migration. Fear of the 'other' has contributed to new fears concerning Muslims in the West, resulting in the relatively new phenomenon of religious discrimination against Muslims as opposed to ethnic racism. In Britain, this has been labelled 'Islamophobia'. However, the arrival of Muslims in the West has achieved little to eradicate ancient fears or prejudices.

Heeren suggests that the historic rivalry has led to an ignorance of the ordinary Westerner towards Islam (Heeren, 1976). However, it is equally true that misconceptions of Western culture and the teachings of Christianity are held by Muslims. It is the intention of this chapter to explore this relationship of misunderstandings by investigating media attitudes towards Islam, both in the press and academic texts. This needs to be understood in the context of an historic relationship and the appropriation of the East in the colonial era that has become known as 'Orientalism' since the publication of Edward Said's seminal text by the same name (Said, 1978). However, very little has been written about a recipient 'Occidentalism'. Both 'Islamophobia' and 'Orientalism' have generated a burgeoning collection of articles and books and some of them need to be assessed.

Historical background

The Prophet of Islam has come under particular vociferous attacks that find their origin in Christian perceptions of Islam as a threat. In the Middle Ages, the Church projected a picture of Muhammad that was an early example of character assassination. It was done to make the Prophet unattractive, even repulsive to the Christian way of life and assert the moral superiority of Christianity over Islam. Thus Muhammad was depicted as an impostor, a murderer, a lover of women with lecherous sexual inclinations for pre-pubescent girls, and a false prophet who had distorted the teachings of Christianity and Judaism to form his own abhorrent sect. The charges laid against his character were always denigrating and usually contrasted him unfavourably with Jesus. Thus such polemic highlighted Muhammad's use of *jihad* as opposed to the pacifism of Jesus, the permission given for polygamy and the number of marriages consummated by Muhammad as opposed to the celibacy of Jesus.

It is true that by the nineteenth century, some of this distortion was being corrected by biographies such as Thomas Carlyle's *Heroes and Hero Worship* published in 1840, but the new focus was on Muhammad as a gifted individual with unique political and military abilities. This slant was to continue into twentieth-century academic texts which introduced more historical reliability but rarely engaged with why Muhammad commanded the religious devotion and veneration of countless millions down through the centuries. At best, he was perceived as trustworthy, genuine, sincere and high-principled, but this humanistic approach failed to apprehend his piety, love of God, wisdom or spiritual insights, so well known to Muslims (Khan, 1978). In addition, the twentieth century has witnessed the growth of Christian Protestant revivalism, particularly in the USA, where increasingly millennialist and dispensationalist tendencies once again revile Islam, this time as the agents of Satan and the protagonists at Armageddon. A new insider medium has appeared amongst such groups, which continue a tradition of ignorance towards Muslims that began with Christian reaction to Islam's advent and success.

The viewpoint that asserts Islam to be the agent of the devil is not so new as perhaps the denizens of the Southern 'Biblelands' might think. It has a distinguished, if equally petty, precedent in the polemical writings of Nicetas of Byzantium in the ninth century, who, in his *Anatrope*, argues amongst other criticisms, that since the God of Muhammad does not accept Christian law, he cannot be the true God and thus it follows that he must be the devil. It was St John of Damascus, born around half a century after the *Hijra* in 622CE who set the tone for Christian disputations with Muslims. John seemed to address Muslim doctrines as if he were dealing with a Christian heretical sect, which some mistakenly believed Islam to be, rather than on its own terms, but more notably he began the long history of scandalising the reputation of Muhammad, seeing him as an impostor who was more interested in sexual conquest and licentiousness than godliness, and who was not beyond using 'revelation' to seduce women towards whom his roving eye took a fancy.

In addition he asserted that Muhammad invented the Qur'an after instruction from a Christian monk on the basic tenets of Judaism and Christianity. John's attitude towards Islam, especially its Prophet, was to be continued as a basic line of attack down through the centuries by Christians of both the Eastern and Western churches, but re-appeared in an especially injurious form in the infamous novel of Salman Rushdie, *The Satanic Verses*, published in 1988 (Rushdie, 1988). The book was particularly injurious to Muslim feelings, because it was written not by a Christian from whom it could be expected, but by someone born a Muslim.

Spanish versions of Muhammad's life also incorporate all of the above themes but sometimes add that Muhammad prophesised that he would rise again from the dead in three days, but when he died his body was eaten by dogs. This is clearly written to compare Muhammad with Jesus and must be seen in the context of the conflicts between Moors and Christians in that region. Daniel, in his masterly exploration of Christian attitudes towards Islam explains that 'Western authors did not set out to shock Muslims with their sac-rilege; they were themselves shocked by what they saw as blasphemy against Christian doctrines' (Daniel, 1993:17). In particular they were horrified by the Muslim denial of the Crucifixion, refusal to accept the divinity of Christ, and the crude dismissal of the Trinity as poly-theism. However, above all they were alarmed by the rapid expansion of Islam and the conquest of Christian territory.

It was probably the latter, the sense of the dangerous 'other', com-bined with a fear of being overpowered by an enemy with whom they shared many shifting borders, that, above all, helped maintain the 'deformed image' of Islam as a dogma of Christian society for many centuries. At the present time, it raises its head again, when once more the threat of the 'barbarian at the gate' is promoted by certain ele-ments of the Christian Right in the USA and the political right in Europe. It is this which, as stated by Daniel,

> led men to prefer, sometimes nonsensical, and often unpleasant and untrue versions of the history of Muhammad and of the tenets and practices of Islam; and that they did so even when sound information was available. (Daniel, 1993:24)

There seemed to be no awareness or sympathy for the range of beliefs that the religions share with each other, and we find some of the most virtuous and best minds of medieval Christianity able to support the Crusades and advocate for them, with no ability to see beyond the idea of the wicked Saracens who had taken the Holy Land by force. However, some of the more discerning may have been surprised by the level of civility, chivalry and knowledge once they became acquainted with the Muslim world.

In short, the following list contains the most common elements of Christian polemic against Islam:

1. *The attack on 'pseudoprophesy'*, where the revelation itself is per-ceived to be false and without any redeeming features. The criteria for proving the falsity of Muslim beliefs were taken from Christian scripture, with certainly no awareness that disproving one sacred text by the 'truths' of another is an absurd exercise which can be played by both parties. The Muslim position towards Christian scripture was softer in content, following the Qur'an's position that the earlier revelations given to Jesus and the Jewish prophets were true but that the subsequent sacred writings have been abro-gated by the Qur'an as they have been 'invented' to some degree by human addition to the divine words.

2. *The claim that Muhammad's life was immoral*, and therefore proof that the revelation was false. The pagan Arabs were presented as woe-fully ignorant and therefore open to the chicanery of a low-born upstart, bent on seducing women and allowing his followers the same privileges, promising them endless sensual delights after their deaths.

3. *The place of violence and power as a constituent of Islam*, in which Muhammad's career and the subsequent military success of the Arabs is compared with the pacifism of Jesus. However, the solu-tion is to use force in opposition to it, and Christians fervently adopted the idea of the Crusades.

4. *Muslim civilisation as a theatre of indulgence*, most explicitly expressed in the idea of loose sexual morals, debauchery and drugs. This often focused on the number of wives and concubines permitted and the laws which regulated marriage, divorce and remarriage. There were both exaggerated and inaccurate descrip-tions of the private morality of Muslims which was considered to be dangerous to Christian virtue.

Thus the Christian variety of Orientalism existed not so much to understand Islam in its own terms but rather to represent it in a deformed manner for the medieval and renaissance Christian. Islam is perceived through Christian eyes as a religion of resistance, which provides a warped discourse in opposition to the doctrines of the Incarnation, the Trinity and the idea of God the Father.

The early Christian denial of Islam's independent status as a new religion, instead seeing it as a heretical sect of Christianity, is echoed by the works of contemporary writers such as Michael Cook, Patricia Crone, Martin Hinds, John Wansbrough and Gerald Hawting, known as the 'revisionist' school of interpretation. Such writers develop a series of arguments based on archaeological and non-Muslim textual sources, which in a variety of ways suggest that 'Islam' only slowly emerged as a new religion which fabricated its early history. They argue that 'Islam' emerged out of sectarian controversies between Christians and Jews in the Middle East 'projected back to an Arabian origin' (Wansbrough, 1977 quoted in Ruthwen, 2004). Such writings need to be placed within the history of Christian suspicions of Islam and orientalist 'scientific' attempts to 'objectively' discover the source of Islam. The latter will be explored below.

However, the position in regard to Christian understandings of Islam was to change with the European dominance of the Orient in the colonial period, when Western fears of Muslim power were diminished by their own resurgence achieved through advances in science and technology. But the relationship was now radically changed as the post-Enlightenment West increasingly transferred its own religious heritage to the private sphere of individual choice, removing, piece by piece, the role of Christianity in the public realm. From the eighteenth century onwards, Islam would be put under the microscope of a different kind of Orientalism, influenced primarily by an attempt to comprehend religion based on the methodology of the natural and human sciences.

Orientalism

Since the seminal work of Edward Said was first published in 1978, scholars in the field of Islamic Studies have been alerted to the dangers of Orientalism. Said simply defined Orientalism as 'a way of coming to terms with the Orient that is based upon the Orient's special place in European Western experience' (Said, 1978:1). Said argued that the European academic study of the East can be criticised as a method of dominating, restructuring and having authority over the Orient. It is both a desire for the exotic arising out of the 'mysterious East', for example, which has always impacted on traditional scholarly approaches to the study of Sufism, and an attempt to impose 'scientific' order on the Orient consisting of categorisation, classifications and typologies, so popular amongst Victorian natural scientists. Perhaps the most pernicious of these so-called scientific theories, the idea of a biological basis for racial inequality, was to provide an alternative way of denigrating the Oriental by explaining backwardness, inequality and inability to match the West's new capabilities. Thus science became the alternative to Christian 'myths' of Islam's degeneracy, yet nineteenth-century Christians stayed in the hunt, supplying a moral-political admonishment of Muslims and other religions of the Orient through the missionary movements. Said, of course, has alerted us to the colonial discourse inherent in all such theories at this period, both Christian and scientific.

Even those, such as Richard Burton, whom Said admits had an unparalleled understanding of the Muslims he travelled amongst, and who attempted to see life from the perspective of the person living in it, was not free of the colonial enterprise. For example, 'Egypt is a treasure to be won' and 'the most tempting prize which the East holds out to the ambition of Europe' (Said, 1978:196). In addition, Burton's Orientalism is not free from the seductive idea of the 'mysterious East' where the constraints of Victorian morality, especially sexual mores, can be loosened. The translation of *The Perfumed Garden*, for example, provides titillation for the repressed in the same way as the Hindu *Kama Sutra* and, in its own way, continues the Christian myth of sensuality and libertine behaviour being an innate quality of the Muslim. Interestingly, depictions of the Muslim female at this period are radically different from those in the contemporary Western media. Instead of the veiled and passive image of male domination and exploitation of Muslim women, so common in our newspapers, the nineteenth-century artist or photographer favoured the languid, sensual, reclining figure, redolent with suggestions of sexual experience and drugged licentiousness. A 'Turkish delight' image predominated, more suggestive of the 'dance of the seven veils' than the 'sexless' images of today.

It is perhaps unfair to accuse all the scholars of Islam in the colonial era as dominating over and redefining Muslim culture and religion in their own terms. The alternative view would be that some of them were colonised by Eastern worldviews, trying to ditch their European socialisation and adopt the customs and religious beliefs of the Oriental, although this is more common amongst those influenced by Indian traditions and Buddhism than Islam. However, all Eastern mysticism, including Islamic Sufism, has always been a certain kind of Orientalist's paradise. Yet it is here that it could be argued that the most distortion has taken place, leading to an appropriation of Sufism, in particular, that disguises its origins in Islam and denies it the possibility of being a living religious worldview with deep roots in traditional Islam. Said, analysing the works of Massignon, a significant presence in the study of Sufism, states that all his work in Islamic mysticism was an attempt to 'describe the itinerary of souls out of the limiting consensus imposed on them by the orthodox Islamic community, or Sunna' (Said, 1978:268). Said's argument supposes that Massignon, a practising Roman Catholic, saw in Islam a primary motivation to declare war (*jihad*) on Christianity, Judaism and internal heresies, but believed Sufism, the mystical path of Islam to be a 'countercurrent' and 'a road towards divine grace' for Muslims (p. 268).

Thus Sufism is appropriated as a kind of Christianised Islam in which Muslims can escape the constraints of orthodoxy. Very little is made of the relationship between Sufism and the path of the *Sunna*, embodied in Hadith and Qur'an, or in the Sufi's fervent love of Muhammad. In addition, Sufism is presented only as the voice of a mystical elite, rather than the living tradition of millions of pious Muslims, especially those outside the Arab heartlands. This approach is echoed by the traditional method of the Orientalist in translating the poetic texts of significant Muslim mystics into a variety of European languages and which has resulted in Sufism being appropriated into the West as a now virtually dead or 'corrupted tradition'. It flourished in Persia, Turkey and India during a particular period of Islamic history and was represented by exceptional men and women who achieved high mystical awareness and expressed it in ecstatic poetry, but has since gone into decline.

Famous examples of this approach are translations of the *Conference of the Birds* by Attar, the works of Ibn Arabi or al-Ghazali, but the favourite of the nineteenth-century Orientalists are translations of Omar Khayyam. Today, these would be replaced by the *Mathnawi* of Jalalu'd-Din Rumi, which has been appropriated to such a degree, that very few of the millions that purchase copies of his poetry are aware of his knowledge of the Qur'an or love for the Prophet Muhammad; it is almost as if he has been uprooted from Islam and reformed as a figure of Western or universal esotericism. Of interest here, is that thousands of North Americans regard Sufism highly, from those who only familiarise themselves with the poetry of Rumi to those who become practitioners, whilst living in a period where Islam is denigrated and once again feared as the enemy at the gate. Yet there is no recognition that Sufism is part and parcel of Muslim life, so successful has been the appropriation. Richard King refers to this process as 'reverse-colonialism', an attempt to essentialise certain forms of Oriental mysticism as prime candidates for a 'universal religion' of the future (King, 1999:140).

Academic discourse

An examination of two passages from two renowned scholars of Islam, Hamilton Gibb writing in 1942 and Montgomery Watt in 1988, reveals an antipathy towards Muslim and Arab culture, that indicates in these two excellent scholars an entrenched stereotyping in regard to the superiority of the Western mind concerning progress and the ability to be rational. First, Hamilton Gibb writing in 1942:

> It is true that there have been great philosophers among the Muslim peoples and that some of them were Arabs, but they were rare exceptions. The Arab mind, whether in relation to the outer world or in relation to the processes of thought, cannot throw off its intense feeling for the separateness and the individuality of the concrete events. This is, I believe, one of the main factors lying behind that 'lack of the sense of law' which Professor MacDonald regarded as the characteristic difference of the Oriental.
>
> It is this, too, which explains – what is so difficult for the Western student to grasp – the aversion of the Muslims for the thought processes of rationalism. (Gibb, 1942:7)

It has to be recognised that Professor Gibb and MacDonald were products of a colonial era and were recipients and participants of a view in regard to the 'native', a term for all colonised people, that branded them as 'other' and essentially intellectually and culturally inferior to the European colonisers. In addition, Gibb's critique of the Muslim as rejecting rationalist modes of thought, or worse, incapable of achieving it, is rooted in a post-Enlightenment dualistic view of rationality and religion in opposition to each other. Muslim scholars have perceived rationality in a different light, utilising it as a tool for interpreting or understanding revelation.

Montgomery Watt, influenced by the attitudes of his mentor, similarly writes over forty years later:

> For Muslim scholars unchangingness is both an ideal for human individuals and societies. Unchangingness is both an all-pervading assumption which colours most aspects of the standard world-view . . . It is thus very difficult for the Westerner to appreciate the outlook of those in whose thinking there is no place for development, progress, or social advance and improvement. (Watt, 1988:3)

Although Watt focused on progress as opposed to rationality, albeit linked in the modern Western psyche as it was the latter's victory over the superstition of religion that led irrevocably to the former, it is in two features that he displays similar thinking to Gibb. First, there is the assumption of an innate difference between the Western and Oriental mind, to the degree that the one is not understandable by the other. The second, leading on from the first is the underlying assumption, not recognised or challenged, that the differences are primordial, belonging to nature rather than economic, social or political circumstances. It is this very primordialism that underlies the work of the current crop of Islamic scholars writing in the aftermath of 9/11, who still posit Western democracy and the values of secular humanism as the pinnacle of human achievement and in the process, still assert the cultural, intellectual, political, economic and material supremacy of the West over the East,. None of this is presented as having anything to do with relations of power, but rather an innate superiority, that leads to analyses that posit Western civilisation contrasted with barbarism (Huntingdon, 2002). Recent events in which several Muslim states have been identified as 'rogue states', the invasion of Iraq and Afghanistan, the torture of prisoners to elicit information, the number of arrests without due legal process in Western Europe and the USA, all helped to generate the growing perception that 'Islam is the new American enemy, a green menace that has replaced the red menace of

the Soviet Union' (Haddad, 2004:99). The sense of Muslim beleaguer-
ment and marginalisation, especially amongst American Muslims,
has been encouraged by the new Islamic scholars, who in reality are
ideologues for Western culture, and who have spared no opportunity
to present Muslims as terrorists and a threat to the United States.
Haddad uses the label 'Islamophobes' for scholars and journalists
such as Steven Emerson, Daniel Pipes and Bernard Lewis (Haddad,
2004).

The resurrection of academic media that denigrate Islam or
suggest in some way that Muslims are inferior to their Western counterparts is an unfortunate corollary to the events of 9/11 and perhaps
forewarns us that the reputation of academia must be challenged by
informed and questioning reading. Perhaps more unfortunate is the
overshadowing of the works belonging to the new generation of
scholarly analysis of Islam and Muslims which were written partly to
offset the distorted images of Muslims and their cultures created by
Islamic scholars coming out of an older tradition of Orientalism. As
stated by Charles Adams:

> These scholars, in general, lack nothing of the historical, linguis-
> tic, and philological qualifications of their teachers and predeces-
> sors, but they have grafted onto this powerful heritage the
> systematic and phenomenological concerns which they absorbed
> at the feet of their mentors in the history of religions. The lamen-
> tations of former years, therefore, now give way to hope and
> optimism. (Adams, 1985:ix–x)

For example, scholars like Annemarie Schimmel have presented
Sufism to us in a way that Muslims would recognise, rather than
the works of translated poetry completely removed from a living
Muslim experience rooted in Islam. Other scholars are trying to
imbed themselves in an understanding of the Muslim through fieldwork, emulating the approach of Burton but hopefully without the
colonial baggage of the nineteenth-century Orientalist.

Islamophobia

It can be seen that any contemporary negativity expressed towards
Muslims, either in the contemporary news media or in acts of prejudice against Muslims, has a history arising out of both explicit

vehemence against Islam originating in Christian fears and ignorance of the new religion and colonial orientalist discourse. Recent attempts to create negative images or reinforce stereotypes have to be seen in the context of this history. Both Orientalism, now in its post-colonial stages, and Christian fears of Islam remain alive in the twenty-first century, especially in the aftermath of 9/11. The Reverend Franklin Graham, the son of the famous evangelist, Billy Graham, chosen by George Bush to deliver the prayers at his presidential inauguration, has continued in the tradition of Christian polemic against Muslims by asserting that 'Islam is a wicked and evil religion' (Graham, 2004). The same school of thought is followed by the US deputy under-secretary of defence for intelligence, General William Boykin, who has described the US as being involved in a 'holy war' against the 'idol' of 'Islam's false god' and a 'guy called Satan' who 'wants to destroy us as a Christian army' (Boykin, 2004). The theme of a false god, possessing no connection to the monotheistic deity of Judaism and Christianity, has been picked up by the Reverend Pat Buchanan, who has claimed that Muslims worship a moon-god revered in ancient Mecca.

Since 9/11 there has been anecdotal evidence of an increase in racist attacks directed at Muslims but studies in 2002 by the University of Leicester show hostility towards Muslims in the city peaked whenever there was a 'terrorist' atrocity. Reported incidents included abuse hurled at children and women, insults on public transport, objects hurled in the street and even a baby being tipped out of a pram. However, the motives for the attacks seem to indicate that they are not the direct consequence of violent activities by extremists but rather that extreme events focus negative views of Islam and allow discrimination to become public. The main criticisms of the perpetrators seem to be that Islam victimises women and that Muslims refuse to integrate (Casciani, 2004). Where such attitudes persist, the question has to be asked to what degree do the popular media promote such attitudes in a plethora of articles over the last decade that put forward such a view of Islam.

Dr Lorraine Sheridan, who conducted the Leicester research, stated that 'the attacks are being carried out by people who don't like Islam, the abuse is more about the religion than race' (quoted in Casciani, 2004). In isolating religion as the cause of discrimination Sheridan has noticed a change in the polemics of racism in Britain, where the discrimination is moving away from abusing ethnic identity to religious identity. This is particularly true in the case of Muslims and led to the respected Runnymede Trust, an independent think tank on ethnicity and cultural diversity, publishing a report in 1997 in which they labelled the phenomenon 'Islamophobia' (The Runnymede Trust, 1997), a term widely used now in Britain and Western Europe to signify anti-Muslim prejudice based upon an unfounded hostility towards Islam directed against individuals or groups because of their actual or perceived religious background or identification. However, this change had been noted earlier by Barker, who points out that 'new racism' is based on supposed incompatability of cultural traditions rather than biological superiority (Barker, 1981), and picked up by Donald and Rattanasi who describe how this perspective of cultural difference bases itself on incompatability of values and lifestyles belonging to different cultures (Donald and Rattanasi, 1992).

In 1997, almost five years before the traumatic events of 9/11, Professor Gordon Conway, Vice-Chancellor of Sussex University, who chaired the Runnymede report, recommended to the British government that changes be made to British law to make religious discrimination and incitement to religious hatred illegal. In the delivery of the final report Conway noted that 'the media, in particular, are commonly Islamophobic. They generate stereotypes of British Muslims which serve to marginalise them in our society' (Conway, 1997). He noted that British Muslims are increasingly subject to prejudice, discrimination, harassment and violence.

It has to be accepted that the European situation is unique in that Muslims are no longer merely within its borders, but belong to the identity of Western Europe no less than any other populations that may have been around for more generations. It is not nationality that is problematic for young British-born Muslims, for example, but rather the degree to which they wish to share in their parents' or grandparents' lifestyle or the extent to which they wish to involve themselves with their religious affiliation. These issues are no less relevant for non-Muslim youth. But, in spite of their sense of belonging, there is no doubt that fear and hostility remain dominant features of the perceptions of those who continue to regard Muslims in the West as a 'fifth column' or 'enemy within the gates', making no differentiation between the new diaspora communities and Muslims in the Middle East or other parts of the wider Muslim world.

Not everyone agrees, as Ian Baruma writing in the *Guardian* in 2002 indicates. Although acknowledging that not everyone looks favourably or without prejudice on Muslims, he argues that most of those who racially bait Muslims are unlikely to be able to tell the difference between Muslims and other minorities such as Hindus or Sikhs. Yet there are very few incidents of vandalism directed at the sacred buildings of the latter communities in the same way as mosques are targeted. Nor have there been such pernicious examples as the Muslim woman whose body was covered in bacon in a mortuary. However, Baruma's main argument seems to be directed at the spectre of Muslim extremism and its threat to Western societies. He argues that both racial prejudice and 'Islamism' are barriers to integration. He states that you cannot be 'a jihadi, at war with the wicked infidels, and a law-abiding citizen of a European nation' (Baruma, 2002).

It is interesting that Baruma is writing before the events of 9/11, and some might argue prophetically, but his focus on a few disenchanted or alienated youth as representative of Muslims in the West and his simplistic option of either being Islamophobic or implicit in the undermining of Western values indicates his stance. Others are more obvious, and the explicitly racist, or as it defines itself, 'racialist' British National Party has conducted its own vociferous far-right media campaign against Western Muslims. Immediately in the aftermath of 9/11 they campaigned for Islam to be removed from Britain and looked upon the street riots in Bradford and other Northern cities, not so much as the result of socio-economic conditions, but as a direct result of Muslim religious propaganda to remove unbelievers from Britain and establish an Islamic state. Chris Allen cites an example of British National Party polemic literature taken from a publication printed in South England aptly entitled *A Cross to bear: Islam out of Britain* as stating, 'Christianity is being crucified on the dark cross of globalisation in favour of a much more virulent Islam' (Allen, 2004). What is of interest in this example, is not so much the anti-migrant stance of the far right, but rather the re-invention of ancient Christian fears of Islam by a racist organisation.

The government responded shortly after 9/11 by stating that it will wipe out Islamophobia. A Home Office Minister, John Denham, addressing an anti-racist conference in London stated: 'We are making it abundantly clear that nothing in the events of September 11 provide any justification for racists in this country to attack, discriminate against, or abuse Muslims. The real Islam is a religion of peace, tolerance and understanding' (BBC News, 29 September 2001).

However, even more recently the national media have reported the findings of the study carried out by the Commission on British Muslims and Islamophobia which warns of Muslim alienation from mainstream society which may 'boil over' into more riots in Northern cities. The report concludes that Britain is 'institutionally Islamophobic' and cites examples of increased intolerance demonstrated by attacks on mosques and individuals, especially Muslim women, since the events of the Iraq war and its aftermath. These are being carried out in the context of a wider political discourse of a 'clash of civilisations' or a 'new global cold war' (Doward and Hinsliff, 2004).

Media

A note of caution needs to be appended to any examination of the 'Islamophobia industry' that it stands in danger of essentialising Muslims, too concerned with the single issue of religious racism to provide an analysis that incorporates the full diversity of Muslim identity and the variety of attitudes to the West. The problem is further compounded by the media. The main concern of Muslims with the Western news media is that they tend to portray Muslims as either terrorists or misogynists. In the case of the former it has disproportionately focused on the views and actions of a violent minority, thus risking stereotyping Muslims as aggressive and anti-Western and ignoring millions who are peaceful citizens of their respective nations. It is essential that perceptions are not created which endow all Muslims with the potential to become violent advocates of *jihad* or with feelings of alienation towards the West. Indeed, media assumptions can be clearly perceived in the quick reaction to attribute the Oklahoma bombings to Muslim extremists. In regard to women, they are far too often presented as passive victims of male dominance and exploitation, a subject that will be addressed in more detail in Chapter 11. The overriding focus is on Muslim dress codes, especially head covering, an issue which is of little concern amongst Muslim women themselves.

As a number of high-profile events take place around the world involving 'suicide bombers', there is little to distinguish between the liberation struggles of the Palestinians reduced to using themselves as weapons against a modern heavily armed and resourced military, and the actions of the al-Qa'eda pilots at 9/11. Without such a nuanced analysis it would appear that Muslims throughout the world are a common problem, to be resolved in a war against 'terrorism'. Of more concern, is the ability of the media to bring the horrors of tragic events into our personal space. Mark Wark has stated that Muslims have been 'inserted as close to home in the West as it is possible to go; right into the living rooms of millions' (Wark, 1994:23). Thus powerful images with the ability to create strong emotional impressions and provoke subsequent reactions are projected but without any analysis or reflection on the individual situation that has provoked the event.

As a consequence, it can become legitimate to perceive Muslims with distrust and suspicion. Even before 9/11 and the subsequent 'war on terrorism', both local and global news focused on Muslims as the 'other'. This was very apparent in Britain where the media focused on a number of key events such as Salman Rushdie, the formation of the Muslim Parliament, riots in Oldham and Bradford, and the fight to win state funding in Muslim schools. Each of these was presented in such a way to promote the image of an irrational and alienated stranger whose values were completely at odds with those of the West. In between these global news events, continuous small items focus on dowry abuse, honour killings, estranged women, children taken to places of origin in divorce cases, none of which are anything to do with Islam but rather ethnic practices often condemned by the representatives of religion as opposed to the tenets of Islam. In addition, since 9/11 there are the continuous news items provoked by the global situation. As the 'newsworthiness' of Muslims and Islam increases, the overall impact is to develop an imagined and distorted construct: a constructed identity which becomes increasingly at odds with Muslim perceptions of themselves and further alienates both Muslims and non-Muslims from each other.

Muslim attitudes to the West

The traffic of misunderstanding has not all been one way, although Muslim polemical discourse against Christianity has not contained either the vehemence or the antagonism directed at Islam. It is difficult for Muslims to be too insulting towards Christianity when it is regarded as a privileged religion in the Qur'an, foremost amongst the 'People of the Book', a former recipient of revelation through a loved and respected prophet and the Gospels. Even in the Muslim empires, Christian minorities were generally protected, even though admittedly with a payment of a tax. In addition, Muslims respect Isā (Jesus) far too highly as a major prophet and 'sign' of God to dispar-age him in the way that Muhammad has been treated. Even at the time of the Crusades, Muslims appeared to recognise that the moti-vations of the attacking force were far from godly, in spite of the papal rhetoric, preferring to label the Crusaders as Franks rather than Christians, a title which appears to disassociate them from religious motives for the war.

Muslim criticism of Christianity has been threefold. First that it has degenerated from a pure monotheism by developing a doctrine of a Trinitarian God. However, here there is misunderstanding of the nuances and sophistication of the doctrine in either Eastern or Western churches; instead Muslims tend to accuse Christians of holding to a belief in tri-theism. The second criticism follows from the first, in that Muslims reject with abhorrence the idea of incarnation, arguing that the idea that God could have sons (or daughters) is anthropomorphism at its worst, moreover it associates someone (Jesus) with divinity, the worst of sins in Islam. The final criticism is that Christians have corrupted the pure monotheism of Jesus, both textually and doctrinally. In this context, Akbar Ahmed, a British Muslim and anthropologist has written, 'an examination of what the contemporary oriental thinks of the occident would reveal images as distorted and dishonest as in the worst forms of orientalism' (Ahmed, 1992:178).

The distortion also occurs when seeking to understand Western secular institutions. The term 'secular' is generally understood as 'godless' which in turn leads to the idea of an immoral society, for it is incomprehensible that any public or private morality could exist in the vacuum of an atheist nation. Indeed, the more sophisticated understanding of secular, as meaning the separation of religion to the private and individual realm rather than the public sphere, is also not appreciated and is seen as an attempt to take God away from the arena where he should be sovereign. Western family law, sexual permissiveness, capitalism based on interest (usury), the attitudes to alcohol, crime rates, pornography, prostitution, homosexuality, and child abuse are all perceived as a sign of a society that has departed from its anchor in God's laws. Although today such views might be perceived as an indication of a more fundamentalist position, which seeks to replace secular laws with the Muslim *shari'a*, an eighteenth-century subcontinent Muslim visitor to Britain recorded in his travelogue that the English were the most unfortunate of people for they had to make up their own laws; this was compared unfavourably to Muslims who had been spared such an arduous and imperfect task by the mercy of Allah who had revealed his own laws to them. Yet Mirza Abu Talib Khan was liberal in his attitudes towards early nineteenth-century British lifestyle, participating in the social life and enjoying being feted by the British public (Visram, 2002:18).

Since the early days of Islam, Muslims have been producing polemical materials which are anti-Christian, and there has been little change in the type of material or the issues that were raised for criticism. What changed were the circumstances of the Muslim world. During the early conquests of Christian territory in Byzantium, Muslims did not need to be defensive but rather to indicate to themselves the shortcomings of the religious beliefs of the conquered. Since the colonial period, polemical literature against Christianity is both a response against missionary activities but also to help assert moral and religious superiority in the face of political and economic decline. In other words, a common feature of the literature, besides its simplistic understanding of Christianity, is that it is written mostly for Muslims not for the purpose of converting Christians.

Perhaps the most well known of contemporary Muslim critics of Christianity is Ahmed Deedat, a South African of Gujarati origin, whose pamphlets, leaflets and videos have gone out all over the world and can be found in virtually every Muslim bookshop. Deedat's comments on Christianity are hardly new, dealing with many of the issues mentioned above, but his language is known for its sarcasm and ridicule. It is highly rhetorical and emotionally charged, referring to Christians as 'crusaders' and 'Bible-thumpers'. Missionary activity is especially derided as 'menace' and 'tyranny', closely associated with colonial and post-colonial ambitions for world dominion by the West. The most detailed study of Muslim polemical literature has been carried out by Kate Zebiri, whose exploration can be divided into five areas of critique:

1. Criticism of the biblical text and interpretation
A common feature of this type of approach is to state that the Bible has many versions throughout the world that contain different renderings of the text, as opposed to the Qur'an which is always exactly the same. It is believed that verses have been removed and added.

Corruption of the text was believed to have taken place in the compilation. Paul is often seen as a villain who took a corrupted version of Jesus to the Gentiles, in the process obscuring Judaic monotheism. It is also argued that a number of Old and New Testament passages prophesy the coming of Muhammad.

2. The 'falsified' Jesus of the Gospels as opposed to the 'real' Jesus of the Qur'an

Stories in the Gospel accounts which insist that Jesus drank wine, or at least attended festive events where wine was drunk, spoke harshly to his mother, or refused to obey the law of God are considered proof that the Gospels are fabricated. Thus, although Jesus cannot be criticised by Muslims because of his special status as a prophet, the Christian version of Jesus, the son of God, can be criticised as he is an invention. Although Muslims acknowledge the Virgin Birth, and the purity of Mary (Miriam), they refuse to accept the Crucifixion.

3. The corruption of Christian doctrine

The main corruption of Christianity is to forsake the worship of God in favour of the Messenger by imposing the spurious doctrine of Incarnation and Trinity upon Jesus' simple monotheism and servitude to God. The main reason for this is said to be the inability of the fledgling Christian community to protect itself against the overwhelming pagan traditions of the Middle East and Mediterranean world. In the struggle for survival the historical Jesus was lost, to be replaced by an esoteric and Gnostic god-figure.

4. Christianity and Western civilisation

In general very few Muslims comprehend the distinction between being Christian and being Western. Western culture is usually identified with Christianity with little understanding that Christians may be equally critical of certain aspects of Western society. A common criticism is the identification of Christianity with colonialism, exploitation and racism. As such it is a white man's religion closely linked to North American and European imperialism. Very little awareness seems to exist of Southern Hemisphere Christianity.

5. Contemporary Christianity

Noticeable by its absence, other than it is seen to be in irreversible decline as contrasted to the inexorable rise of Islam. There is certainly no awareness of the diversity of Christianity, the creativity and sophistication of its thought, partly because very few Muslims, even amongst the educated, study texts written by Christians for Christians. Muslim bookshops tend to stock anti-Christian polemics or books written by non-Muslims which are speculative but also seem to provide evidence that endorses a Muslim position (Zebiri, 1997:50–84).

Muslim literature that criticises Christianity is certainly more confrontational in the twenty-first century than Christian materials on Islam. However, two cautionary notes need to be considered. First, the fact that for certain Islamic movements there is no distinction made between Western imperialism in the post-colonial context and Christianity. Secondly, some forms of Christianity, most notably in the USA, with its strong Protestant evangelical traditions which often display forms of millennial dispensationalism, remain strongly anti-Islam and still produce literature that draws upon medieval themes. Zebiri notes that there are signs of change in Britain, where the Islamic Foundation promotes the study of Christianity 'via its own source materials instead of indulging in cheap polemics' (Zebiri, 1997:89).

Conclusion

Any conclusions concerning media representations by Muslims and Christians of each other, or secular media representations of Muslims, need to be examined in the context of both the history of relations between the cultures of Europe and Muslim civilisation and the contemporary situation of post-colonialism, especially since the events of 9/11 have dramatically transformed the context worldwide.

Clarke, writing in 1997, believed that the 'master-myths of polarity and complementarity between East and West may be at last in the process of out-running their usefulness'. He considers that both terms, 'East' and 'West', have lost whatever coherent meaning they may once have had (Clarke, 1997:225). Promoting an optimistic version of globalisation, Clarke argues that, worldwide, ideas and institutions are being transformed by 'cultural and political energy' whose origins lie in the West. In this respect, he agrees with Francis Fukuyama's position that in the post-communist era, Western institutions and political ideals will spread throughout the world.

The optimism of Clarke and Fukuyama is sometimes contrasted

with Huntingdon's 'clash of civilisations' thesis. However, Fukuyama's optimism originates in the economic boom of South-East Asia, now joined by China. So far there is little evidence of Muslim nations benefiting in the same way. Bedevilled by corrupt regimes, they remain amongst the world's poorest communities, thus provid-ing ammunition for those who would seek solutions in conspiracy theories and external threats of a war on Islam. Huntingdon's thesis is located in tensions between the Muslim world and the West and thus contributes to the body of orientalist literature that has histori-cally promoted divisions. What is certainly significant, is that even when one removes the politicisation of Islam, Muslims are returning to their religion and its traditions around the globe. They may well form the strongest resistance to the globalisation features proclaimed by Fukuyama, and do not tend to see them in the same optimistic light. It is not necessarily because they oppose the economic benefits of Western consumer society, but because they see in it deficiencies that all the world's great religious founders warned against.

The media of the religious and the secular are part of this struggle for the world-soul and very little of their output is objective or informed. In Britain, the tabloid newspapers fuel Islamophobia as part of their vociferous campaign to demonise the migrant and the outsider. On the other hand, the writers of the liberal broadsheets pro-mote their own orientalist fantasies, fearing being accused of being racist or Islamophobic, or right-wing in a post-colonialist discourse. At its worst, this kind of writing presents Islam as the last torch of spiritual light in a world of ill-gotten comforts and atheism.

Behind it all is an essentialising of the Muslim world – an inability to recognise that behind the stereotyping which depicts Muslims as different and dangerous, is the lived experience of millions of human beings, diverse and sometimes difficult, but who seem to be able to draw upon the spiritual resources of their religion, and who are also able to recognise its shortcomings. As stated so succinctly by Bruce Lawrence:

In the 1990s most Euro-American journalists continue to echo the sentiments that drove European kings and their subjects to launch their crusades almost a millennium ago, crusades whose enemy was Arab Muslims. In the aftermath of the Cold War the enemy, once again, has become the one Islam, the militant, unyielding, violent face of 'Arab' Islam. Whether one picks up a popular book claiming to represent 'Western cultures and values' under attack from Islam, or lead articles of the *New York Times*, such as the recent 'Seeing Green: The Red Menace Is Gone. But Here's Islam,' the message is the same: Islam is one, and Islam is dangerous. (Lawrence, 1998:5)

For those writing after 9/11 the temptation is even greater to demonise, marginalise and distort, to pose Western freedom and civilisation against Muslim superstition and ignorance. In such an environment, the old myths and fabrications reappear in new forms and then the temptation for those on the liberal left who resist colonialism and corporate capitalism is to enlist Muslims to their cause, and to paint too rosy a picture, that conveniently forgets gender issues, homophobia, and social injustices in the Muslim world. In short, Orientalism, in both its negative and positive aspects, still rules the roost when it comes down to media depictions of Muslims. As one Muslim friend of mine recently commented, 'and there I was, thinking being a Muslim made me a member of the human race!'

CHAPTER 3

Doctrine and Architecture:
manifestations of tawhid

Muslim sacred architecture can be explored in order to throw light on Islam's central doctrine of tawhid *(God's unity and uniqueness). Through such an exploration of mosques and shrines, it is possible to highlight the tensions between immanence and transcendence that exist in divergent forms of Islam. In this chapter readers will be introduced to concepts of both traditional and orthodox views of* tawhid *and how the architecture of mosque and shrine outwardly manifests interpretations of Islam that tend to veer towards an emphasis on either immanence or transcendence in their apprehension of the divine. Simultaneously, readers will be introduced to the close relationship that exists between sacred space, architecture and perceptions of Divinity.*

Introduction

Writing in the *Guardian*, William Dalrymple describes a visit to a shrine close by Peshawar on the North West Frontier of Pakistan centred around the tomb of a seventeenth-century Muslim mystic-poet, Rahman Baba. Dalrymple describes how the tomb has been used for centuries by poets and musicians who would sing mystical love songs by moonlight (Dalrymple, 2004). Shrines such as the one described by Dalrymple are duplicated throughout the Muslim world, although, depending on the location, music and singing may or may not be encouraged. The presence of such shrines, containing the remains of Muslim holy men and, occasionally, women, provides an alternative network of sacred space that complements and sometimes rivals the millions of mosques that co-exist alongside them in the villages, towns and cities of the Muslim world.

Although value judgements made by certain forms of Islamic activism condemn the shrines, and even some scholars hive them off to 'folk' or 'popular' religion, an investigation of their architectural features and religious practices in comparison with the mosque reveals different understandings of the primary Islamic doctrine concerning God, that is *tawhid*, the unity and uniqueness of the creator; the two aspects of divine oneness. The doctrine of *tawhid* is embodied in the first clause of the *shahada*, the great witnessing of Islam's monotheism, which proclaims *la illaha illa'Llah* – there is no god but God. At a first glance, it appears to be an apparently simple statement but one which offers the possibility of a number of interpretations, ranging from the simple condemnation of polytheism to sophisticated modern interpretations of divine sovereignty and its implications for the political organisation of the state. However, it would be a mistake to consider *tawhid* as merely a rejection of idols. If there is a negation contained in the notion of *tawhid*, it refers to anything which is given primary significance in human affairs and therefore denies God the sole sovereignty and loyalty of his human subjects (Vahiduddin, 1979:75). As taught by Maulana Mawdudi, the famous twentieth-century revivalist from Pakistan (d.1978), the negative in the first clause of the *shahada* goes far beyond the worship of plural gods, but rather asserts that there is nothing that should be put in the way of divine rule. Mawdudi emphasised man-made political systems as idolatry, but an alternative worldview in Islam provides a more spiritual interpretation of the *shahada* which looks at the inner realm of surrender defined as reintegration with the divine will through self-purification and is more likely to see human ego glorification and self-will as worship of false gods.

Tawhid and its implications

But above all else, *la illaha illa'Llah* is the primal statement of the divine describing its own reality; a basis for the understanding of *tawhid*, first and foremost embedded in the being of God, undeniably one and incomprehensibly unique, and then manifested in nature, human relationships, social organisations, worship and ritual and even the material dimension of the religion. Kenneth Cragg once described Muslims as the 'people of the point' (Cragg, 1987:7). He was referring to the geographical locus of the Ka'aba in Makkah as the point in which the emotional focus of all Muslims is directed in prayer. Five times a day millions of Muslims around the globe face towards Makkah, whilst those in Makkah itself face towards the Ka'aba, thus creating geometric patterns of human beings all directed towards one point, a feature which is unique in the world's religious history. It is said in Muslim myth, that the circumambulating of the Ka'aba replicates the movement of the angels in adoration around the throne of God. In addition, the Ka'aba takes on significance as it is believed to be the site established for the worship of the one true God by Adam, the primal man and prophet, and then renewed by Ibrahim when he visited Hajar and Ishmael, and finally reclaimed by Muhammad as a victory for monotheism from the pagan Arabs who had installed their idols in the shrine.

But the idea of the 'people of the point' can be taken much further to explore the way in which Allah's oneness and uniqueness is manifested in human affairs to create unity. As Allah is one, so has he created one religion (*din*) for human beings to worship and submit to his sovereignty. This is the religion known as Islam by Muslims, and which includes the lineage of biblical prophets, up to and including Jesus (Isa). But it goes far beyond even this. Allah, it is believed, has revealed his true religion to numerous individuals throughout time and to all cultures; thus one religion has been shown to humankind, each time either distorted by culture or lost to polytheism and the worship of false gods. Although the Qur'an acknowledges the diversity of human beings, it is in the worship of the one God that unity is rediscovered and maintained.

This unity of religion is manifested in revelation, continuously renewed through messengers, and sometimes when required a divine book, both acting as agents to draw human beings and their creator even closer to each other by providing the details of how human beings should live on the earth in harmony with the divine will. All of this is premised in the unity of human nature, the idea of *fitra*, the primordial, divinely given being of the human creature, the natural or instinctive being. Thus Islam does not posit the idea of a corrupted being fallen from grace through original sin but rather a person prone to forgetfulness and weakness, but whose innermost being is altruistic and drawn towards godliness, epitomised by the possibility of complete submission and obedience. The idea of *din* (loosely translated as religion), especially in the historic manifestation of Islam, as introduced by the Qur'an, the final book, and Muhammad, the final Messenger, is to work with *fitra*, supporting it, encouraging it and providing the means to overcome human weakness and forgetfulness of God. Thus the Qur'an describes Islam as *'Din al-fitra'*, the religion most closely associated with the primordial nature of human beings. As stated by Saadia Chishti, 'an adherent of Islam, according to this definition, is acting according to the primeval instinct already present in him' (Chishti, 2003:77).

The unity of God is also replicated in human community. The Qur'an promotes the concept of community not in a Western socio-logical sense, but rather as a group of people, a tribe or a nation, that are united not by blood ties, language, culture, food or customs, but by their relationship to God. All other outer markers of community identity would ideally be established through the process of obedi-ence to God's revelation; thus eating habits, dress codes, family struc-tures, governance and ritual would be determined primarily by religion, although cultural diversity would be recognised as long as it did not contradict the primary loyalty to God. The ultimate mani-festation of such a community would be the whole of humankind living in accordance to God's will.

In concrete terms, unity is demonstrated through the ritual life of the Muslim. Although individual prayer is not discouraged, it is in communal unity that Muslim religious life is fully implemented. Although the *du'a* prayers, individual prayers or group prayers of supplication, take place daily in the mosque, before and after the *salat*, it is in the ritual of the latter that the spirit of *tawhid* is discovered. Muslims gather in rows, shoulder to shoulder, facing towards Makkah, repeating with each other a series of movements and words, culminating in prostration, an act of submission before the over-whelming awesomeness of Allah's unity and uniqueness. In the month of Ramadan, the sacred time when the Qur'an was first revealed, when the barriers that divide the divine world from the creation are thin and easily bridged, all adult Muslims should fast, and millions do, abstaining from drink, food, and sex from the hours of sunrise to sunset. In *zakat*, the divine imperative to provide for the needy, the thrust towards community, is strengthened.

But, arguably, the most marked series of ritual actions to demon-strate and to encourage the sense of unity takes place on the annual Hajj, the pilgrimage to Makkah. In a series of activities, beginning in and culminating in the circumambulation of the Ka'aba, millions of Muslims, male and female, of all nations and cultures, rich and poor, try to surrender their individual identity into the religious *gemeinschaft* by wearing the same garb, a single white cotton sheet, and shaving their heads whilst performing identical ritual acts. Each performance re-enacts a special mythopoeic moment in the relation between God and humankind, uniting each Muslim into a sense of oneness that bridges a sacred past and the present time, overwhelming the usual human divisions of culture, language, status and wealth. Thus the rituals of the Hajj cement the bonds of community in an epiphanic imminence, whilst also strengthening the individual in his or her relation with their creator and encouraging a return to *fitra*. As stated by Abu Majid: 'The concept of unity is exemplified in the performance of the congregational and Friday prayers, pilgrimage and the *qurban*, or sacrifice, where collective efforts are required (Majid, 2003:470).

Unity then is paramount in Islam and has to be sought in social structures, ritual observation, family life and within each human being. Not only is God to be declared as one, incorporating within the declaration a deep distrust of Islam's sister monotheism of Christianity, which on the surface seems to have risked the integrity of *tawhid* through the doctrines of Trinity and Incarnation, but also humanity and all existence is rooted in the idea of divine unity. The recognition of difference is not denied but rather affirmed as long as it fades before the overwhelming presence of the majesty of God. Thus *tawhid* indicates not only a puritanical monotheism but also an awareness of wholeness in human affairs, nature and the individual human psyche.

Thus it is to *tawhid* that Muslims ideally look in order not only to discover the nature of the divine, but to create political systems, a theosophical understanding of human nature, the dynamics of community living and respect for other beings. As stated by Othman Llewellyn:

> Among the essential aspects of *tawhid*, the affirmation of God's oneness, is to recognize that God is the one and only Lord of every created being. Therefore every single creature must be treated with *taqwa*, or reverence towards its Creator, and to serve the Lord of all being, one must do the greatest good one can to His entire creation. (Llewellyn, 2003:188)

Transcendence and immanence

Although some Muslim writers have mainly focused on the oneness of God in the context of opposition to polytheism, or more specifically placing something created either by God or human agency, whether an object or an ideal, alongside God thus usurping his supremacy as the sole object of human worship, others have gone further and promoted the idea of 'all-inclusiveness'. Although there are dangers in this approach to *tawhid*, in that monotheism can easily become pantheism or monism, the Qur'an itself speaks of Allah as both immanent and transcendent. Certainly the primary mood of the Qur'an is on transcendence, a remote Supreme Being who exists beyond his creation but yet brings all creation into existence through the primal command 'Be' and to whom all beings exist in submission, each in their allotted place and role; but the Qur'an also declares that Allah is closer to human beings than their jugular veins.

For many Muslims, especially those belonging to religio-political movements such as the Wahhabis, the fear of diluting *tawhid* results in an emphasis on transcendence to the exclusion of considering Allah's immanence. In such forms of uncompromising monotheism the emphasis is on the uniqueness of God, his absolute 'otherness' or incomparability to anything in creation. As noted by Frederick Denny, Islamic ritual is the expression of doctrine (Denny, 1985:64) and so is architecture. In this respect, ritual and architecture unite with each other to protect Allah's transcendence. No images or representations of the sacred or even likenesses of Muhammad are found in the mosque or in Muslim sacred art. Only the unaided imagination can reach out to the divine being, but even that would be considered a risk by the strictest adherents of Islamic monotheism – leading to the danger of creating a false image within the mind itself.

The act of ritual prayer provides the unique physical movements to demonstrate submission and servitude, which then make a concrete expression of *tawhid*. At the same time, the mosque is kept deliberately empty of any images or forms that may distract from Allah's overwhelming transcendence or assist in creating anthropomorphic conceptions or visualisations of the divine presence.

On the other hand, as stated by Said and Funk, the emphasis on transcendence can lead to forms of orthodoxy where love and intimacy in the relationship between creator and created are almost completely ignored. They both argue that this can lead to forms of Islam where *tawhid* is understood as remoteness, downplaying ideas of the unity of existence or the reflection of divine attributes in the human. In such paradigms, peace is perceived as merely the absence of war or the lack of civil order and there is likely to be a political element to the interpretation of *tawhid*, developed from a theology of sovereignty (Said and Funk, 2003:168) that spills over into Islamic political theory.

Yet immanence is there in Islam. Although Islam is a religion of divine majesty, Allah is also manifested to his subjects through beauty and love. Love, by definition, requires a personal God who is able to be intimate with his people and the Qur'an states: 'And He is with you wheresoever you may be' (57:4). In spite of the overwhelming emphasis on the incomparability and omnipotence of God, the Qur'an indicates that he is both *tanzil* (far) and *tashbih* (near). For many Muslims, the spirituality of Islam is discovered in the presence of Allah within his creation. The Qur'an describes Allah as *al-Muhit*, the all-encompassing (4:126) and *al-Mawjud*, the ever-present (10:32). Thus it is possible for the Muslim to find the divine presence throughout creation, and at the deepest level Allah is ultimately the universe itself, for he creates out of his own being rather than *ex nihilo*. Allah is the ultimate reality, the truth (*al-Haqq*) of existence (*al-Wujud*). For the Sufis, the mystics of Islam, the preoccupation is on the unity or oneness of the divine being, rather than his uniqueness, and is best understood by the idea of *wahdat al-wujud* (the unity of existence). Sufism will be explored in Chapter 7, but suffice it to say at this point that the emphasis on divine unity and the belief in Allah's intimacy with the created leads to a different understanding of God, humanity and nature. In this paradigm, love predominates and peace is understood as a state of being where the human being lives in accordance with *fitra*, experiencing the divine presence both within the purified heart and without, in harmony with nature. In such a paradigm the whole universe has been created for worship rooted in experience of the divine presence. At its ultimate expression, *tawhid* is a human experience of oneness with the divine being rather than a statement about the nature of God. For the Sufi, the experience of *tawhid* is the culmination of a life spent in remembrance of Allah possibly resulting in ecstatic intimacy. The transformation of the simple statement of the oneness of God into an experience associated with a spiritual elite, able to attain a state where they are transformed to such a degree that they cease to exist before the overwhelming presence of God, offers a radical reinterpretation of *tawhid*. The danger is that it leaves the ordinary believer's understanding and practice of Islam, although sufficient, in a lower category of experience and comprehension. This effectively provides a two-level understanding of the Prophetic revelation in which the mass of Muslims operate only on an exoteric level of understanding and practice, with an elite able to achieve an esoteric possibility of oneness.

Although the term *tawhid* is not found in the Qur'an, the principle of God's oneness is imbedded in the central message of the revelation and is proclaimed on numerous occasions. The Qur'an states on thirteen occasions that Allah is the 'sole divinity', and in a further twenty-nine instances proclaims *'la illaha illa huwa'* (there is no divinity other than He), a variation on the first clause of the *shahada*, that is also known as *kalimat al-tawhid* (Gimaret, 2001). Islam has even been called *ahl al-tawhid* (the way of unity) by some Muslim authors and jurists.

The embodiments of *tawhid*
The mosque

The English word 'mosque' is a derivative of the Spanish 'mesquito' but the Arabic original is *'masjid'*, a place of ritual prostration, the act of submission that acknowledges the awesome presence of God's unity. The simplicity of the mosque reveals the majesty of early Islam's ascetic monotheism, and although court architecture and the variety of cultures in which Islam has been imbedded have produced splendour and magnificence of design and construction, the basics of the ideal of simplicity remain unchanged. Even to this day, countless village mosques replicate the same basic architectural features that would have been found in the earliest mosques.

The first mosque was built in Medina to house the Prophet and his family and was erected to Muhammad's own specifications. It was primarily a home for Muhammad and his family and a community centre for the growing number of Muslims. The *Encyclopaedia of Islam* describes the edifice as a 'near-square enclosure of some 56 x 53 metres with a single entrance; a double range of palm-trunk columns thatched with palm leaves was added to the *qiblah* side, with a lean-to for destitute Companions to the south-east and nine huts for Muhammad and his wives along the western perimeter' (Samb, 2001). Certainly the first Muslims prayed there but there is no evidence that it was considered a place of prayer and it would be in keeping with Muhammad's vision of the earth as a place of prostration that he had no intention of creating a special sacred space for Muslim worship other than the Ka'aba in Makkah (Samb, 2001).

However, the simplicity of the structure was in keeping with both Muhammad's personal life and the ascetic monotheism of early Islam.

Over 80 per cent of the interior was open courtyard and it was this that became the first feature of the early mosques. This emptiness would reflect the doctrine of *tawhid*, as it imposed no conception that could anthropomorphise the deity. However, the emptiness of the courtyard fitted precisely the requirements of Muslim ritual prayer and the large communal Friday gatherings. It was not until 673CE that the mosque in Amr at Fustat provided a place from which the call to prayer could be made (Samb, 2001). It was not until as late as the ninth century that covered arcades were added to provide shade. However, the addition of a covered area over the *qiblah* known as the *musalla* was not undertaken to reinforce the idea that one part of the mosque was more sacred than another, as this would provide a hier-archical notion to the geography of sanctity that would contradict the ideal of equality and unity of all creation before God. Yet the *musalla* did provide a new model for the mosque where the courtyard itself could disappear, and the mosque itself could be enclosed and cov-ered. Thus the dome over the *qiblah* became the covering for the mosque itself. Later, when Islam became the religion of an empire, mosques were built under the patronage of the rulers but simplicity and harmony remained the central features.

The architectural features of a mosque replicate the main function of the edifice as a place of ritual prayer held five times a day and the special gathering of the community on Friday when the sermon (*qutbah*) delivered by the *imam* takes place. The central place of ritual prayer in Islam dictates the features of the mosque. Prayer requires *wudu*, the ritual purification, a secondary ritual in which head, ears, nose, mouth, feet and arms are washed in a prescribed fashion. Once in a state of ritual purity the worshippers can declare their intention to Allah, made to ensure sincerity of worship. Thus mosques will commonly have a water supply situated at the entrance, usually in the courtyard, or in the case of mosques in Western countries, a series of specially constructed wash places off the lobby before entering the prayer-hall. However, in places where water is not available, such as in the desert, sand can be used for *wudu*, the ritual cleansing. The only other required feature is the *qiblah*, the ornamental arched niche set in the wall that faces towards Makkah and which gives the direction of prayer. Commonly, mosques will contain: a *minbar*, a raised platform from which the *imam* delivers the Friday sermon; a minaret, from which the prayer call (*adhan*) goes out to the local people to remind them that it is time to pray; and a dome. None of these are essentials but have become traditional features. The simplest structure of a mosque would be the temporary *masjids* made by nomadic people in the desert, where a rectangle is drawn in the sand and one side of the rectangle is marked as the *qiblah*.

In two respects, the mosque's features reflect *tawhid*: the first is the absence of any images of the deity or principal figures significant in the formation of the religion. Essentially, the mosque is a space, an empty arena to provide room for worship. In many of the larger mosques of the Middle East and South Asia, where climate permits, this space may be outdoors with only the *qiblah*-facing wall containing the dome. The empty space has nothing to detract the worshipper from ritual prayer, but more significantly provides no means by which the imagination can reach out to visualise or conceptualise the awesome uniqueness of Allah incomparable with any aspect of creation. The only decorative feature will be the Arabic calligraphy from verses of the Qur'an.

The second feature is the way in which the mosque turns the worshipper towards worship through focus on a single point. This one-pointedness reflects the manifestation of *tawhid* as unity. In this case, unity is expressed as the one-pointed concentration of the human faculties upon God and the sublimation of the individual into the community of worship. The *wudu* and the stating of intent allow for the turning away from the world, a gathering together of the individual's outwardly focused mind and body to a renewal of the promise to submit. Entering the prayer-hall, the *qiblah* provides a point of direction but does not in any way suggest that it is the focus of worship. The worshippers will form lines, shoulder to shoulder, performing the rituals of submission together behind the *imam*, whose role is to maintain unison and concentration rather than to intercede in any way on behalf of the gathering or even to be a leader of the community of worshippers.

Mosques do have other functions besides prayer. They sponsor Qur'anic recitations, are an area for retreats during Ramadan, collect and distribute donations for charity, and provide the space for marriages and funerals. In addition, many of them will also supply religious education – instruction in the Qur'an, Hadith and Islamic law, often maintaining small schools – and act as locations for visiting preachers, but the primary function is prayer (Esposito, 2003a).

can be argued that the mosque does not constitute a sacred space and that no one mosque is superior to another. The Qur'an is insistent that the creation itself is sacred and Muhammad is said to differ from all other messengers of God in that there is no sacred territory associated with the revelation entrusted to him. Indeed, Muslims are free to pray wherever they are, and there are some who suggest that even the architectural features of the mosque only symbolise the wider creation, the dome, for example, being compared with the shape of the heavens above the earth.

As stated by Westcoat, 'the sacredness of mosques differs from that of shrines by virtue of their role as places for collective community prayer directly with Allah, with no intercession by saints' (Westcoat, 2003:521). Westcoat also points out that the mosque is in close accord with the Qur'anic theology of Paradise in that it provides a space where the individual can direct their behaviour towards the attainment of reward in the afterlife. This confirms the idea that the mosque provides an environment to concentrate the mind of the worshipper primarily on *tawhid* as the uniqueness of God. There is no suggestion here of intimacy and union with the divine but rather distance is maintained from Allah who offers only the reward of the attainment of Paradise to the faithful rather than his own presence. As we shall see, the *mazar* or shrine offers a sacred space with a very different paradigm of relationship with the divine.

The mazar or qubbah

Most shrines are built upon the tombs of Muslim holy men, and sometimes women, the most auspicious being those that contain the remains of Muhammad's Companions, earlier prophets and the countless *awliya* or 'friends of God'. Often described in English as 'saints', the *awliya* are more commonly known as Sufis. The graves of the holy are visited by millions of Muslims who seek their spiritual blessings (*baraka*) and their ability to intercede with Allah on behalf of the petitioner. Some village shrines, built over graves that contain the bodies of the particularly pious, are very simple affairs, no more than elaborate gravestones, but some of the famous shines of well-known Sufis are very elaborate, where raised tombs are housed in mausoleums able to provide space for petitioners to offer prayers that request intercession and to circumambulate the remains of the saint. The complexes can contain satellite tombs of relatives and disciples, including the hundreds of graves of descendants and successors who have administered the shrine complex down through time. In addition, the site may contain a mosque, communal kitchen areas for feeding pilgrims and the needy, guest houses, administration offices, and religious schools. The most popular sites are visited by millions every year.

Although the shrine will be visited by the committed on a regular basis, the main occasion for gathering will be the *urs* or death day of the saint, known as a 'wedding day' for it is the day in which he or she met with Allah. On such festivals, hundreds of thousands can attend the more well-known shrines in the Muslim world, especially those in the Indian subcontinent. It has been commented by some scholars that the shrines particularly offer an alternative location of worship for women who have marginal status in the mosque (Esposito, 2003b). There may be an element of this in female attendance at shrines or it may be that women are more likely to seek the intervention of the holy to assist their petitions in times of family crisis. However, it should not be assumed that shrines are places where only females participate, for, on the contrary, tens of thousands of men also attend especially at the time of *urs*. Yet it is true that women are often seen in abundance in deep and prolonged prayer around the outer walls of the *mazar*.

The ritual activity around a shrine is very different from that which takes place in a mosque, and so are the architectural features. Whereas the mosque protects Allah's transcendence, the tomb-shrine seems to come dangerously close to worship of the human. The most common practice is to take fine coverings, usually coloured green and sometimes embellished with embroidered verses of the Qur'an or sayings of the Prophet, and to lay them on the tomb thus covering the saint's remains. In the Indian subcontinent the petitioner will usually shower the tomb with rose petals. The pilgrim often bows at the feet end of the tomb and offers up *du'a* prayers, private prayers independent of the ritual *salat*, often to make petitions requiring the saint's intercession.

The functionaries at the tomb are not *imams*, but usually the family descendants of the original saint. They provide prayers for the petitioners at their request and supervise the rituals, often supplying the materials used in veneration in exchange for donations. They may also offer counsel for special problems and even healing in the name of the saint. However, countless small rural shrines will be unattended except by petitioners.

Pnina Werbner identifies the rituals of the subcontinent shrine as duplicating the rituals of a wedding. She describes witnessing the occasion of early ritual veneration of the grave of Zindapir, a well-known Pakistani Sufi who died in 2002. She writes:

> Since his death however, the wedding theme has come to be enacted in practice very clearly through the placing of *chaddars* on the grave. The men approach the grave carrying the *chaddar* by its four corners so that it is raised horizontally above the ground, much as the *chaddar* is carried to be placed over the bride's head during the *mehndi* ritual. As they process through the *darbar*, people throw rupee banknotes intended as *nazrana* or *sadaqat* on to the horizontally held cloth, just as they do at *mehndis*. The procession arrives at the grave singing, before the men jointly cover the raised mound, much as a bride would be covered. Rose petals and other garlands of flowers or bank notes are also thrown on the grave, just as they are at weddings. (Werbner, 2003:253)

The network of shrines at the tombs of saints provides religious sites that can be argued to be a sacred space within Islam. Pilgrims to the shrines expect an inner transformation or a change of circumstances that results from contact with the sacred. Eade and Sallnow describe the process as a series of transactions or sacred exchanges which they label 'sacred commerce' (Eade and Sallnow, 1991:24). Through the process of sometimes elaborate ritual, the blessings of the saint in the tomb are transferred to various objects which can then be taken away from the shrine to the pilgrim's home and used to revitalise their life and also distributed to the local community of Muslims, especially those devoted to the saint. These may consist of rose petals, blessed water, coloured threads to tie around the wrist, verses from the Qur'an, or pieces of cloth and other objects that may be associated with the saint or unique to his tomb.

This sacralisation of objects has to be understood within the context of both sacralisation of space and the sacralisation of person. It is, first and foremost, the living saint who has purified himself and the space around him who provides a very different articulation of *tawhid*. The saint will have embarked initially upon a process of self-purification and conquest of the *nafs* (self, ego) through remembrance of Allah's names, retreats, ascetic lifestyle, prayer and fasting. He or she will also have lived under the discipline and spiritual authority of a Sufi.

The classic pattern is for the saint to undergo a migratory journey to promote Islam in the land of 'infidels', sometimes even into a 'wilderness' where he will live an austere lifestyle dedicated only to remembrance of Allah. In either case, the surrounding space, spiritually 'conquered' in the name of Islam, becomes sanctified by the saint's presence and the location of his miracles. The journey is transformatory for the saint, relocating him outside of *'dunya'* (worldly life) and secure in the *din* (way of Allah), but also for human beings who come into contact with him. Thus he becomes not only a conduit for human beings seeking a closer relationship with the divine, but also for God's grace to flow into the world. Although his first priority will be to take those who approach him closer to Allah, he is also likely to be known as a healer of the sick, both mental and physical. However, the saint should not be worshipped or confused with God himself but his intimacy with God can permit veneration. There are those in the Muslim world who feel that the borders between worship and veneration often become blurred.

Thus the sacralisation of the person is based on a different comprehension of God that can sometimes lead to conflict with various self-proclaimed orthodoxies. For the Sufi mystic, *tawhid* is understood as the annihilation of the self into the overwhelming presence of the divine, discovered first and foremost within the human heart. Jalalu'd-Din Rumi (1207–1273), the most well known of the mystics of Islam writes:

> The real Workman is hidden in His workshop,
> Go you into that workshop and see Him face to face
> Whosoever seeks Him without is ignorant of Him.
> Come, then, into His workshop, which is Not-being.
>
> (Whinfield, 1979:71)

The 'Workman' and the 'workshop' are found within the purified human heart, in an act of annihilation of the self and of all phenomenal being, in which every thing disappears except for the presence of the being of God. The person who is able to conquer both inner and outer nature is described by another pre-eminent Sufi, Ibn Arabi as the 'Perfect Man'. This transformed person attains a state of unity with God and thus becomes a centre or pole for the sacred located in the human. For Rumi, such a personage is far preferable as a site of sanctity to Islam's official sacred spaces.

> The sage said, 'Whither are you going, O Bayazid?
> Where will you bring your caravan to a halt?'
> Bayazid replied, 'At dawn I start for the Ka'aba.'
> Quoth the Sage, 'What provision for the way have you?'
> He answered, 'I have two hundred silver dirhams;
> See them tied up tightly in the corner of my cloak.'
> The Sage replied, 'Circumambulate me seven times;
> Count this better than circumambulating the Ka'aba';

Rumi goes on to explain why:

> Of a truth that is God which your soul sees in me,
> For God has chosen me to be His house.
> Though the Ka'aba is the house of His grace and favours,
> Yet my body too is the house of His secret.

> Since he made *that* house He has never entered it,
> But none but that Living One enters *this* house. (p. 89)

The living saint is the embodiment of grace. Pnina Werbner describes the characteristics of Zindapir, the living Sufi she stayed with in Kohat, Pakistan:

> The saint literally glows with *faiz* (grace). He can project it at will, transferring it at a glance to a trusted *khalifa*. It shines with his munificence and beneficence, an inner quality which his appearance and facial expression reveal. (Werbner, 2003:251)

But if the saint is powerful in his lifetime, it is nothing compared with his power and authority after death. The saint is believed to be alive in the grave and a hundred times more powerful. A common saying states that if the power of the saint is so extraordinary when the space he embodies is only confined to the circle immediately around his feet, then imagine how much it is amplified when increased to the size of his reclining form in contact with the earth. This saying indicates how the sacrality of the saint is transferred and embodied in the earth itself which then becomes the embodiment of his sanctity. Tomb shrines not only contain the physical remains but also familiar objects of the saint's daily life. In the larger shrines, satellite sites that commemorate places significant to the events of his life are visited by pilgrims. These may be the place of birth or the site of a miraculous event. These also become sacred locations containing objects able to transmit spiritual blessings. In the mystical theosophy of Muslim sainthood, the true saint transcends this world. In a state of self-purification and abnegation, he travels at death to the highest realms of existence, where he is believed to commune with both Prophet and God. He is given a new transformed body which lives forever. As stated by a disciple of Zindapir and recorded by Werbner:

> Sufis are alive in the grave and their bodies are left untouched in the earth. Their souls are active, they can hear and see what is happening, they can help people after their death. They do not die. (Werbner, 2003:202)

The saint alive in his tomb is a bridge between the petitioner and the transcendental Allah, a link between microcosm and macrocosm, able to intervene on behalf of the needy, for in his lifetime he was filled with the divine presence, possible because the inner world of the human being replicates the proximity of creator and creation. Thus a new arena for intimacy is created in which a transcendental being is given immediacy and proximity through the sacralising of person and geographical space. The remoteness of God established by *tawhid*, when defined as uniqueness, is overcome not by Qur'an and Prophet as is usual in Islam, but rather by the transformation of a person, then extended to territory which is transformed into a space for Allah. Werbner comments that it is 'the divine transformation in space which is the ultimate proof of the divine transformation of the person' (Werbner, 2003:43). After his death, the power of the saint is amplified at his tomb and in the objects that surrounded his life.

Conclusion

The differences discerned in an examination of mosque and shrine are more than superficial, and point to a doctrinal dispute primarily imbedded in the emphasis placed on the two aspects of *tawhid*. Although *tawhid* points towards uncompromising monotheism, the two elements that are constituted within it, namely uniqueness and unity, have divided the Muslim community religiously and ideologically. As stated by the *Oxford Dictionary of Islam, tawhid* is an essential feature of Islamic thought in the contemporary period, as it provides the way forward to assert Islamic unity in a Muslim world torn apart by nationalism, ethnicity, tribalism and post-colonial problems. The *Dictionary* states '*Tawhid* has emerged as a powerful symbol of divine, spiritual, and socio-political unity' (Esposito, 2003c).

Throughout Muslim history, the political significance of *tawhid* has been noted by activists. The thirteenth-century jurist Ibn Taymiyya asserted the emphasis on God's uniqueness and transcendence, passionately declaring Allah to be the creator, sovereign, judge of the world who had set the parameters for human beings. Thus the response to such a divinity was obedience to the divine will through correct religious practice and full implementation of the *shari'a* in every aspect of life, both private and public. Thus social organisation and statecraft are to be guided by religion, and the spiritual and political realms are interlinked through the expression of collective virtuous behaviour according to the teachings of the Qur'an.

The message of Ibn Taymiyya has become increasingly significant in the modern era. It was picked up by the eighteenth-century Arabian reformer Muhammad ibn Abd al-Wahhab (d.1792), who was the first to recognise the revolutionary implications of *tawhid* for revitalising a Muslim world that he perceived to be in a state of decay. The blame for the condition of Islam was laid squarely at the feet of those who had corrupted the understanding of *tawhid* by compromising Islamic unity through their veneration of tombs, belief in intercession of prophets, angels and saints, and an experiential knowledge of unity that challenged the authority of the Qur'an. In his successful attempt to purge Muslims of popular accretions that he considered unIslamic, he drew together the tribes of Arabia in a solidarity based on their allegiance to religion, an echo of the original Islamic achievement under the Prophet. The result was the destruction of countless shrines and tombs in Arabia and the establishment of the modern state of Saudi Arabia, committed ideologically to the promotion and defence of Islam on the Wahhabi model.

Others were to use *tawhid* as an attack on tradition, but it was the crisis created by colonialism, nationalism, secular ideologies and the failure of the Muslim world to attain parity with the West's economic and political dominance that led to the articulation of a worldview based upon *tawhid* that would lead to Islam's recovery and revitalisation. The basic argument of the new twentieth-century radicals such as Sayyid Qutb and Maulana Mawdudi does not depart far from Ibn Taymiyya or Muhammad al-Wahhab. Ideologically it still asserts that society must reflect divine unity through communal submission to the revealed will, but the key difference is that modern Islamic governments had to be the expression of Islamic law. Thus the focus of contemporary Islamic reformers is political unity based upon the unity of all Muslims rooted in a conservative understanding of *tawhid*. The revivalists have spawned two movements, the eighteenth-century Wahhabis who continue to flourish through a number of movements worldwide and the twentieth-century Salafis, who in addition to being anti-West, condemn the practice of saint-veneration at their tombs as an heretical innovation.

So it would seem that in order to draw fully upon the unitive political possibilities of *tawhid*, Muslims will need first to resolve the ancient conflicts that exist with regard to religious understandings of *tawhid* that can still divide the Muslim world. The Wahhabis and Salafis remain a revolutionary reforming force to be reckoned with, but their brand of 'protestant' Islam is rooted in a monotheistic understanding of a transcendent God, unique and other from his creation, who primarily communicates with the human being through the revelation of *shari'a*, the divine law, obedience to which leads to submission. The Sufis, on the other hand, look to *tawhid* as oneness, an inner experience of unity in which the purified heart sees its Lord. So far the two have proved to be incompatible with each other's commitment to their interpretation of Islam.

But bridges do exist, except for those who claim a strict and narrow orthodoxy. The tombs of the Sufis and the Companions or family of Muhammad provide an alternative space to that of the mosque and the *ulema*. The trained *imam* may be able to intellectually provide an exegesis of the Qur'an or preach on the superiority of God's final revelation at the Friday sermon but the saint is regarded as the exemplification of the Qur'an. The mosque can be a place of prayer and education, but the tomb shrine provides the location for the human quest for support and sympathy beyond the realm of the normal when everyday solutions fail.

To some degree the countless shrines provide a counter-culture to the official Islam of the *ulema*, bringing the rewards of mystical contact with the divine into proximity to the common people. Sufis and *ulema* can compete, as we see in later chapters, but they can also subsist with each other in a symbiotic relationship in which the *ulema* require the patronage of the Sufi and the latter needs the support of the *ulema* to keep him in the fold of orthodoxy, or at least within traditional Islam. The tombs provide a bridge between pure mysticism and the more conventional mosque-based Islam and provide sites where common or 'popular' religious practices can be integrated into the norms derived from Qur'an and Hadith. As long as the *shari'a* and the outer focus of Islam are upheld by the supporters of sainthood, there is no reason why the unity of Islam cannot be maintained.

CHAPTER 4

The Shari'a: the law of God or a cultural construct?

Here the tensions exist not so much between competing Muslim communities but between Muslims and Western academic scholars who have written on Islamic law as a cultural construct rather than as the final and complete revelation of God. In addition, the popular media tend to present the shari'a *as only Muslim criminal law, a very small part of the whole. This chapter will focus on how Muslim law is constructed and the various views of Western and Muslim academics regarding its historic development. The debate will centre on the processes of construction, assessing the significance of the Qur'an, Hadith,* ijma, qiyas *and* ijtihad *to Muslims and the tensions that can exist between law construction influenced by human politics, economics and social change and the claim that the* shari'a *is the inviolate and final law of God.*

Introduction
In an article in the *Guardian*, Ali Dizaei, a chief superintendent in London's Metropolitan Police wrote that:

> The British public can be forgiven for believing that, once one enters the Middle East, sensitive, innovative and efficient policing is replaced by that of corrupt, camel-hoarding officials and feudal warlords who chop off the hands of thieves and stone adulterers to death. The implication is that Islam and harmony do not mix . . . (Dizaei, 2004)

Dizaei overturns our usual perceptions of law and order in Muslim society in a perceptive article that demonstrates how millions of

Muslims succeed in staying true to their religion 'but thrive under peace and revere it' (Dizaei, 2004). However, Dizaei, as a police officer interested in the working practices of his colleagues in Dubai, focuses on criminal law. Yet Islamic law, known as the *shari'a*, is far more than that. He is right to point out that Western perceptions dwell on archaic laws concerning punishment for offenders, with little realisation of the full implications of Islamic law and its radical differences from secular law in the West.

Criminal law or *Hadd* (pl. *hudúd*) is an aspect of *shari'a* law, and does comprise of: i) *sariqa* (cutting off the hand for theft); ii) *zinà* (caning or execution for fornication and adultery); iii) *qadhf* (slander or false accusation of fornication and adultery, punishable by caning); iv) *haraba* (highway robbery or rebellion, for which the punishment is amputation of the right hand and left foot, exile, imprisonment, or sometimes execution by crucifixion); v) *shurb al-khamr* (alcohol consumption, punishable by caning); and, sometimes vi) *al-ridda* (apostasy, which is punishable by death). Even so, it should be understood that the punishments prescribed are rarely implemented in most Muslim nations, including those countries that have opted to maintain a more traditional approach to their legal systems.

Within Muslim understandings of law, the *shari'a* is perceived very differently from Western perceptions of law. Literally, it is the 'watering-place', connoting it as an essential requirement for human existence. *Fiqh*, the science of jurisprudence, the codified norms developed from the foundations of the Qur'an and the Hadith, is a fully articulated, functional expression of the totality of Islam. The body of *fiqh* is meant to be universal – that is, it incorporates every conceivable human action. *Fiqh*, then, provides for Muslims the practical understanding and implementation of how to do God's bidding; to live one's life in the most moral and ethical way, considered far too important to leave to the vagaries of human reason and therefore, requiring obedience to the will of a compassionate God known to human beings through revelation.

The ultimate purpose of the *shari'a* is the common good, the welfare of all creation but particularly human beings, who have the stewardship of other creatures. The judgements of the *shari'a* are based on scriptural revelation and their goal is to maintain wholeness and harmony, both at an individual and collective level. As defined by Abdul Said and Nathan Funk:

The principal concern of the Shari'a, or law of Islam, is the maintenance of proper, harmonious relationships on and across all
levels – between the individual and God, within the individual,
within the family and community, among Muslims, between religions, and with all of humanity and creation. (Said and Funk,
2003:160)

However, as we shall see, although the law in its entirety must remain
anchored in the transcendent, from which its moral imperatives
derived, there is a tension between the eternal law of God, revealed
by a sending down (*tanzil*) in the Qur'an, and the systematic creation
of a fully worked corpus of law in Muslim history. It has been up to
human beings to utilise their moral and intellectual faculties to construct and reconstruct God's law through the process of *fiqh*. There are
dangers in this process, as recognised by Nomanhul Haqq:

And a dynamic process of ever-new *shari'a* constructions it is,
since human knowledge could never claim, nor is it capable of
acquiring, epistemological certainty or finality. (Haqq, 2003:139)

Generally, one of the challenges facing the monotheistic religions,
especially Islam and Judaism, is how to resolve the difficulties
created by a belief in a single act of God in which he intervened in
human history through revelation of a divine law, to which the
chosen recipients are beholden until the end of time. A revelation
judged to be comprehensive, but revealed in a localised cultural
milieu and geographical space, in a particular event taking place in a
moment of time, contains tension with its universal applicability as it
moves through time and across territories. There are also challenges
between divine immutability and the constant mutability of human
society. These challenges have been sharpened by the rapid changes
that have taken place in the twentieth and twenty-first centuries.

The monotheistic God of Abraham, Moses, Jesus and Muhammad
is marked by his knowledge of past, present and future. Therefore a
single revelation that is not going to be repeated by future updates
must contain within it all the knowledge required by human beings
until the end of time. Yet both the Torah and the Qur'an were revealed
to a particular people (the nomadic Jews and the tribes of Arabia) at a
particular point in the development of human beings, where human
knowledge, even though God may be omni-prescient, was limited to

both a particular culture and the mores of the time. Yet for those who believe in the revelation it must be comprehensive, going beyond its apparent particularity and answering the questions of the faithful in all aspects of life, even when the religion moves forward in time and across geographical space, subsuming cultures and civilisations remarkably different from the original recipients.

The apparent solution, short of admitting cultural relativity to God's word, is the need for specialist interpreters who are able to search within the hallowed text, applying it to new situations but not interpreting it. In other words, skilled practitioners seek to discover the content that God would have already placed in the revelation, because certainly he possessed knowledge of the human future. In the case of Islam and Judaism, where it is believed that God provided a comprehensive way of life revealed as a binding covenant between human and creator, and a legal contract with a Lord who is both Judge and Sovereign, such specialists are more jurists than priest. Their area of expertise is jurisprudence and they are not intermediate between humankind and God.

However, jurisprudence in modern Western societies is usually regarded as the science or philosophy of human law rather than skill in understanding God. Yet Islam went on to become the foundation of nations, empires and a civilisation where the law of God was developed to become the law of the land. Those who had the training to interpret the original revelation contained in the Qur'an and the sayings and deeds of the Prophet as recorded by his Companions, the body of literature known as the Hadith, as well as the corpus of law developed by their predecessors, were not merely philosophers and theologians but functionaries of the legal system, both making decisions and passing sentences in law courts.

For the system to work, ordinary Muslims had to be assured that their judges and scholars were not diluting the word of Allah and creating a legal system based on their own judgements, however skilful and learned they may have been deemed to be. In addition, the scholars themselves needed to be secure in the knowledge that time-honoured practices existed for the application of God's law to new situations that protected them from human interpretation or error. The revelation was sacrosanct so the processes of law-making had to be trustworthy. Although the title of this chapter suggests a dichotomy between the revelation of the law of God and a law-making process involving interpretation, the contrast of the two is a concern for 'insiders', not necessarily the judgement of the 'outsider' scholar who may well consider all such activity to be uniquely human. Yet it was, and remains to this day, an urgent imperative for the Muslim to distinguish the two. The choices are simple: either the original revelation was not complete and needs to be supplemented by human law-making, an unthinkable conclusion to the believer; or the original revelation and its subsequent development were both somehow equally the activity of God. Another possibility to be considered by Muslims would be that the original revelation was of divine origin but the subsequent creation of a body of law was a human construction, as prone to error as all human activity.

The difficulty is that the Qur'an itself does not appear to contain a prescription for every human activity and actually has very little to say even on statecraft and jurisprudence outside of personal family law. Even though the Qur'an is supported by the four volumes of Hadith that contain the Prophet's actions and deeds, for he was considered to be an exemplar of obedience to the divine imperative, the genius of the first generations of Muslims was to codify this into a system of jurisprudence. It would regulate not only the lives of Arab tribes but the far more sophisticated conquered territories of the Byzantine and Persian Empires, and succeed in maintaining the trust of most Muslims that the revelation had been placed in safe hands for most Muslims.

The process of developing this system of jurisprudence, however, went far beyond a legal system. The *shari'a*, as it came to be known, provided a comprehensive categorisation of God's commands and recommendations that was able to regulate every aspect of human existence from 'worship and ritual equal with legal rules, political, toilet, greetings and table manners' (Schacht, 1952). Schacht later claimed that 'Islamic law was the core and kernel of Islam itself' (1964:1). Fazlur Rahman states, 'It is the Way, ordained by God, wherein man is to conduct his life, in order to realise the Divine Will' (Rahman, 1979). Islamic law does this by prescribing all human activity, including how and what to eat, when to wash, what clothing to wear, how and when to perform religious rites, including fasting and prayer, commercial transactions, relations with non-Muslims, rules of warfare and crime.

The Qur'an

For Muslims it is axiomatic that the Qur'an is untouched by any human input, and contains only the unadulterated word of God.

Muhammad is only the human voice, uttering something that he received from the divine realm via Jibreel, the angelic messenger known to Christians as Gabriel. The Qur'an, revealed to Muhammad over a twenty-two-year period, is pure and is believed to have been pre-existent in Paradise, from where it was commanded by divine will to descend to Muhammad, the last of the prophets. For Christians tempted to compare Jesus with Muhammad, this is a mistake, for it is the Qur'an that comes closest to the role of Christ in Christianity. The inspiration of the Qur'an goes beyond the message and extends to the actual sound of the recitation, which is literally hearing the spoken words of God. Thus there is an eternal Qur'an, the word of God that remains eternally with him, the Qur'an that was revealed to Muhammad on the first command to 'recite' and which was then spoken by him to others as he preached. It is then extended on to the hearts of the listeners and their recitation of its verses, and finally in the inscription of the recitation, the production of the earthly book, which in turn continues to be recited and memorised by the faithful. It is the central tenet of the Muslim understanding of revelation that in this process the Qur'an remains unchanged, unlike, it is believed, the sacred texts delivered to the Jews and Christians. Thus it remains the last and ultimate scripture, the fullest testament of God's will and it is the responsibility of the Muslim community to protect its integrity.

The verses of the Qur'an can be divided into those delivered at Makkah and those revealed in Medina. The earlier Makkan revelation essentially contains ecstatic and fervent verses on the oneness and uniqueness of God, a criticism of idolatry, the need for worship and submission and the absolute inescapability of death and judgement. These are supported by examples from the lives of earlier prophets, especially those prominent in the Jewish worldview. It is only after the *Hijra*, the migration to Medina in the face of Makkan persecution, and the subsequent invitation to Muhammad to become a leader in that city, that we find the Qur'an providing judicial and communal directives, especially those concerning family law, for the fledgling Muslim faith community.

Although the visual world of the Qur'an obviously draws upon the terrain of the desert Arab and its analogies belong to their everyday activities in the marketplace and the desert, Muslims are not dismayed by this evidence of particularity. They, after all, believed themselves to be the recipients of the final revelation and the replacement of the previous 'People of the Book' as God's new people. They expected God's omniscience to be aware of this and teach submission, wonder, reverence and gratitude through examples familiar to them. Nor was it a problem that the Qur'an engages with actual events in the life of Muhammad, sometimes even his domestic life. Although the book has an eternal existence, when it is revealed it engages with actual events in the life of its recipient. Islamic theology was later to call this *'Aszab al-Nuzul'* – occasions for the calling down of revelation, rather than the cause.

During the life of the Prophet it is said that he recited the Qur'an shortly before his death and that each new verse was identified and given its place in the overall structure of the existing revelations. These verses were then recorded by selected scribes on any object that could be used for transcription. It is also confirmed that several of the Companions wrote down the text for their own use and several hundred others memorised its contents.

If there was a problem period when the Qur'an was at risk, it must have been on the death of Muhammad, when the human source of revelations was no longer around to consult on matters of clarity, or to interpret personal or social issues of the early Muslims from its content. In addition, it had to be held in trust that the revelation was now completed. Although Muslims are certain that the verses had all been collected and memorised if not actually inscribed in totality, the information that Abu Bakr, who took on the leadership of the community and called for the final text to be written, had to destroy rival versions, would suggest to outsiders that the process of compilation was not as risk-free as Muslims would like to confess.

It was Umar Ibn al-Khattib who urged Abu Bakr to ensure the security of the text as the original Companions died either peacefully of old age or in armed struggles. The first authenticated version was presented to Abu Bakr by Zayed Ibn Thabit and was kept in the residence of one of the Prophet's wives. As the Muslim territory expanded copies were made of the original and sent around the Muslim world (Perspectives, 1997). Although there was the possibility for inaccuracy, addition or omission to occur in this process, we must also take into account that oral culture contains individuals with remarkable powers of memory. There would have to have been agreement between those entrusted with the awesome responsibility to maintain Allah's words passed on to the Prophet of God for the benefit of all humanity. This was too important a task to fail because of disagreements over the content.

Hadith

A more problematic issue would have been the inescapable fact that on the surface the Qur'an does not deal with every circumstance in life. However, it must somehow contain in some form all that is necessary for every human eventuality if it is the final revelation of God's will. After all, when eternal rewards and punishments were at stake, only an unkind deity would leave such matters of ultimate import to human reason or conscience. Both faculties, however honed by experience and inspiration, were imperfect tools for determining God's will and thus the divine mercy provided revelation, so that nothing was left to chance.

To interpret the Qur'an carried risks but wasn't there already a perfect exemplar who had lived by its tenets and explained its meaning to his community throughout his life? Thus the early Muslims turned to the Prophet of God to further their understanding of how to live by the revelation. Imitation of the Prophet became crucial to the life of the devout and in time some realised that it was crucial to collect his words and record his deeds.

It would only be human nature for the close Companions of the Prophet to remember his deeds and words and live by them. He had, after all, been their teacher and guide. However, it would also have been human nature for his words and deeds to proliferate like Chinese whispers as the Arab expansion brought in thousands of new subjects converting to the religion of their conquerors. As new situations became more complex, governance more sophisticated, morality more diverse, so many must have used, probably sincerely although perhaps at times cynically, examples from the Prophet's career to justify their actions and re-order societies now in the domain of Islam. In time, it became an imperative to sort the wheat from the chaff and try to determine the accuracy of the multitude of sayings regarding Muhammad. If such statements were going to be used as the first line of support for the Qur'an's revelations, Muslims needed to be able to ensure that they were genuine. One simple test was already there; they must be in harmony with the words of the Qur'an itself. Muhammad's role as arbiter and exemplar brooked no contradiction with its content. But what of situations where the Qur'an appeared to be silent?

Certainly the transformation of a religious movement to an empire and world civilisation would have encouraged some Muslim rulers and even religious authorities to collect and possess traditions that were favourable to supporting their claims. Scholars would have utilised the sayings to remind Muslims of their religious duties, claiming authority back to the Prophet through use of his words. The caliphs, especially those of the Umayyad dynasty trying to regulate an empire, would not have been shy of invention for political purposes and the various schools of interpretation developing in the first century of Muslim history would have collected Hadith that supported their respective theological positions. In an early twentieth-century study, Margoulieth argued that the civil war between Ali, Muhammad's son-in-law, and A'isha, the Prophet's youngest wife, would have spawned Hadith to justify the position of the protagonists (Margoulieth, 1914). Even earlier at the turn of the nineteenth century, Goldziher argues that the Hadith were the result of religious, historical and social developments in the first two centuries of Islam (Goldziher, 1890).

However, this situation of proliferation had not always been so, even though the Companions probably did record and memorise the sayings of their beloved Prophet and spiritual guide, it is said that Muhammad forbade the recording of his words as they may have resulted in Muslims being confused between them and his utterances that were part of the as yet uncodified Qur'an. The third caliph, Umar ibn Abd al-Aziz, forbade the recording of Hadith (Rahman, 1979), but the Prophet's death and the codification of the Qur'an provided Muslims with a clear knowledge of its contents and any confusion with Muhammad's extempore statements could then be avoided. Thus the obstacles were removed and by the end of Islam's first century Hadith were beginning to proliferate. Tradition also states that it was the third caliph who began the process of sending out emissaries throughout Muslim territory to record the sayings and deeds of the Prophet.

A serious dilemma now existed for Muslim scholars and religious leaders. There was no question of Muhammad's ex-cathedra authority as already the idea of the Prophet's infallibility was developing as doctrine. This belief was given authority by the tradition that asserts that Muhammad's beloved wife Ayesha, when asked the question

what it was like to live with him, replied it was like living with the
Qur'an. Even though many of the Prophet's words were additional to
revelation, Muslims could not conceive that he could possibly contradict it. The Qur'an itself supported this position with the verse that
states, 'And what the Prophet gives unto you take it, and what he for-
bids desist from it' (Qur'an 56:7). On the other hand, it was essential
to create a means of resolving which statements or deeds attributed to
him were genuine. Only then could the *Sunna* (the way of the
Prophet) come to exist as the second most powerful influence on
Muslim life after the Qur'an, and supplement the revelation.

Although the *'sunna al-nabi'* was surely practised by the
Companions during Muhammad's lifetime, replacing the ways of the
ancestors that provided tradition to the Arabs with a new prophetic
imitation, still in the first two centuries of Islam scholars embarked
on a vigorous exercise to collect and authenticate the traditions associated with Muhammad's name. There are disagreements amongst
Western scholars of Islam concerning the dating, for example whether
there was only oral transmission in the first century or whether
oral and written collections took place simultaneously, but the main
distinction between the Orientalists and Muslim scholars is over
authenticity and reliability not dating.

Margoulieth argues that memories were becoming weak, the names
of intermediaries who carried the tradition forward had been forgotten and the exact words lost. Schacht also talks about loss of memory
and material and even falsification by political leaders. Certainly the
problem of jurists and theologians working with state patronage, and
the benefits it brought, would have meant decisions being made to
support policy. Others rigorously rejected state-sponsored Islam as a
political dilution of the Prophet's way of life and looked for contradictory statements as evidence for their own claim to religious purity.

The Muslim solution was to create collections of sayings and deeds
of the Prophet whose reliability is based on the links in the chain of
transmission. Thus each individual Hadith consists of two parts; *matn*,
the content and *isnad*, the chain that linked it back to a Companion
and then the Prophet himself. The scrutiny of the chain became
almost as important as understanding the content in the development
of the authoritative *Sunna*. Establishing the character and reliability of
the chain became known as the Science of Justification and
Impugnment. To this day, a debate over right doctrine or action
between Muslims will not only utilise rival Hadiths but each protag-

onist will seek to prove that the *isnad* of his Hadith is stronger than that of his rival. Each *isnad* has been classified as weak, truthful, unknown and completely trustworthy. Finally, after this process of classification, six collections of Hadith were established as authentic; those of Abu Da'ud (d.275), Al Tirmidhi (d.279), al-Nas'ai (d.303), Ibn Maja (d.273), Muslim ibn al-Hajjaj (d.261) and Muhammad ibn Isma'il al-Bukhari (d.256). Amongst these the collections of Muslim ibn al-Hajjaj and al-Bukhari are regarded as the most authoritative amongst the Sunnis. Rahman notes that the collection of al-Bukhari is considered to be second only to the authority of the Qur'an itself (Rahman, 1979:63–64). The Shi'a created their own collection in which the chains of transmission consisted of the infallible *imams* who inherited the leadership from Ali and the Prophet's grandchildren.

The general rule was that the *Sunna* could not contradict the Qur'an but where Hadith conflicted with each other, then it was the *isnad* that provided the next link in affirming authority. Thus in the process of authenticating the chain, it also became important to develop a category of knowledge that was concerned with the reputations and character of the narrators. The science of assessing *isnad* gave rise to *Asma al-Rijal* (the names of the men), a collection of biographies that looked at veracity and reliability through exploration of the lives of the narrators. A typical *isnad* would state in direct speech 'A related to us that B and C had informed him that D had asked the Prophet of God . . .' The character of the person who asked the question of the Prophet was ensured as it would be a Companion or close family member.

The process was rigorous; not only were elaborate systems developed to test the chain but any tradition which occurred before more than one witness, must be reported by several narrators. For example, if a gathering of Companions were present when the Prophet pronounced on something, but only one narration was provided, the Hadith was not acceptable. Doi mentions that the process was so vigorous that out of 600,000 traditions collected, only 7,397 were selected by al-Bukhhari (Doi, 1984:54).

It was not only the *isnad* that were subject to scrutiny: the *matn* were also under a critical process that observed the following conditions:

1. The Hadith should not be contrary to the text or the teachings of the Qur'an or the accepted basic principles of Islam.
2. The Hadith should not be against the dictates of reason or the laws of nature or common experience.

3. The Hadith should not be contrary to the Traditions which have
   already been accepted by the authorities as reliable and authentic
   by applying all the above principles.
4. The Hadith which sings the praises and excellence of any tribe,
   place or person should be generally rejected.
5. The Hadith that contains the dates and minute details of the future
   should be rejected.
6. The Hadith that contains some remarks of the Prophet which are
   not in keeping with the Islamic belief of the Prophethood and the
   position of the Holy Prophet or such expression as may not be suit-
   able to him, should also be rejected. (Doi, 1984:55)

Mention should also be given to the important and highly venerated
Hadith al-Qudsi. These are Hadith whose chain consists of only
Muhammad, who then refers to having heard Allah himself state
something. However, although the meaning and contents are from
Allah, the form of wording is by Muhammad, thus distinguishing the
Hadith al-Qudsi from the contents of the Qur'an. A typical Hadith of
this type will begin with 'Said the Messenger of Allah, that Almighty
Allah said'.

Thus the traditions of the Prophet came to exist as a second source
in addition to the primary root of the Qur'an, and as a sacred text in
its own right. Together the Qur'an and the Hadith provided a root
from which law could be derived. Where the Qur'an was specific, no
further elaboration was required; where the Qur'an gave only universal principles, the *Sunna* (the way of the Prophet gleaned from the
Hadith) provided specificity; where the Qur'an revealed commandments, Muhammad provided examples of practice; where the Qur'an
was general, prophetic explanation and example filled in the detail.
Thus Qur'an and *Sunna* provided the authority which is believed to
be unchanged throughout time and circumstance. For either to fail
would effectively reduce Islam from God's sovereignty to a fallible
human half-truth, as happened with the revelations that came before
them. However, there were new circumstances and problems that
arose in the course of time when the solution appeared to receive no
guidance from either Qur'an or *Sunna*.

In addition to the above problems, the jurists of Islam were faced
with the challenge of producing, from the essentially religious and
ethical contents of the Qur'an and Hadith, a comprehensive legal system that could cope with the complexities of ruling an empire that

was rapidly gaining territory and would eventually extend from Europe to India. In order to achieve this aim, three mechanisms were developed to ensure that the spirit of the revelation was maintained.

Ijtihad

The belief in *ijtahad-nabawi*, the capacity of Muhammad to resolve problems that were not discussed in the Qur'an, because it was believed that the prophetic intelligence is endowed with wisdom and greater intelligence than permitted to ordinary human intelligence, had provided the means to authenticate the Hadith as another primary source of authority. However, individual but qualified scholars were also to begin the process of developing responses to new situations by going to the Qur'an and the Hadith. Doi argues that the first three generations of Muslims only went to the Qur'an and Traditions of the Prophet (1984:64) but a Hadith clearly states that where necessary individual interpretation is permissible.

> When the apostle of Allah intended to send Mu'adh ibn Jabal to the Yemen, he asked: 'How will you judge when the occasion of deciding a case arises?' He replied, 'I shall judge in accordance with Allah's Book.' He sked, 'What will you do if you do not find guidance in Allah's Book?' He replied, 'I will act in accordance with the *Sunna* of the Messenger of Allah.' He asked, 'What will you do if you do not find guidance in the *Sunna* of the Apostle of Allah and in Allah's Book?' He replied, 'I shall do my best to form an opinion and spare no pains.' The Apostle of Allah then patted him on the breast. (Nyazee, 1994:3)

However, to control the undesirable possibility of individual interpretation that was not rooted in wisdom or inspiration, the jurists were restricted to utilising the two processes of *ijma* and *qiyas* as a means of undertaking *ijtihad*. These two methods became the secondary authority for determining Islamic law based upon interpretation of the primary sources of Qur'an and *Sunna*. *Ijtihad* is not considered to be a source of laws, only the primary authorities can be that. Nyazee describes it as an 'activity, a struggle, a process to discover the law from the texts and to apply it to the set of facts awaiting decision (1994:287). However, there can be no *ijtihad* where the text is so clear that it does not brook interpretation. The first interpretation is literal where possible, after that analogy is used and finally the jurists can seek to discover the spirit of the law.

Ijma

Ijma refers to the consensus of the community on matters of law and practice. Its authority arose from the saying attributed to Muhammad that 'my community will never agree on an error'. Thus *ijma* is authorised by the *Sunna*. In practice, it was not the totality of the Muslim population that exercised the right of *ijma*, far too unwieldy in the new circumstances of a world civilisation, but rather groups of religious scholars and jurists, many of them selected by the Umayyad rulers and assigned the task of producing legislation from the Qur'an and the practice of the Prophet. Originally *ijma* was probably practised by the Companions of the Prophet, or at least tradition assigns that activity to them.

These religious leaders discovered that there was already in existence a vast body of agreed practice and this was drawn upon in subsequent attempts at analogical reasoning to interpret correct practice in new situations. Once *ijma* had been linked back to Qur'an or *Sunna*, even if innovatory, it could be declared not only as authentic practice but also infallible, by utilising the idea of the inerrancy of the majority and the validation of the scholars.

There is difference of opinion regarding the validity of *ijma* undertaken by the early Muslims. According to some jurists, it was only the Companions of the Prophet who could sanction *ijma*. Others argue that only the *ijma* of the Companions cannot be overturned by anyone except jurists who were their contemporaries. The Maliki school of law looks to the people of Medina and their established practice; others, including some Hanbalis, stated that only the first four caliphs produced *ijma* that was binding. Others considered that it was not binding if produced more than one generation after the Prophet. The Shi'a considered *ijma* produced by the *ahl al-bayt*, the household of the Prophet, his family members, to be binding.

However, it is agreed that any *ijma* which is soundly based on the text of the Qur'an and the *Sunna*, cannot be abrogated by any subsequent consensus. Equally, no *ijma* can be produced that contradicts the text of the two primary sources of law. It is only where *ijma* has been created in the public interest that it can be replaced by future jurists seeking the public welfare in new situations. Doi points out that *ijma* can be divided into two broad categories: *Ijma al-Azimah* (regular consensus of opinion) and *Ijma al-Rukhsar* (irregular consensus of opinion). In the first there is no dissent by any other jurist but in the latter there is contrary opinion by some scholars (Doi, 1984:67). He further explains that *ijma* is sub-divided into *Ijma al-Qawl* (verbal consensus of opinion), *Ijma al-Fi'l* (the consensus of opinion on an action performed by a jurist) and *Ijma al-Sukut* (the silent consensus where no other jurists express an opinion on the words or actions of another but choose to remain silent).

Qiyas

Tradition claims that it was Ibn Hanafi, one of the four founders of the schools of law, who first introduced the legal principle to deduce the correct interpretation of Islamic law by the process of applying the Qur'an and *Sunna* to new situations by the use of analogical deduction. Although the Qur'an may not mention particular modes of transport for example, it may well say something about other modes of transport. By applying a deductive process to the existing verses covering transport, it is possible to enlarge the body of law on transportation and arrive at a Qur'anic interpretation of the new situation. The fundamental principle behind both *ijma* and *qiyas*, is that if any jurist (*mujaddid*) pronounces on an issue, it must be able to be accepted as the *hukm* of Allah, a command that is sacred and to be obeyed, even though it has been discovered by the jurist.

Qiyas works by first taking a particular word and examining its general implication. For example, the Qur'an uses the word 'fie' when referring to children's relations with parents. The exact verse is 'Say not "Fie" unto them nor repulse them, but speak to them a gracious word' (Qur'an 17:23). However, commonsense dictates that the verse is not only referring to one word of abuse, but rather all aggressive language to parents is prohibited. Thus *qiyas* is the process of seeking the general from the particular but also the higher order from the lower; for example, if such language is forbidden to parents, then surely physical abuse of parents is also prohibited.

Analogy can also work by seeking to find generic types from specific words. For example, wine (*khamr*) is forbidden in the Qur'an. Although specific, if treated as a generic it can refer to all forms of intoxicant or substances that veil the mind or remove clarity.

The four schools of law (*Madhhab*)

Through these means the jurists were able to develop and systemati-
cally categorise and tabulate a body of law that could regulate public
and private life amongst the Muslim populations, but maintain the
conviction that the *shari'a* was identical to the revelation. By the third
century, the four Muslim schools of law, that of Hanafi, founded by
Abu Hanafi (d.150), Hanbali, founded by Ahmad Ibn Hanbal (d.241),
Shafi'i, founded by Muhammad ibn Idris al-Shafi'i (d.216) and Maliki,
founded by Malik ibn Annas (d.179) had been established and then
adopted respectively by various geographical and cultural regions.

The Hanafi school is the largest school, followed by the occupants
of West Asia, Lower Egypt and the Subcontinent. The Hanbali are
dominant in northern and Central Asia and their teachings were
revived in the eighteenth century by the Wahhabi movement in
Arabia. The Maliki movement is currently the largest in North and
West Africa and Upper Egypt and finally, the Shafi'i are based in Cairo
and Baghdad.

Each school came into being through focusing on a different aspect of
the current body of revelation at the time of founding. For example, the
Shafi'i developed the principles of jurisprudence by allowing the verbal
tradition of Hadith to take precedence over local customary traditions,
whereas the Maliki were founded on the principle of relying on living
traditions in Medina as long as they were supported by the Hadith.

The codification of the law undertaken by the founders of the four
schools into an organised and disciplined body of knowledge
achieved by deduction and consensus created a structured discipline
of Islamic jurisprudence that utilised a unique Muslim methodology.
Comprised, according to the four authoritative schools of law in the
Sunni tradition described above and one for the Shi'as, of commands
that were safely derived from the Qur'an and *Sunna*, decisions concerning legal precedents that required a legal ruling could be taken
from this body of law. From this point onwards, decisions could be
taken by going to the body of knowledge known as *fiqh* (understanding), rather than going direct to the Qur'an and the *Sunna*. After the
creation of *fiqh*, largely based on the authority of *ijma* and *qiyas*, the
ulema, as the jurists were known, declared the door of *ijtihad* closed.
From this point forward, the jurists of Islam became experts on the
science of *usul al-Fiqh*, studying the body of law developed by their
predecessors rather than going straight to the Qur'an and *Sunna*. A

limited form of *ijtihad* was permitted where scholars could interpret laws already existing in their own school. However, not all scholars throughout the history of the Muslim world have accepted the authority of the *ulema* to close the doors of *ijtihad*, especially in the modern period. Some have argued that the decision to close the doors of *ijtihad* arose out of the exceptional circumstances of the Mongol invasion, when Baghdad was threatened with destruction. However, the decision by the *ulema* of Iraq can be challenged as made under duress or panic, and that no one had the authority to stop the process of *ijtihad* (Doi, 1984:69).

Fiqh, however, became the domain of the *ulema*, and its study was promoted in a vast network of schools, usually attached to a mosque, known as *madrasas*. Established by the twelfth century, the *madrasas* contributed to the unity of the Muslim worldview and the maintenance of the *shari'a* after the collapse of the Abbasid Empire and the disintegration of the caliphate after the invasion of the Mongols. In an eight-year course, the *ulema* of the *madrasas* taught their successors to become *imams* in the mosques and go on to make judgements in Islamic law themselves. Thus the *shari'a* came to be a comprehensive system based upon the revelation laid out in the Qur'an and the *Sunna* of Muhammad and interpreted by the founders of the four Muslim schools of law.

Thus a central tenet of Islam, that only Allah is sovereign over human affairs and has the right to determine the correct course of action for human beings, was validated into a pragmatic system that could provide Muslims with both a workable legal framework for society and a conviction that they had a blueprint for existence that accorded with revelation. In fact, for many Muslims, *shari'a* is synonymous with Islam itself. Literally meaning 'the way to a watering-place', an apt metaphor in desert lands, it became the way to implement Islam in daily life and to feel that one was on the straight path described by the Qur'an in its first *sura*, al-Fatiha, almost a credo for the devout.

In the two hundred years following Muhammad's death, various Muslim commentators had developed a comprehensive system of right and wrong actions based upon the revelation in the Qur'an and the precedents set by the Prophet's deeds and actions. As a result of this process all conduct could be judged as obedience or disobedience to the divine law. The law of God was enshrined into the legal structures of Muslim territory. Not only would Muslims fear the wrath of a just creator, who would punish wrongdoing with hellfire, but they would also find themselves facing legal penalties for breaking the law of the land.

Yet, in the first instance, the Islamic law is religious rather than legal. It exists as a system of do's and don'ts which express the reality that God is sovereign (Geaves, 1999:164). However, flexibility is built into the system, first by the relationship of the law with local customs. The customs of occupied territory were fully explored and permitted to the degree that they complied with the injunctions implicit in the revelation. This combination of local law (*urf*) mixed with *shari'a* provided Muslim society with the means to accommodate local culture as it moved around the world either through conquest or migration.

In addition, the early scholars of jurisprudence acknowledged that the codification had to provide the space for personal discovery and that for the system to be truly all-encompassing it had to go beyond acts which were either forbidden or permitted. A five-fold categorisation of actions was developed as follows:

i) *wajib* – obligatory acts which Allah has commanded and where failure to follow leads to punishment in the afterlife. Such prescriptions are found in the Qur'an.

ii) *mandub* – actions which are recommended and whose performance brings reward but omission is not punished. Such actions are far too many for the Qur'an to record but may be found in the *Sunna*.

iii) *ja'iz* – actions to which Allah is indifferent and is not concerned if they are performed or not. There can be no reward or punishment for either their performance or omission. These are probably not mentioned in the revelatory literature.

iv) *makruh* – actions which Allah frowns upon but which are not forbidden. Restraint is rewarded but performance is not punished. Once again such actions are more likely to be described in supplementary literature.

v) *mahzur* – actions which are prohibited and it is forbidden to indulge in them. There is no reward for avoiding them but performance is punished. Such actions are found in the Qur'an.

Categories ii, iii and iv allow for individuals to develop their personal conscience and thus bring a journey of personal discovery to the world of *halal* (allowed) and *haram* (forbidden) prescribed in the *shari'a*. Rahman points out that this system came to be known as 'resoluteness and relaxation' (*azima* and *rukhsa*) and provided the vehicle for Muslims to search in their own hearts (Rahman, 1979:84).

Thus, a comprehensive system of law was developed and became the norm and the ideal for Muslim societies, providing the flexibility for both cultural difference and individual conscience, but also at the same time supplying a code of behaviour for all Muslims to be certain that they were obeying the will of God. Muslim family law, criminal justice, business and trade obligations, and rules of warfare were all developed on the basis of revelation. Thus a unique form of government was developed, if not always implemented, in which rulers were not considered to be legislators, or even custodians of divine law, although ideally they should be the latter.

Opponents and contradictions

In reality, certainly since the time of the Umayyads, conflict was to develop between the *ulema*, as custodians of God's law, and the various rulers of Muslim territory. The sultans, amirs and caliphs were far from religious figures, although some individuals may have been, and they often wished to impose a form of imperial absolutism over their people. The rulers' desires to establish their own autocratic will and exercise absolute power were bound to conflict with the ideal of Allah as the only lawgiver. Throughout Muslim history, absolute rulers tried to find ways to circumvent the restrictions of God's legal strictures, especially those concerning morality, and the *ulema* vied with them to prevent the dilution of the *shari'a* or to keep the *shari'a* at the centre of the lives of ordinary Muslims.

Since some of the *ulema* were prepared to accept state patronage it was not clear-cut, and individual members of the *ulema* could always be found to rubber stamp the ruler's wish and interpret the law accordingly. Sunni jurists, less susceptible to the emotive calls for justice against tyrants demanded by the Shi'a, decreed that it was not acceptable to revolt against immoral caliphs as long as the ruler accepted that the *shari'a* was implemented and that the religious practices of Islam and Muslim family law were left alone. In reality, in most parts of the Muslim world two parallel systems of law existed side by side. Rulers were allowed to develop their own regulatory systems but generally the term *shari'a* was avoided in favour of ordinances. John Esposito describes this process:

> As a result, Islamic society possessed a dual system of law and
> courts (*Shari'a* and Grievance), religious and secular, with
> complimentary jurisdictions. *Shari'a* courts were increasingly
> restricted to the enforcement of family laws. The Grievance
> courts dealt with public law, especially criminal law, taxation,
> and commercial regulations. (Esposito, 1988:87,88)

The compromise was not accepted by everyone. There were those
who placed less emphasis on the implementation of the exoteric
demands of the religion and pursued a path of inner piety and
purification. Their objections were not with expressions of Muslim
life achieved through implementation of its revelatory prescriptions
but with the corruptions of the imperial Muslim state and the absence
of inner intent amongst those who offered up blind allegiance to religion. Driven by a desire for deep and intimate relations with Allah
they attempted to return to the purity and simplicity of the Prophet's
time, modelling themselves on the lives of his Companions. Seeking
a mystical closeness they sought for ways to combine the exoteric
with the esoteric, and rejected the outward obedience to the law if it
was not allied with right intention.

There were other critics, who perceived the law as diluted by the
acceptance of the two-tier system and the compromises that arose from
the alliance of the *ulema* with the rulers. In addition, they were sometimes suspicions of the processes in which law had been constructed by
concessions to existing customs or even the very processes that had
created the *fiqh*. Such figures demanded the right to engage in *ijtihad*
and return to the sources of Qur'an and *Sunna* to determine *shari'a*.

Conclusion

Thus it is not only non-Muslim scholars, without any obligation to
acknowledge the divine origins of Islam, who have queried the
process of constructing the *shari'a*. Western scholars of Islam have
introduced a strong note of caution in regard to the processes of the
early jurists and rulers in the authenticity of the traditions that were
collected and the relations between law-formation as a political
exercise and the development of Muslim theology (*kalam*). Muslim
scholars have been more optimistic, even if like Rahman they still
observe a degree of caution towards the process. Following Goldziher
and other early twentieth-century Orientalists, most contemporary

Western scholars remain sceptical, preferring to suggest that the traditions that comprise the Hadith reflected more the views of the early generations of Muslims as they grappled with statescraft than the life and teachings of the Prophet himself.

Muslim scholars have rarely challenged Qur'an and Hadith or the processes of collection and recording but they have sometimes attempted to use a discourse that distinguishes the divine elements of Qur'an and *Sunna*, the *prima facie* revelatory truths from the processes of law-making that might have introduced a human element. The solution is a dismissal of tradition and return to the Qur'an and *Sunna* for answers and a reassertion of the right of the qualified jurist (*mujaddid*) to engage in *ijtihad*.

This critique reached its fullest expression during the colonial period of the nineteenth and early twentieth centuries when Muslim nations found themselves dominated by European powers. In many cases, the division between *shari'a* and Ordinances provided a means for colonial powers to govern Muslim populations. European legal codes were introduced, but where these were perceived as workable or equitable and the practice of Islam was not interfered with and Muslim family law permitted, nothing much was changed from the rule of Muslim sultans or amirs. Sometimes conditions were even improved and reforms introduced that benefited local populations.

However, it was in this period and in the time that followed, when Muslim nations achieved their independence, that the most questioning of the nature of the *shari'a* and its relationship to the maintenance of the state took place. Increasingly the call for an Islamic state governed by full implementation of *shari'a* law became the rhetoric of radical transformation of Muslim society, even though historically it is unlikely that such a social system ever existed and would prove to be elusive.

Nyazee states that the word 'evolution' will always be controversial when used in the context of the *shari'a* as it evokes images of a human process in the collation of Allah's commands and the efforts to produce a model society based on them (Nyazee, 1994:111). This is, after all, exactly what the Qur'an accuses the recipients of earlier revelations of doing and thus creating the cause for a final revelation. Nyazee argues that

> those who feel the *shari'a* was laid down once and for all may reject the idea of evolution in Islamic law. Their objections are

partly justified. But as Islamic law is meant to apply to every aspect of Muslim life in all ages, it follows that it has to evolve and grow like any other legal system so that it may be able to cater to the demands of the changing times. (Nyazee, 1994:111)

Nyazee believes that the *shari'a* was created with flexibility built around a central immutable core, and thus was able to grow to become a complete legal system through the processes that have been described briefly above. He believes that although the Qur'an and *Sunna* are inviolable and eternal truths, the development of the modern state requires Muslims to develop new laws. Not all agree by any means. But both the followers of a conservative position, such as those influenced by Mawdudi or Sayyid Qutb, and those more in harmony with Nyazee's position, can agree that considerable creativity will be needed to develop a uniquely Muslim constitution for their body of nation states as they seek to maintain the spirit of the Revelation, the requirements of the Qur'an and *Sunna*, but to join the remainder of the world able to demonstrate an Islamic example of justice, equitability and progress. However, debarring the use of extreme methods to combat perceived Western neo-colonialism, which will surely provoke equally aggressive counter-attack and resistance, it must be the Muslim people themselves who develop the creative ways to integrate the voice of God into modern judicial systems and methods of governance.

CHAPTER 5

The Umma: an homogenous unity or deeply divided?

Having introduced the idea of divergent views in the previous chapter, the following exploration of the Muslim concept of umma *(community) will assess the dynamic relationship that exists between the ideal of a sacred community and actual experience as manifested in the contemporary Muslim world. It will be argued that the tension between the two moulds and shapes the actions that transform Muslim society. In the process, those factors in Islam that promote a sense of unity will be contrasted with the lived reality of a fragmented or diverse series of worldviews that exist within the larger framework of the Muslim world.*

Introduction

Muslims often claim that Islam has no division between the sacred and the secular, but the division of *din* (religion) and *dunya* (world) certainly manifests itself through the dynamic tension of a number of consequent dualities. Foremost amongst these is the titanic struggle between good and evil which began with the creation of the first human being and will continue until the Last Judgement and the vindication of God's faithful. Connected to this central duality is the dichotomy between the ideal and the real that is central to the Muslim sense of struggle or *jihad*.

Every religion to a degree is faced with the challenge of an ideal lifestyle: states of consciousness or codes of ethical behaviour as exemplified in sacred texts or the lives of sacred founders and their imitators. Yet nowhere is this so articulated in doctrine or worldview than in Islam. The ideal for all human beings is comprehensively established in the final revelation of Allah, the Qur'an and the lifestyle of God's messengers, but most particularly the behaviour of Muhammad, the seal of prophethood.

Yet many Muslims regard the history of Islam from the time of the Prophet to the present as a series of challenges to meet the ideal. For some, those who have been successful in doing so are only the original Companions of Muhammad; others regard the *salafa*, the first three generations of Muslims, as a demonstration of the closest to the ideal life in submission to God. For those who aspire to come close to Allah, joined in intimate communion through piety and remembrance, the *awliya*, the mystics of Sufism, provide the ideal. However, despite the differences over where the ideal can be found, millions of Muslims would agree that the religion of Islam is perfect, manifested in the lives of a religious elite, but that most fall short through weakness and forgetfulness, enticed away from the revelation of a merciful and benevolent creator by the distractions of the world.

The ideal is sought not only by individuals but also at the level of society. The majority of Muslims would surely agree that the community created around the centrality of the Qur'an and the leadership of the living Prophet in Medina manifested the ideal society. Muslim societies since that period can be seen to represent the 'real': pragmatic attempts that are usually perceived as falling short of the Qur'an's vision of community. However, Muslims do not give up hope that the ideal is obtainable for it is a central belief that Islam is both practical and achievable.

The community in Medina is significant because Muhammad was able to weld together, out of Arab tribal societies steeped in traditional customs and ancient rivalries, a new and revolutionary grouping of people whose central unifying identity and codes of behaviour were based on submission to God and obedience to God's final Prophet. To achieve this, the first Muslims drew upon the Qur'an's revelations to build a progressive understanding of *umma* (community), which elaborates upon the ideal of a community defined as a people who are linked together by revelation. Paret describes the Qur'an's concept of *umma* as 'some kind of ethical or religious body of people with whom God works in history to fulfil the divine plan of salvation (Paret, 1987:1015).

The idea of *umma* is linked with divine judgement and an imperative for all beings, even the animals, to be gathered together at the final day.

> There is not an animal that lives on the earth nor a being that flies
> on its wings, but forms communities (*ummat*) like you. Nothing
> have We omitted from the Book and they all shall be gathered to
> their Lord in the end. (Qur'an 6:38)

However, Allah's mercy and compassion ensured that a warning is
provided to the free-will creations, that is the human and the *djinn*, so
that they may be saved from the hellfire and enjoy the rewards given
to God's faithful. But Muslims traditionally believe that it is communities that are judged, as well as individuals, each one standing before
the divine throne behind their messenger who will petition on their
behalf. Thus the warning is conveyed by human messengers,
amongst whom an elite are chosen as recipients of Allah's revelation
in the form of a divine book. Thus an *umma* may also be defined as a
people who have been provided with one or more messengers.
'Before thee We sent Messengers to many nations (*ummat*)' (Qur'an
6:42).

But the succession of prophets from Adam to Jesus was met by deri-
sion and disbelief by the majority. 'Then We sent Our messengers in
succession; every time there came to a people (*umma*) their messenger,
they accused him of falsehood' (Qur'an 23:44). In addition to being
the recipients of a divine warning delivered through a human messenger, perhaps the primary definition of an *umma* is that of a people
who surrender to God's will. Thus, oddly, Ibrahim (Abraham) is
unique in the Qur'an as a community of one, a microcosmic model of
the ideal for all others. 'Abraham was indeed a model (*umma*).
Devoutly obedient to Allah, and true in faith, and he joined not gods
with Allah' (Qur'an 16:120).

Before the advent of Muhammad and the Arabian revelation,
Ibrahim's model was most fully exemplified in the Jewish and
Christian communities marked out as special by the Qur'an's desig-
nation of *Ahl-i Kitab* (People of the Book). In fact, before the revelation
of the Qur'an, it is believed by Muslims that the Jewish people had
been blessed by many warnings which included three prophets who
had heralded the arrival of a divine book: Moses and the Torah, David
and the Psalms, Jesus and the Gospels. Yet still the Jews turned away
from God's straight path. However, they are not completely condemned, as the Qur'an asserts that there is possibility of a saved
remnant within the wider communities of Jews and Christians. 'Not
all of them are alike: Of the People of the Book are a portion that stand

for the right; they rehearse the Signs of Allah all night long, as they prostrate themselves in adoration' (Qur'an 3:113).

The idea of a saved remnant, a righteous minority within the wider religious community, is met with again in a different context of a group within Islam itself, but we will meet up with that revolutionary and potentially explosive possibility later. Generally speaking, although acknowledging the idea of a saved remnant within the older communities of God, Muslims tend to see them as superseded by Islam, drawing upon the following verse to substantiate their belief: 'That was a people (*umma*) passed away. They shall reap the fruit of what they did, and you of what you do! You shall not be asked about what they did' (Qur'an 2:141).

The idea of Islam existing alongside the previous revelations but renewing them was transformed in Medina into the belief that the previous communities of God had been replaced by Allah's final revelation to a new chosen people. It would seem that originally Muhammad hoped for recognition by local Christians and Jews but as this was not forthcoming, especially from the neighbouring Jewish tribes, he turned away from them. Instead his energy was directed to the Muslim community, the Qur'an providing its adherents with unique prayer rites, fasting, pilgrimage and charitable responsibilities. The direction in which Muslims prayed was moved from Jerusalem to Makkah. 'Our Lord make of us Muslims, bowing to Thy will, and of our progeny a people (*umma*) Muslim, bowing to Thy will; and show us our places for the celebration of due rites; and turn unto us Thy mercy' (Qur'an 2:143).

Muhammad was to be the example for the Muslims, and the Muslims in turn would be the example for the world, thus taking on themselves the old covenant given to the Jews. 'Thus We have made of you an *umma* justly balanced that you might be witnesses over the nations, and the Messenger a witness over yourselves' (Qur'an 2:143).

Thus the final development, the finished product of the *umma*, is manifested in Islam, the last and complete embodiment of the will of God encapsulated in the Qur'an and embodied in the Prophet as its exemplar. The People of the Book, the historic forerunners, are given up on, even though individuals amongst them are acknowledged. 'You are the best of peoples (*ummat*), evolved for mankind. Enjoining what is right, forbidding what is wrong, if only the People of the Book had faith; among them are some who have faith, but most of them are perverted transgressors.'

But perhaps the greatest transgression of all was the loss of unity in a religious community and its fragmentation into sects. The first Muslims were aware of this in Christianity and feared it happening among themselves. The unity of the *umma* is the social embodiment of *tawhid*, reflected in the individual human being by signs of inner purity, obedience to God's will, one-pointed worship and a final state of unity wherein the person ceases to war with itself. If the surrendered human being is the microcosm of God's own transcendent unity, then the *umma* is the embodiment of that unity manifested in human society. Fragmentation, especially religious fragmentation, is an indication of a community at war with itself, a loss of Islam itself. The Qur'an praises the unity of the Muslim community but warns of its loss in future generations.

> Verily, this *umma* of yours is a single *umma* and I am your Lord and Cherisher; therefore serve Me and no other. But later generations cut off their affair of unity one from another; yet will they all return to Us. (Qur'an 21:92,93)

It is possible that all was not well even during the life of the Prophet, at least not towards its end. As tribes came in from the desert to offer Muhammad their fealty, he knew enough of his own society to realise that the desert tribes always sought the patronage of the strong for protection. His victories against his opponents in Makkah ensured that he would be regarded as a strong leader and thus he understood that the newcomers' motivations were suspect, no longer religious but imitating the old systems of patronage that had always been a part of desert survival. The Qur'an echoes his misgivings and begins to introduce verses addressed to hypocrites. It is at this point that the idea of a righteous remnant reappears, but this time it is addressed to the Muslims not the People of the Book. 'Let there arise out of you a band of people inviting to all that is good, enjoining what is right, and forbidding what is wrong. They are the ones to attain felicity (Qur'an 3:104). Later, we shall see how the significance of this verse becomes important in the contemporary period, as a number of revivalist movements set themselves up as a righteous vanguard to renew Islam and purge the community.

The myth of unity

It has become almost compulsory for Muslims to defend their faith as
unitary when faced with Western observers. On numerous occasions
I have visited mosques to be told that Islam unlike Christianity is
undivided. However, closer scrutiny reveals a number of divisions,
not just between the first major schism of Sunnis and Shi'a but also
within both these major groupings. The intensity of the divisions
reveals itself in a number of struggles and conflicts going on throughout the Muslim world. Some of these have ancient histories but are
revitalised under the crises of modernity and other pressures unique
to the contemporary period.

Muslims maintain the myth of unity for it is difficult to admit that the
final revelation is bedevilled by the diseases of its predecessors. After
all, Muslims cannot look to a solution in which Allah sends a new
prophet or a new revelation. It is now hard and fast doctrine that
Muhammad is the seal of prophethood and no new religion of God can
come to rescue the Muslim *umma* from its dilemmas. Yet more discerning Muslims are aware that problems have arisen throughout history;
and so the belief has developed that a special figure, known as *mujaddid*, arises every one hundred years to renew the community. This is
supported by a saying of the Prophet that declares, 'God will send to his
umma at the head of each century those who will renew its faith for it.'

The process of renewal of the faith to keep it to the pristine purity
of the original revelation is contained in the two concepts of *islah* and
tajdid. *Islah* is mentioned in the Qur'an in the context of the warnings
of the prophets to their respective communities to return to the ways
of God. *Tajdid* refers to the process of renewal. Thus throughout the
centuries there have been those who have called for renewal and
worked to restore Islam to their own understanding of the contents of
the original message and its implementation. Implicit in such
renewals is the understanding that the community is divided and
requires purging of un-Islamic behaviour or accretions that are foreign to the faith in order to restore unity. The division of Islam into
sects is implicit in the saying attributed to the Prophet, where it is stated that his community would divide into seventy-two sects with only
one maintaining the true Islam. Obviously each movement feels itself
to be that one and its competitors to be the heretical remainder. Yet,
the saying itself provides the stimulus for sectarian movements to

appear as each new reformer and his followers see themselves as the one that maintains true Islam.

A number of Western scholars studying Islam in the twentieth century have maintained the myth of Islamic unity enshrined in the vision of *umma*. Gibb provides us with a classic definition of *umma* in which he states:

> It consists of a totality of individuals bound to one another, not by kinship or race, but of religion in that all the members profess their belief in one God, and in the mission of the Prophet Muhammad. Before God and in their relation to Him, all are equal, without distinction of rank, class or race. (Gibb, 1963:173)

Yet such a unity based on religion rarely existed in spite of the ideal. As we have already seen, even during Muhammad's lifetime, tribal loyalties were difficult to subsume into an overarching Muslim identity based on belief in one God and a common set of ritual practices. After Muhammad's death, Abu Bakr, the first caliph, had to fight against tribal rebellions. There are those, even amongst Muslims, who see the events after the death of Muhammad as a re-establishment of the supremacy of the Quraysh tribe, the old enemies of the Prophet, as the aristocracy and rulers of the Umayyad caliphate, certainly after the death of Ali, the fourth caliph. The political fragmentation of unity was fiercely fought out amongst the various factions, and three out of four of Muhammad's successors as leaders of the Muslim community met violent ends. A'isha, his favourite wife, was to lead Muslim forces in civil war against Ali's supporters. In addition to the political differences over the leadership of the community there were underlying religious tensions concerning who could be regarded as the true Muslims. In Chapters 6 and 7 we shall look in more depth at the development of both the Shi'a and Sufi alternatives, both initially appearing in reaction to the Umayyad dynasty, although for distinctly different reasons.

The rapid expansion of Islam was to bring its own problems of integrating people whose religions and cultures were far more sophisticated than and markedly different from the tribes of Arabia. The Islamicisation of Persia, an ancient and proud culture with its own religious heritage of Zoroastrianism, in particular created rivalries with the Arab Muslims. Although Gibb may speak of unity before God, in all other aspects such as class, ethnicity, gender, wealth and place of birth, Muslim society could not maintain the consciousness of *umma* as an overriding unity. Arab Muslims certainly regarded themselves as superior to the new converts, especially those whose language was not Arabic, for had not God chosen to reveal his final revelation to the world in that medium, therefore showing his favour to the Arab people. The Persians, on the other hand, and those from the conquered Byzantine Christian territory, were not likely to acknowledge the cultural supremacy of tribal peoples from a desert backwater.

Even the *ulema*'s classical division of the world into *dar al-Islam* (the territory of Islam) and *dar al-Harb* (the world of war) did not stop various Muslim forces under the command of warlords from trying to conquer and re-conquer Muslim territory. India was invaded again and again by Muslims from Central Asia even after it had become Muslim territory. In fact, the mighty Moghul Empire was certainly weakened before the advent of the British due to the sacking of Delhi by Nadir Shah.

In addition, class divisions bedevilled the unity of the Muslim community. Indian Muslims even developed their own social hierarchies reflecting the Hindu caste system that they condemned. Thus those who could claim descent from the Prophet's family, the Sayyids, were at the peak of the hierarchy, with those who had descended from the original Arab conquerors or traders next. At the bottom of the hierarchy were indigenous Indian Muslim converts. Thus the following statement made by Charles Adam in 1983, twenty years after Gibb's comments, needs also to be viewed critically. Adams states:

> The Islamic society is bound together by ideological harmony, composed of individuals with various ethnic-linguistic and racial backgrounds. What distinguishes individuals in such a socially diverse society is not their ethno-linguistic and racial characters, rather, it is their identification with the Islamic ideology. (Adams, 1983:120)

Even in Britain, where a relatively new Muslim population has successfully forged an identity based on Islam, and where they could be said to have identified with 'Islamic ideology' over and above 'ethno-linguistic and racial backgrounds', ethnicity has not been subsumed. Certainly there is a desire for a united Muslim identity based on religion: an actualisation of the *umma* ideal, which reaches out to a global Islamic resurgence for inspiration and feelings of unity. Yet, in reality, there is little sign of trans-ethnic communication. Muslims of Pakistani, Bangladeshi, Turkish, Malaysian, Yemeni, Palestinian, Iranian, Iraqi and other places of origin remain in their own enclaves, attend their own mosques, marry within their own national groupings and maintain their own customs. The divisions are actually more finely tuned than simply national backgrounds and loyalties. Amongst British Pakistanis there are intense loyalties and rivalries between Mirpuris from Azad Kashmir, Punjabis, Sindhis, and those whose families migrated from India at Partition in 1947 and who are not native to the territories that became Pakistan.

Yet there are politico-religious movements that attempt to promote an ideology that transcends ethnicity and to unite Muslims together under the banner of religion. It is within these movements that one does find young Muslims from across the ethnic divides, consciously identifying with a trans-national Islamic identity and seeking to restore the unitary vision of the *umma*. It is also amongst such movements that one finds radicalisation, although not necessarily of a violent propensity.

Adams, in his description of Muslim transcendence of difference, was writing on the religious teachings and political activities of Maulana Mawdudi, the great twentieth-century ideologue and critic of the West. Although his description fails to meet the norm of the Muslim world, it certainly echoes Mawdudi's own position and that of his followers in the subcontinent, or fellow-travellers in other parts of the Muslim world. Mawdudi's ideology was worked out in response to the apparent superiority of Western culture and the success of its institutions throughout the Muslim world and must be judged in the light of colonial and post-colonial Muslim responses to Western domination.

Islam and nationalism

Throughout the eighteenth and nineteenth centuries the impact of European expansion began to be felt throughout most Muslim territory. Economic control in the eighteenth century gradually became political and military domination in the nineteenth (Donohue and Esposito, 1982:5) and returned full circle to economic and political domination in the post-colonial era of the latter half of the twentieth century. Muslims increasingly found themselves living under the domination of Christian or, even worse, secular rulers from the rising powers of European nations. The *ulema* were found to be inadequate to deal with the new situation, preferring to cling on to their old traditional ways, retreating to the mosques and the Muslim seminaries (*madrasa*), a domain where they could retain control. Essentially schooled in the *madrasa* system, with a curriculum unchanged since the medieval period, they were increasingly challenged by a superior European technology and military might that was founded upon economic power and the new discoveries of science. In addition, they had to deal with a new worldview rooted in philosophical and political history that had given rise to democracy, nationalism and secularism. The Muslim crisis arose primarily from the fact that they were powerless to stop the European powers from taking control of Muslim territory. In the old medieval conception of *dar al-Islam* and *dar al-Harb*, Muslims could realistically consider that one day the world would become the former, but now *dar al-Islam* itself seemed to under threat. This provoked a crisis within the faith which the rigidly traditional religious leaderships were ill-equipped to resolve. With an educational methodology based on *taqlid* (blind imitation), innovation and adaptation to the new situation was difficult and foreign domination by non-Muslims raised questions concerning the health of Islam and the reasons for the apparent loss of divine favour which appeared to no longer provide success to the *umma* as it had in the past.

The problem of inner decay had already been prominent in the minds of a number of Muslim thinkers and reformers, but now they had to consider the possibility of Muslim civilisation being unable to survive this new external threat. Most of the responses to the crisis agreed upon the necessity of Islamic revival in order to restore the past glories of the Muslim *umma*, but there was disagreement concerning the means of achieving this. These disagreements, although initially intellectual responses, were to polarise into positions that politically and religiously divided the Muslim world to the present time. Jamal al-Din al-Afghani (1838–1897) and Muhammad Abduh (1849–1905) were to become the leading proponents of a position that proclaimed that Muslims could rediscover their power by rejuvenating the morality and ethics of Islam but meanwhile learn from Europe the developments that had been made in science and technology. The crucial element was to restore the glory of Islam by reviving the essentials of the faith. Then Muslims could go on to reform their legal, administrative and educational institutions and once again compete favourably with the new power of Europe.

The position of these Muslim activists and thinkers raised a number of important concerns in regard to interpreting Islamic jurisprudence and the methodology of Muslim education. In order to establish the essentials of the religion, interpretation of the Qur'an and Hadith was required in which independent reasoning (*ijtihad*) was utilised. But the *ulema* had rejected *ijtihad* in favour of *taqlid* in the tenth century when they decided that the codification of Islamic law was essentially complete. Muslims were to follow past precedent as elaborated by the early jurists and new problems were to be resolved by studying the established legal texts of the four schools of law. Esposito argues that this stance, taken in order to establish the existing law as sacrosanct, left Muslim society inflexible to changing situations (Esposito, 1988:85). However, even in earlier periods, prominent Muslim scholars and religious luminaries had set a precedent of ignoring the *ulema* and undertaking *ijtihad*. Prominent figures such as Al-Ghazali (d.1111), Ibn Taymiyya (1263–1328), Shah Wali-Allah (1702–1763) and Abd al-Wahhab (d.1792) had all claimed the right to practise *ijtihad* in their respective times, in order to revitalise Islam. Although holding diverse interpretations of Islam, they had all argued that properly qualified Muslim scholars should be able to go direct to the Qur'an and the *Sunna* to provide a renewed vision rather than merely studying the legal texts (*fiqh*).

In contrast to both these views, the liberal and modernist reformers of the nineteenth and twentieth centuries believed that creative interpretation of the Qur'an and *Sunna* was open to all Muslims in order to discover the way to adapt Islam to the changing conditions of modern society, thus permitting legal and social reform. These reformers accused the *ulema* of holding back progress by being out of touch with the modern world. Key modernists, for example Sayyid Ahmad Khan in India, worked closely with the British rulers and advocated an essential agreement between the values of Islam and the Western world. He called for a thorough reinterpretation of the Qur'an that acknowledged its metaphorical and cultural content rather than more literalist interpretations.

Divided in response to the Western threat, the reformers of all camps accused the *ulema* of holding back progress by being out of touch. For the modernists, the clerics inhibited the development of the Muslim world through their inability to learn from the modern world.

To the revivalists, they held back any possibility of Muslim renaissance through their inability to go beyond blind imitation in their adherence to tradition, and thus their failure to revive the fortunes of the *umma*. The revivalists asserted their right to *ijtihad* in order to discover the essential truths of the revelation and the Prophet's example and through implementation restore the glories of Islam. In return, the *ulema* retaliated by accusing both groups of reformers of introducing innovations (*bida*) from the Christian world which would corrupt Islam.

A new intellectual class of Muslims, educated to Western standards, taking on the values of the colonial powers and lacking the religious outlook of the reformers, gradually developed to challenge the authority of the *ulema*. Influenced by nationalism, they stressed loyalty to the nation rather than the *umma*. Rifa'a Badawi Rafi al-Tahtawi (1801–1873), an Egyptian writer resident in France for five years as the *imam* to a student mission, and influenced by French ideals of republicanism, appears to be the first to have introduced the idea of the fatherland (*watan*) and patriotism (*wataniyyah*) into the Arabic medium (Donohue and Esposito, 1982:11). More significantly, in the milieu of the rapidly collapsing Ottoman Empire, the Muslim sociologist Ziya Gokalp (1876–1924) propounded the theory of Turkism. He saw Islam as a source of ethics which could be adapted to the needs of the time and the service of the nation, but religion and nation had to be separated for the common good of both. He argued that it was possible to retain Islam's fundamental values and principles but to develop a modern Turkish national culture in which religious law would be replaced by secular law. Islam would remain in place as a national state religion that would primarily function to supplement Turkish culture and national identity. It could be used to develop connections with the wider Muslim world but the interests of the Turkish nation must always be paramount. For such thinkers, the nation was a natural integrated unit which through the medium of a common language and a distinctive cultural identity, brought together diverse ethnic and religious identities and welded them into a distinctive unit where the primary loyalty was to the *watan*.

Thus a heated debate on the nature of the state and the question of loyalty took place throughout the Muslim world. Each Muslim nation arrived at its own individual solution but there is no doubt that the twentieth century was to witness a fundamental shift of territorial loyalty to the nation state. In this respect the concept of *umma* was to take on a new symbolic meaning, more amongst the Muslim minority communities than in the Arab heartlands. For the Arabic-speaking nations *'umma'* was a term used in everyday language to denote various types of community. Where Arabic was not spoken as everyday language and Muslims lived alongside other communities, the ideal of the *umma* came to be a very powerful cultural and religious symbol which could be drawn upon to promote Muslim identity against the majority population of the respective nations (Geaves, 1996:24). In addition, throughout the latter half of the twentieth century, it also took on an ideological significance as a new kind of Muslim revivalist struggled to impose the values of Islam over the ideal of nationalism and patriotism to the fatherland.

This situation was further complicated by the success of Western-educated elites in seizing control of the newly emerging independent Muslim nation states after the end of World War II. Irredeemably weakened by several years of total warfare, the European powers were not able to resist the growing political struggles for independence across the world. But, ironically, those who led the various resistances to colonial domination were educated in the schools and universities of the very rulers from whom they sought emancipation. Thus the new governments embraced the ideals of secularism, socialism and nationalism that they learnt from their former rulers. Legal codes were put into place that owed more to the various European systems than to the Muslim *shari'a*. In addition, the secular ideal that separates religion and politics, placing the former firmly in the private individual domain rather than public institutional life, conflicted with the Muslim worldview, which regarded all aspects of life as part of God's domain. Secularism and the ideal of the nation state were for some in opposition to the classic Muslim ideal of an overriding Islamic identity of a united community of believers. However, it should be remembered that this was an ideal not a reality and many Muslims had throughout history given their primary loyalty to rulers, tribal leaders, or empires which had often been in conflict with other Muslims elsewhere.

Throughout the nineteenth and twentieth centuries in most Muslim nations the *shari'a* was modernised by the replacement of traditional Islamic legal codes with those from the legal systems of the former European colonial powers. In some places, even Muslim family law, the heart of the *shari'a* consisting of the laws of inheritance, divorce and marriage expressly addressed by the Qur'an, and the major force for governing the social lives of Muslims everywhere in the Islamic world, began to be tampered with by the new Muslim rulers even though usually left intact by the former colonial rulers. An Islamic rationale was provided by Muslim governments wishing to reform their legal codes, who proclaimed the right to practise *ijtihad* in order to revitalise the Muslim world in line with modern Western nation states. The *ulema* either cooperated with the governments by working as state-sponsored *imams* in government-built mosques and *madrasas* or alternatively felt powerless to halt the process even while they viewed it as profoundly contrary to the revelation of God enshrined in the Qur'an and Muslim tradition.

The new Muslim nation states have inherited all of the above problems of governance since their independence and have not been able to challenge the dominance of Western political, economic or military power. So far, they have not been able to create a society which claims the allegiance of all their people, nor have they established themselves as the primary locus of Muslim identity, although since the revolution in Iran it could claim to be the first of the Muslim nations to approach this ideal. Generally, the state has sought to appropriate to itself those loyalties which Muslims ideally would have given to the universal religious community established by Muhammad, yet this has not been fully successful. This is further complicated by the artificial borders of a number of Muslim nations carved out in the twentieth century, where different ethnic groups with a distinct identity exist within the frontiers of individual nations. Such groups are not always successfully assimilated within the ideal of the nation state. For example, the Kurdish populations of Iraq and Turkey or the populations of Indian Muslims that migrated to Pakistan during Partition in 1947 have not been fully integrated into their respective nations. In other countries there are tensions between rival religious groups such as Shi'a and Sunni Muslims, as is the case in Iraq.

Besides the conflicts between the Western-influenced ruling classes and the traditional *ulema*, there exists a third major division. The massive injection of European ideas gave impetus to the Islamic revivalist groups whose central tenets had always included the idea of removing foreign cultural accretions to revive Islam by restoring its pristine purity. Although similar movements had existed in the past they tended to criticise Sufi adherents of Islam as the innovators who introduced alien religious practices into the religion, but, in the twentieth century, revivalist movements appeared with an agenda to remove Western influences from Muslim nations. The leaders of these tightly knit, well-organised movements did not belong to the *ulema* and, unlike the earlier revivalists and reformers, they were not formed around the teachings of *madrasa*-trained members of the *ulema*. Prominent examples of such movements are *Jamaat-i Islami* founded by Maulana Mawdudi in the subcontinent and the *Jamaat al-Ikhwan al-Muslimin* founded in Egypt by Hassan al-Banna. Such organisations rejected both nationalism and the hidebound, ineffective traditionalism of the *ulema*. They fought against the idea of loyalty to the nation state, or at least those that were founded upon principles derived from the West. Instead they asserted that the primary loyalty of Muslims should be the global community of Islam, even if initially it meant the overturning of Muslim governments and their replacement by an Islamic state. Reinterpreting the old label of *jahiliya* (ignorance), used for the decadent condition of the pre-Islamic Arab society, they asserted that such a state of godlessness now pervaded the whole of humankind, including those societies which would normally be called Muslim but who do not implement the *shari'a*. Thus a simple choice was advocated between loyalty towards Islam and participation in *jahiliya*. The common demand of the revivalists was addressed towards Muslim nations to implement the *shari'a* in its entirety and revolutionise their governments and society to become Islamic states freed from Western influence.

Maulana Mawdudi

The foremost ideologue of the Islamic state was Maulana Mawdudi (1903–1979). Ishtiaq Ahmed describes him as 'the ablest theoretician of the Islamic state in the Muslim world' (Ahmed, 1987:33). A closer look at Pakistan reveals the tensions that were appearing in a number of Muslim nations. To the Muslims of the subcontinent, the attainment of a state of their own was a religious as well as a political event. The constitution of the new state built in an Islamic ethos as part of its *raison d'être* but ironically this was to create problems as the ethos of Islam clashed with the logic of Muslim nationalism. There were those who believed that the new nation had been created for the sole purpose of showing the world a model Islamic state that was based on the sovereignty of Allah rather than the secular ideal of the sovereignty of the people, which was probably closer to the vision of Jinnah, the founder of Pakistan.

The new state of Pakistan needed to establish an industrial base and this required the expansion and dissemination of modern skills through an education system that was secular and not dependent upon a received religious wisdom. On the other hand, the ideological underpinning required to successfully establish a common national identity and sense of patriotism had to be imparted to various ethnic groupings with distinct local cultures and languages. Both these transformations of Pakistani society were a challenge to traditional views. Whereas the ideal of the *umma* could be utilised to unite various ethnic groupings under one identity, it did not necessarily sit easily with the ideology of the nation state. In addition, Islam itself was divided between Sunnis and Shi'as. Amongst the Sunni majority, traditional shrine-based Sufism was dominant but its leadership was intensely locality based and other-worldly in orientation. The Sufi *pirs* with their strong devotional followings had been challenged since the eighteenth century and nineteenth century by reform movements in India, with their agendas to reawaken Muslim society based on a more literal interpretation of the Qur'an. These historic divisions continued to cause tensions in the new Muslim state of Pakistan.

The *ulema*, both those loyal to the *pirs* and those loyal to the older Indian reform movements, had failed to come to terms with the modernisation process; increasingly the urban educated sectors of the population saw them as superstitious and clinging on to outmoded traditional ideas which were irrelevant in the world of new techno-logy and discoveries. However, the secularisation of culture which accompanied the processes of urbanisation and the development of modern science and technology, was seen by many as the heritage of the West and as a legacy of the colonial world which had been thrown off at independence. Yet freedom had not liberated the new Muslim nation from the colonial influence of the Western powers; for many, it had only changed the form of the oppression. The modernists were suspected of having compromised with the post-colonial exploiters and the old Islamic reform movements, with their message that Islam needed to be cleansed of outside cultural influences, were now part of the established *ulema* and perceived as backward.

Stepping in to the vacuum, Mawdudi recreated the reform message in a new form, arguing that a purified Islam needed to be practised within the confines of an Islamic state which would provide the correct ideological framework for the nation to address modernisa-tion. He argued that Islam was the better alternative to both Western imports of either capitalism or socialism. Thus, in one stroke, he politicised the message of Islam within the context of contemporary struggles for power.

Mawdudi was to politicise religion through his theology of sovereignty. He persuasively argued that the need for an Islamic state rose from the nature of the universal order, where God's laws govern all creation. It is only human beings that suffer from the delusion of independence. Nature is under the sway of Islam because it obeys God's natural law, but human beings have the capacity to obey or disobey. In order that they make the correct choice there is revelation. Human behaviour is therefore governed by revealed law just as the universe is ruled by natural law. The law which governs human behaviour is fully revealed in the Qur'an and the *Sunna* of the Prophet. The key to understanding Mawdudi's ideas on the necessity of an Islamic state is his interpretation of the *shahada*, the witnessing to Islam required in order to be a Muslim. He saw the problem of history not as humanity's denial of the oneness of God but rather as an unwillingness to recognise the sovereignty of God. Mawdudi interpreted the *shahada* as a statement which not only proclaims the uniqueness of God as the creator or sole object of worship, but also expresses the uniqueness of God as the master, sovereign, Lord and law-giver. Thus God alone has the right to legislate and command human affairs.

> In the former, (western democracies) the people make their own laws; in the latter (Islamic democracy) they have to follow and obey the laws given by God through His Prophet. In one the government undertakes to fulfil the will of the people; in the other the government and the people alike have to do the will of God. (Mawdudi, 1948:31)

It is this revolutionary interpretation of the *shahadah* which provided Mawdudi with his main critique of the intrusion of Western ideas and philosophies into Muslim society. Secularism, nationalism and Western models of democracy are all based on the Enlightenment ideal of the sovereignty of the people. Mawdudi revolutionised Muslim politics by arguing that the acceptance of any other authority as sovereign is a form of *shirk*, and as such raises that authority to the status of being a partner with Allah. The great moral evil of the age, he declared, consists of accepting other sovereigns such as 'the will of the people' or the laws created by worldly rulers and setting them up in competition to the rule of God.

> What distinguished Islamic democracy from western democracy is that while the latter is based upon the concept of popular sovereignty, the former rests on the principle of *Khilafat*. In western democracy the people are sovereign, in Islam sovereignty is vested in God and the people are his representatives.
>
> (Mawdudi, 1948:31)

Thus true Muslims should band together to resist such 'idolatry' and strive for the creation of an Islamic society, as well as maintaining individual righteousness. For Mawdudi, the imperative of Islam directs individuals to develop a community of faith which promotes social change by creating a society fully obedient to God's law. Mawdudi called this state the 'Caliphate based on the Prophetic Pattern' or *Khilafah 'ala Minhaj al-Nabuwah* (Ahmad and Ansari, 1979:20). It has no power to make new laws, but will work within the limits prescribed by Allah through fully implementing Islamic law without any compromise with Western legal codes or the ideologies implicit in nationalism, secularism and Western-based democracies.

> Legislation in an Islamic state should be within the limits pre-scribed by the *shari'a* (divine law). The injunctions of God and His Prophet are to be accepted and obeyed and no legislative body can modify them or make any new laws which are contrary to their spirit. The duty of ascertaining the real intent of those commandments which are open to interpretation should devolve on people possessing a specialised knowledge of the *shari'a*.
>
> (Mawdudi, 1948:32)

For Mawdudi, a Muslim society that either creates its own constitution or borrows legal or constitutional frameworks from outside Islam breaks its covenant with God and therefore loses its right to be considered Islamic.

Interpretations and challenges to unity

	Sufi movements	Wahhabi-type reform movements of the nineteenth century	Revival movements of the twentieth century: (Salafi or neo-Wahhabi)
Shahada	The emphasis is on immanence. The clause *La illaha illa'llah* is interpreted with a slight monistic or pantheist emphasis. That is, there is nothing but God. The focus is on oneness – one without a second. Divine Unity insists that there can be no duality.	Interpreted in the traditional manner as opposition to idol worship and polytheism. Allah was known about and even worshipped by pre-Islamic Arabs along with idols. The revelation is an attack on polytheism – no god but God, this *shirk* (making others equal to God) becomes the greatest sin.	Mawdudi interpreted the clause 'there is no god but God', with apolitical dimension. He insists that it is a statement of relationship not fact. The relationship is one of sovereignty. Islam is about submission to an almighty sovereign and achieved by obedience to the revelation. Thus the *shahada* is made political and all non-Muslim ideologies are idolatry (*shirk*). Thus Western imports such as socialism or democracy should not be imported into Islam.
Qur'an	The eternal word of God and the primal source for the revelation. However, there is an esoteric approach to its interpretation.	The eternal word of God and the primal source for the revelation but emphasis on the exoteric – traditional jurisprudence is accepted as a valid and trustworthy addition to the revelation.	The eternal word of God and the primal source for the revelation but emphasis is on the exoteric. However, tradition is denied and Muslims should go directly to the Qur'an. The emphasis is on self-understanding and *ijtihad* is permitted for authorised scholars.
Muhammad	The Prophet is regarded as pre-existent – all creation comes into existence for his birth to take place. He is the exemplar of spirituality and the ultimate mystic. He is the recipient of prayers of intercession. The inner teachings of the Qur'an are exemplified in his closeness to Allah.	The chosen mouthpiece of God – human but just, pious and righteous. He provides the exemplar for correct behaviour and practice.	The chosen mouthpiece of God – human but just, pious and righteous. He provides the exemplar for correct behaviour and practice. There is a major emphasis on the Prophet's political and social aspects – he created the ideal Muslim society in Medina. The role of statesman and prophet of God are inseparable.

In the following chapters we will be exploring in more detail some of the major divisions in the Muslim religious and political spectrum, including Shi'as, Sufis, Wahhabis and some of the twentieth-century revivalist movements. In regard to the contents of this chapter, it is sufficient to indicate that there are major differences of interpretation on a number of issues. I have chosen to briefly highlight key areas of controversy only within three arenas; the *shahada*, that is the basic statement of Muslim belief and allegiance; the Qur'an; and Muhammad. This selection is based on the fact that these three are considered to be essentials for all Muslims, and would be fundamental areas where Muslims would like to affirm agreement.

Conclusion

It can be convincingly argued that the integrated community of believers submissive to the will of Allah as proclaimed by the Qur'an has not existed since the death of the Prophet, but that has not prevented Muslims through the ages from chasing the ideal and attempting to renew the original vision. However, sectarian divisions over the question of authority split the community, and the various aspects of the Prophet's charismatic authority were passed onto several different institutions. The *umma* was maintained by the political authority of the caliphate and by the *ulema* who codified and preserved doctrine into a system of law. The Umayyads transformed the *umma* into an Arab dynasty and under the Abbasids the *ulema* and the caliphate separated from each other, and eventually the caliphate itself had ceased to exist in all but name, finally disappearing at the end of the Ottoman Empire. Independent Muslim kingdoms came into being, and the *ulema* managed to hold the Muslim world together through the *shari'a*, but they themselves were divided by differences of belief and were unable to maintain their hold under the challenge of European civilisation.

Throughout Muslim history, devout Muslims have been concerned with the question of what constitutes the true *umma* and how it should be maintained. Exactly who constitutes this category of true Muslim has been a source of contention ever since the Prophet's death. This debate has been exacerbated by the conflict between the respective values of Islam and the West. The result has been the division of the *umma* into many factions, each justifying their position by various interpretations of the message of Islam. Gibb stated that 'the first lesson learned by them was that the community must not be identified with or confused with political regimes. Thus political division in no way impaired the unity of the *umma*' (Gibb, 1963:174–175). He argued that the central doctrine of *tawhid* justifies Islamic totality and universalism. The aim has always been to establish a highly integrated and united *umma*. In reality, Muslim sectarianism has its roots in the political divisions of the *umma* and the various attempts to restore unity that in themselves create new factions. These factional differences in the community are in direct opposition to the ideal of universalism which is preached to Muslims everywhere.

Despite all this, however, ordinary Muslims can look to the wider Muslim community and feel that they belong to it even though it is divided into various competing factions whose differences can lead to violence and civil war. Montgomery Watt takes up this position and states:

> Beyond all these considerations it remained a fact that the ordinary Muslim could look at the great Islamic society or community and feel that he (sic) belonged to it and that it was in a sense his – that it did not belong to one or more ruling groups however great their power might be. (Watt, 1961:174)

In particular, there is a sense of belonging which is maintained through the unity of Islam's ritual or cultic practices. The *salat*, Hajj, and Ramadan provide Muslims with a strong sense of religious communion that cannot be repeated in any other world faith community. In addition, in spite of the diversity of Muslim cultures, I often tell my students that if I was to be transported to any Muslim nation, I would know within minutes that I was in a Muslim environment. There are, however, powerful groups of Muslims who insist that this cultural similarity is not enough. They say that Islam has to be a fully comprehensive way of life, taking its inspiration from the life of the Prophet and his Companions. Their definition of *umma* is far more exclusive, insisting that Islam's diversity be moulded into a homogeneous entity, first through full implementation of the *shari'a* in all Islamic states, and then eventually breaking out of the confines of nation states into a revived caliphate.

CHAPTER 6

Martyrdom: the Shi'a doctrine of suffering opposed to the Sunni doctrine of 'Manifest Success'

Whilst providing an historical overview focusing on the division between Sunni and Shi'a Muslims, this chapter will explore the attitudes towards martyrdom in both traditions, assessing how these attitudes arise out of doctrinal interpretations developed from attempts to comprehend the different historical fortunes of the respective movements within Islam. It is to be hoped that a deeper insight into Muslim attitudes on martyrdom will be gleaned from the content. In the process of exploring these different attitudes to martyrdom, the chapter will define how the two traditions diverged politically and socially as each experienced a diametrically opposite response to the Qur'an's theology of 'Manifest Success'.

With the media packed with coverage of 'suicide bombers' virtually on a daily basis, ranging from the devastating attacks on the World Trade Center, now known throughout the world as the events of 9/11, to the regular explosions in Iraq or Israel, the phenomenon of martyrdom as part of armed struggle or *jihad* seems to be ubiquitous in the Muslim world, in spite of the evidence that it was first used in the modern period as a 'terror' strategy by the Tamil Hindu secessionists in Sri Lanka. The impact of the images of carnage and devastation on our television screens can help to produce a stereotype of Muslim behaviour as innately violent, which feeds into bigotry and can create a fear of the 'other' amongst the general populace.

Yet martyrdom in Islam has not been part and parcel of the psyche of the majority of Muslims throughout history. The Sunni majority have never espoused it, even though justification for it is given in some verses of the Qur'an. Rather it has always been more commonly associated with the passions aroused by the deaths of the leaders of the Shi'a minority throughout their own unique history that has given rise to a cult of martyrdom particular to that branch of Islam.

The Qur'an mentions martyrdom in the context of the first Muslim deaths at the battles of Badr and Uhud, which occurred after the *Hijra* to Medina, and involved both the Makkan and Medinan converts to the new faith in armed struggle with superior forces that opposed them. In order to further our understanding of how attitudes to martyrdom diverged amongst the Sunni and the Shi'a in the first centuries after Muhammad's death and went on to influence contemporary events, it is necessary to understand the significance of the doctrine of 'Manifest Success' that developed during the period of the two battles and how this influenced theological positions in regard to the relationship with God and events in the world. Malise Ruthwen, in the same context, refers to Islam being 'programmed for victory' and argues that it is a 'triumphalist faith' (Ruthwen, 2004:39).

However, it is essential to see how this impacted differently on both the majority Sunni and minority Shi'a communities in their subsequent religious manifestations. Ruthwen points out that the Shi'a never shared in the triumphalism of their Sunni compatriots, but instead developed, like Christianity, 'myths and theologies for dealing with failure' (2004:39). Yet, I will argue eventually that one key to understanding the current phenomena of 'suicide terrorists', who are predominantly drawn from the Sunni majority, is that since the decline of Muslim power in the face of Western political supremacy, Sunni 'triumphalism' has been seriously challenged. The consequence is a drawing closer to Shi'a sensitivities and their theologies of 'suffering'.

In Islam, as with Christianity and Judaism, God works with humanity in history, accompanying them through the peaks and troughs of fortune to eventually establish his will. It is the hope of the true believer that he emerges finally victorious alongside his faithful but longsuffering community or remnant at the end of historical time before the final Judgement Day. It is in an examination of these ebbs and flows of fortune that we can get a clue as to how theological positions and subsequent practices develop in both the Shi'a and Sunni communities; supplying them with divergent worldviews with regard to success and failure, yet accommodated within the over-arching framework of Islam's commonality.

Muhammad's period of intense ridicule and revilement from the Makkan merchants had been confirmed in the Qur'an as the lot of God's prophets, drawing upon a number of examples from Jewish religious history and also citing Jesus' inability to win the authorities to his side. In doing so, the Qur'an suggests to the fledgling Muslim community, struggling with doubt, that the abuse and ridicule aimed at the Prophet and his message was normative for the messengers of God and that their suffering could be taken as proof of the authenticity of the new revelation.

However, the *Hijra* (migration) to Medina had transformed Muslim fortunes. Muhammad's position after this formative event was one of influence and status in the oasis settlement of Medina. The Battle of Badr, against an overwhelming Makkan force, provided both the first Muslim deaths in battle and a surprising victory that was considered miraculous and was perceived as provided by God's special dispensation to his new chosen community. The Qur'an was to declare that angels fought alongside the Muslims: 'Remember you implored the assistance of your Lord, and He answered you; "I will assist you with a thousand of the angels, ranks on rank"' (Qur'an 8:9).

This success was to bring about an important change in the theological position developed in Makkah, and from this date forward (624CE) the majority of Muslims would regard victory and success in the world as proof that they were God's final community of revelation. Once more, the Qur'an noted the transformation.

> Call to mind when you were a small band, despised throughout the land, and afraid that men might despoil and kidnap you; but He provided a safe asylum for you, strengthened you with His aid, and gave you good things for sustenance: that you might be grateful. (Qur'an 8:26)

Successes there were, and the next two centuries would see Islam became a major religious force in the world and the Arabs a significant civilisation. Even the great empires of Persia and Byzantine would collapse under the weight of Islam's growth, and Christian Europe itself would be endangered.

The linking of God's special favour and worldly success was not a new theology: it can be found in the biblical writings of the Jews and has influenced certain forms of Christianity from time to time. It can be found today, especially in North America amongst certain evangelical circles, in the form of 'prosperity theology', a belief that the acceptance of Jesus Christ as a personal saviour leads to material well-being and success. It is a natural development of the kind of monotheism that perceives God as working alongside a special community selected as part of the plan for human salvation. The Qur'an called the phenomenon 'Manifest Success' or 'Manifest Victory'. 'Verily We have granted you a Manifest Victory that Allah may forgive you your faults of the past and those to follow; fulfil His favour to you; and guide you on the Straight Path' (Qur'an 48).

However, such a theology has a problem with failure. Does material misfortune mean that God's favour has been withdrawn? If the withdrawal of grace is permanent, the religious community has no further justification for existence but if it is temporary, then the believers must seek reparation, the means to restore divine favour. The evidence of the return of God's favour will be a restoration of material well-being. Thus the theology of 'Manifest Success' demands that all future failure be seen either as a test of God's faithful in adversity or a sign that in some way the believers were lacking in the required submission, faith or obedience.

Soon after the Battle of Badr, Muhammad led a force of Muslims against the Makkan merchants who were seeking vengeance for the defeat at Badr. The two enemies met at a place called Uhud. The Muslims met with heavy losses including the death of Hamza, the uncle of the Prophet, and even Muhammad did not escape without injury. The Qur'an was to state, 'How else could God know who were true believers, except by observing who persevered in the face of adversity' (Qur'an 3:136). The fault of the Muslims was that they disobeyed the Prophet who wished to remain in Medina and persuaded him to engage the enemy against his wishes.

Martyrdom

Thus it is not surprising that the Qur'an provides its most comprehensive section on martyrs after the Battle of Uhud. Once again, Muslims have paid the ultimate price for their faith and lost their lives, but this time not in the environment of success as at Badr. At Uhud it was in a subdued atmosphere of recrimination and disobedience to the Prophet's instructions. The significance of this is reflected in the number of verses in the chapter *al-Imran*, in all around forty *ayats*. The lessons of the battle are reflected upon and Badr is recalled as the example of God's intervention on behalf of the faithful. 'Allah made it but a message of hope for you, and an assurance to your hearts: there is no help except from Allah, the Exalted, the Wise' (Qur'an 3:126).

But in reassuring the faithful concerning the setback at Uhud, Allah explains: 'Such days of varying fortunes We give to men and men by turns: that Allah may know those that believe, and that He may take to Himself from your ranks Martyr-witnesses to Truth' (Qur'an 3:140). Thus the cycles of fortune require responses from the faithful; especially Allah will look to those who remain steadfast under fire.

> How many of the Prophets fought in Allah's way, and with them fought large bands of godly men? But they never lost heart if they met with disaster in Allah's way, nor did they weaken in will or give in. And Allah loves those who are firm and Steadfast. (Qur'an 3:146)

For those who remained 'steadfast' and lost their lives, eternal reward is promised in the afterlife. 'Think not of those who are slain in Allah's way as dead. Nay, they live, finding their sustenance in the Presence of their Lord. They rejoice in the Bounty provided by Allah' (Qur'an 3:169–170).

Sunni success

In these two battles, Sunni Muslims found a pattern that was to re-emerge again and again throughout history. When confronted with political setbacks and military failure, the *ulema* or religious reformers demanded religious revival as an attempt to regain God's favour. Significantly there was no challenge to the doctrine of 'Manifest Success' until the invasion of the Mongols in the thirteenth century destroyed the centres of Arab Muslim civilisation. The shock to the Sunni mentality resulted in self-reflection, the religious seeing the downfall of the dynasty caused by its profligate behaviour and departure from the ways of the Prophet and the first Muslims. They called for religious revival to revitalise Muslim fortunes and return the community to its supremacy. Fortunately for them, Allah seemed to heed their call as countless numbers of the godless barbarian hordes embraced Islam. The religion was able to recover but at the cost of Arab civilisation and its place at the heart of Muslim culture.

Henceforth three empires would dominate the Muslim world until their collapse under the weight of the emerging European powers from the eighteenth century onwards. None of the three were Arab – the Moghuls in India were Turkic from Central Asia, the Safavids were Persian and the ruling powers of the Ottomans were Turks controlling the old Arab heartlands. However, for the Sunni world, the Ottoman and Moghul Empires were sufficient in their magnificence to reassure Muslims that all was right between them and God. Yet the fall from power that resulted from European colonialism was to be the biggest shock of all – for the new imperial powers brought before Sunni Muslims the vision of a revival of Christian authority – a religion which God was supposed to have supplanted by Islam as his new community of salvation. The response throughout the eighteenth and nineteenth centuries was a succession of regional religious revivals, for defeat could only be interpreted as a sign of God's disfavour. To restore favour to his last community it was necessary to be self-critical, and seek revival and the reform of Islam.

The Shi'a

Yet the Shi'a story was always significantly different. Not for them the repeated patterns of revival to recover 'Manifest Success', for, on the contrary, they had never had it in the first place. A despised minority in the wider Sunni world, they remained caught in the theology of suffering that had belonged to all Muslims in Makkah prior to the *Hijra*. The Medinan transferral to a theology of triumphalism passed them by.

The origins of the Shi'a division go back to an incident that took place not long before Muhammad's death, when he was returning to Medina from his farewell pilgrimage to Makkah. The Prophet and his Companions stopped near a pool called Ghadir Khumm. It is said that after asking them if it was true that he was closer to them than they were to themselves, he said something of major significance for the succession. It is believed by the Shi'a that Muhammad took his son-in-law and cousin, Ali, one of the very first Muslims, by the hand and said, 'He, of whom I am the patron, of Him Ali is also the patron.' To many this signified that Ali was Muhammad's chosen successor (Brown, 2004:101).

It would neither have been a surprising decision nor an unpopular one. After all, Ali was married to the Prophet's daughter, Fatima, and was the father of Muhammad's grandchildren. Even the Qur'an seemed to endorse the specialness of Muhammad's family and direct bloodline. 'And Allah only wishes to remove all abomination from you, Ye Members of the Family, and to make you pure and spotless' (Qur'an 33:33).

In Shi'a conviction, Ali was blessed with a charisma similar to Muhammad's own: one who shone with Allah's light on his countenance. Shi'a tradition states that Muhammad came to know that Ali was his successor when it was revealed to him on the Night Journey, the mystical ascension to the divine presence (Brown, 2004:101).

However, it was not to be. On the Prophet's deathbed, when his family were gathered around him and thereafter performing the rites of death, the elders of the tribes met and chose Abu Bakr, another of the first Muslims and close Companion of the Prophet. Abu Bakr had the advantage of being of the Quraysh, the foremost tribe in Makkah and fitted the image of the desert ideal of leadership. The appointment of Abu Bakr as the caliph (*Khalifa*), one who would stand as regent in the absence of the Prophet of God guiding the community forward in obedience to the Qur'an but without the prophetic powers of Muhammad, began a succession of leaders that would become the Sunni caliphate. Yet there were those who never accepted the decision, believing it to be in opposition to the Prophet's wishes and these people became known as the Party of Ali – Shi'at Ali.

However, Ali himself appeared to accept the authority of Abu Bakr and peace was maintained for a while. Abu Bakr died two years later in 634CE, having consolidated the community. He was succeeded by Umar, the second caliph, who died in 644CE as a result of being stabbed by a Persian slave. But, in spite of his violent death, Umar consolidated the doctrine of 'Manifest Success' in that during his decade as caliph he was able to conquer significant territories belonging to both the Persians and the Roman Byzantine Empires. The territories of present day Syria, Palestine, Egypt and Jordan had all fallen into Muslim hands. Perhaps most significant of all was Palestine, for symbolically it represented the two earlier revelations of Judaism and Christianity and now it was *dar al-Islam*, Muslim territory. It must have seemed as if God was giving everything to his new people and reassuring them of their destiny.

After Umar came Uthman, one of Muhammad's many son-in-laws.

Once again Ali and his supporters bowed to the decision to bypass their claims to his leadership but it was probable that resentment was now rising amongst them, for Uthman cannot be said to have had the same level of popular support as the previous two caliphs. Assassinated in 656CE, Uthman became the first of the Muslim leaders to fall at the hands of fellow believers and thus it can be seen that divisions opened up soon after Muhammad's demise. He had been an old man on his appointment and never seemed to have the control over the now rapidly expanding Arab empire that had been managed by his predecessors.

It was not only the supporters of Ali who were discontented. Some of the pious remembered that Uthman's family had been early opponents of the Prophet and even though he had married two of Muhammad's daughters he seemed close to the Makkan aristocracies, especially the Quraysh, the great enemies of the early days of Islam. He placed their leaders in key positions and allowed them once again to control Arab affairs, but this time from within Islam. He also appropriated funds from the conquests to his own use, even though they were supposed to be shared equally amongst the warriors. Finally he produced a definitive version of the Qur'an authorised by committee. Nigosian suggests that this antagonised the pious whose oral traditions varied (Nigosian, 2004:19). The dissatisfaction grew, the insurgents in the army asked Uthman to step down as caliph, he refused and was killed. The breaking of the Prophet's command that Muslims should not draw weapons against each other was to have profound and lasting impact on the Muslim community.

Now, at last, some in the Muslim community turned to Ali, who was appointed the fourth caliph. But not everyone remained happy with the choice and serious problems were to create havoc with Ali's time as caliph. First Muhammad's widow and the daughter of Abu Bakr, the outspoken A'isha, objected and argued that Ali was part of the plot to kill Uthman. Trying to heal the wounds in the Muslim ranks, he decided not to seek revenge on Uthman's killers but rather to look for arbitration to settle matters. Thus he provoked the wrath of both those who sought revenge and of Muhammad's youngest wife, Ayesha. Civil war broke out between the forces loyal to Ali and an army raised by A'isha. Ali was victorious and banished Ayesha to Medina.

But more problems were to follow. Ali decided to move the centre of the caliphate to Kufah, a town in Iraq where he had more support.

However, this time he was attacked by Mu'awiya, the governor of Damascus and cousin of Uthman. Mu'awiya was a member of the Umayyad clan of the Quraysh tribe and as such would have been politically opposed to Ali's caliphate as it undermined the gains made by the Quraysh during the caliphate of Uthman. The battle was indecisive but one of the conditions of the truce was that Ali should submit the caliphate to arbitration. Ali agreed and thus helped to create a new faction who challenged his legal right to treat the caliphate in such a way, seeking arbitration rather than the command of God. This group became known as the Kharijites (the Seceders) who developed into a number of radical movements, having in common the belief that piety was the only qualification for leadership of the community. In 661CE, his power reduced, Ali was to fall to a Kharijite assassin's knife.

Thus ended the rule of the four caliphs who had been amongst the foremost of the Companions of Muhammad, and it is traditional belief that the period of their rule continues the golden age of Islam when the authenticity of the revelation was maintained. This period has been designated that of the four 'rightly-guided' by Sunni Muslims. Ali's death brought the caliphate into the hands of Mu'awiya, and the empire once again moved its centre to a new location in Damascus. Thus a dynasty came into existence, known as the Umayyad Empire, during which the Arabs consolidated their power from the borders of India to North Africa. But many felt that, as with the parallel example of Constantine making Christianity the religion of the Roman Empire, the heart of Islam had been ripped out. The pious tried to keep alive the lifestyle of the Prophet and his Companions, avoiding the excesses and worldliness of the ruling dynasty, but in many ways the Quraysh could be said to have achieved victory over the egalitarian religious revolution that had destroyed their power in Makkah.

The rebellion of Hussain

Whatever the historical events may have been surrounding Ali, there is no doubt that for the Shi'a, he and the surviving direct descendants of Muhammad, the *ahl al-Bayt*, the 'People of the Household', all become significant figures of their religious imagination. Of the Prophet's four daughters only Fatima outlived him and she died one year later in 633CE. The wife of Ali, she appears as a luminary for the

Shi'a. Known as the 'luminous' or the 'radiant', her life was soon to be elevated by the devout. Surrounded by miracle stories concerning her birth, life and the birth of two sons, who were believed to have been born through her left thigh, she is known as *batul*, a pure virgin. It is said that she never menstruated and Annemarie Schimmel reminds us that in many respects Fatima, after the martyrdom of her son Hussain, becomes the equivalent for the Shi'a of Mary's role as Mater Dolorosa (Schimmel, 1985:18). Sickly throughout her short life, her suffering and purity become emblematic for the fate of the *ahl al-Bait*.

Worse was to come, as Ali himself next fell to the assassin's knife. The Shi'a developed the theological and political position that Ali should by right have been the first caliph, handing on to the 'People of the Household', the Prophet's direct family descendants, thus giving the leadership of the Muslims over to a rule of the bloodline which mysteriously contained some of Muhammad's spiritual power and authority. The Sunnis, on the other hand, acknowledged the authority of the caliphs, even if some of them may have been less certain of those that came after the first four. In many ways, what took place was a classic sociological dilemma that occurs at the death of a founder and the loss of charismatic leadership. The Umayyads were content to accept the more institutional leadership of the community, begun with the more rational choice of Abu Bakr. The shift from charismatic leadership to a fully institutional leadership takes place gradually for most Sunnis with the first four caliphs providing a bridge between the two types of authority. As we shall see in the next chapter, not all Sunnis felt this way and some were able to resurrect charismatic leadership through the institution of sainthood. The Shi'a, on the other hand, utilised the doctrines of the pure and unsullied 'People of the Household' to retain charismatic leadership and resist the dominant institutional power established by the Umayyads.

After Ali's death, the Shi'a may have been inclined to accept pragmatically the reality of Umayyad power but only with the retention of a sense of grievance. It is a central belief that Ali and Mu'awiya made a sacred pact after the battle between their forces in which Ali agreed to Mu'awiya's succession to the caliphate but only if he renounced the right of his son Yazid to follow him. On Mu'awiya's death, the leadership of the Muslims was to revert to the grandsons of Muhammad, Hassan and Hussain.

Whatever the truth, it is believed that Hassan, the elder of the two grandsons, was persuaded to relinquish his claim to the caliphate,

and retired into exile in Medina where he died in strange circumstances. According to the Shi'ite version of the tale, he was poisoned
by the Umayyad leadership. Thus the tale of the woes of the family
continues: destined to be martyred and deprived of their birthright as
the Sunnis grew from strength to strength. But the real fateful story
that grips the Shi'a religious imagination, in effect marking out their
differences from the Sunnis and providing the myth for a theology of
patient suffering, is discovered in the tragic circumstances of the
death of Hussain, the Prophet's sole surviving grandson.

After the death of Mu'awiya in 680CE, his son Yazid inherited the
caliphate, thus beginning a hereditary dynasty. The details vary
according to which side is telling it. One version states that Yazid
placed a repressive general to subdue Ali's stronghold in Kufah. It is
said that the Kufans called for Hussain to liberate them, promising to
support his right to the caliphate. Hussain was intercepted on his way
to the rescue by forces loyal to Yazid and persuaded to move in another direction. He then departed for Karbala where he set up camp on 2
October 680CE (the second day of Muharram). Other accounts claim
that Hussain marched on Damascus from his father's old stronghold
in Kufa with a force of seventy-two loyal followers, believing im-
plicitly in Allah's promise to bring victory to the righteous even by
miraculous means as described in the Qur'an after the defeat at
Uhud. After arrival in Karbala, he was trapped by the Umayyad
armies of Yazid under the command of Umar ibn Sa'ad, who insisted
Hussain could not leave unless he submitted to the authority of Yazid.

Whatever the truth, Hussain's small force was attacked in Karbala
on the tenth day of the Muslim month of Muharram by an overwhelmingly superior army comprising five thousand armed troops.
In Shi'a accounts, the fighting raged all day on the tenth day of
Muharram, a day to be known henceforth by the Shi'a as *Ashura*. By
the afternoon, Hussain remained defiant, cradling his own dead son
in his arms, only to be cut down with his last surviving companions.
Those who survived were beheaded. Hussain's widow, Zaynab, and
his surviving son, Ali, were brought in chains to Yazid who gloated
over his victory for days over the decapitated head of Hussain.
Eventually the widow and her son were released.

Thus it is believed that a wicked and ruthless tyrant came to usurp
the caliphate that rightfully belonged to the family of the Prophet.
This motif would run throughout Shi'a interpretations of history.
Henceforth the Shi'a would view the mainstream of Sunni Islam,

although ostensibly successful and the majority of Muslims, as representative of an illegitimate and degenerate empire that could never be the true people of God. The escape of Hussain's son, Ali, from the slaughter ensured the survival of the true inheritors of Islam, the direct line of the Prophet, replete with their special powers inherited through his bloodline that permitted them to know the inner secrets of the Qur'an, and thus qualified them to lead the faithful. For the Shi'a these were the true leaders of the community, known as the Imams and differentiated from the Sunni *imams* who are merely leaders of the prayer. Amongst the Ithna'ashariyya, the Twelver Shi'as as they are known, still the dominant group in Iran and Iraq, there are believed to be twelve Imams beginning with Ali. But all Shi'a groups are united in acceptance of the first six Imams. They are as follows:

1. Imam Ali Ibn Talib, the cousin and son-in-law of Muhammad.
2. Imam Hassan ibn Ali (d.669), the son of Ali and brother of Hussain.
3. Imam al-Hussain ibn Ali (d.680), the son of Ali, the *Sayyid ash-Shuhada*, the 'Prince of Martyrs'.
4. Imam Ali Zayn al-Abidin (d.713), the son of Hussain, and supposedly quiescent in the struggles between Shi'a and Sunni.
5. Imam Muhammad al-Baqir (d.731), the son of Ali Zayn al-Abidin, a significant scholar, attributed with the development of Shi'a laws and doctrines.
6. Imam Ja'far al-Sadiq (d.765), the son of al-Baqir, also quietist and scholarly in his approach to the caliphate. It was during his period that the Shi'a doctrine of the infallibility of the Imams was developed.

After this period, the Shi'a community split into two concerning the succession, with the Isma'ilis preferring Ja'far's eldest son. However, the Twelvers look to the younger son, Imam Musa al-Kazim. The succession then continues down through to the twelfth Imam, Muhammad al-Mahdi, who contains all the hopes of the Shi'a faithful for final vindication and success.

Shi'a hopes were raised for a while when the Abbasid revolution against the Umayyads called for and won their support. The Abbasid dynasty, which overthrew the Umayyad caliphs in 750CE, had its origins in another branch of the Prophet's family. Abu Hashim, the son of Muhammad ibn al-Hanifiyya (d.700) who was the step-brother to Hassan and Hussain, built up strong support in Kufa. On his death in 718CE, the Abbasid family, descendants of Muhammad's uncle al-Abbas, claiming to be the legitimate successors of Abu Hashim, took over the movement. With a stroke of genius, the Abbasids recruited Shi'a support with the message of an imminent coming of 'the preferred one from the house of Muhammad' (Brown, 2004:102). The Shi'a understood this to mean their Imam and joined the successful rebellion. Once in power, the Abbasids found the support of their erstwhile allies a problem and repressed the Shi'a with a significant degree of brutality. The key players who had participated in the rebellion against the Umayyads amongst the Shi'a were murdered.

The cult of martyrdom

Although the end of the hated Umayyads may have made it appear as if the Shi'a were finally being vindicated, the betrayal by the Abbasids who were considered allies must have convinced many of their ranks that the suffering and injustice would continue forever. The Shi'a's embracing of a cult of suffering based upon their sense of being Allah's righteous minority struggling against the sins of the world would be reinforced by their conviction that all their infallible Imams, the true servants of Allah from Ali to the eleventh Imam, were victims of violence by their enemies. The sense of being under continuous threat led to the practice of *taqiyya* (dissimulation), whereby Shi'a leaders and their followers could conceal their true beliefs to avoid persecution by their enemies. However, this pragmatic decision was deemed insufficient to avoid martyrdom and when the twelfth Imam provided no direct progeny, the significant doctrine of *ghayba* (occultation) appeared, in which Allah protected his last Imam by taking him to a special place of concealment.

This event was supposed to have occurred in 874CE and after this date a succession of official representatives known as *babs* intermediated mystically between the Imam and the faithful. In 941CE, the period of the greater *ghayba* began, where the Imam is *incommunicado* until his return as the *Mahdi* at the end of time to bring final vindication. Since that time, the Twelver Shi'a have been provided with authoritative teachings by the *fuqaha*, the religious scholars titled as *ayatollahs*, who interpret and transmit the Qur'an and collection of Hadith used by the Shi'a and implement Islamic law.

However, it is in the death of Imam Hussain that one most clearly sees the Shi'a's embracing of a cult of suffering in which redemption is found in the ultimate sacrifice of the pure and selfless grandson of the Prophet. If Ali, at times, appears to be more prominent as a spiritual leader than Muhammad himself, it is in Hussain that the Shi'a discover the embodiment of their fate and their hope for ultimate success. The event of Hussain's death known as the *Ashura* became the focus for a special kind of 'passion' piety that is expressed in heart-rending poetry and processions and dramatic re-enactments of the events that mark the annual occasion of Muharrum, a festival of mourning.

The festival combines a number of emotional features: first of all, there is shared mourning relived in intense rituals; secondly, there is a sense of Shi'a guilt for they had failed to rally round the Imam when he came to the aid of beleaguered Kufa, leaving him to his fate in Karbala; thirdly, there is a sense of hope and vindication that Hussain's tragic fate will redeem the Shi'a faithful; but fourthly, there is a veneration of martyrdom. The events of Karbala represent for the Shi'a the idea that to be a martyr is the ultimate fate of those who maintain the true faith.

Sometime in the eighteenth century, the passion play, known as the *ta'ziya*, materialised, in which the events of Hussain's life are re-enacted and commemorated and Shi'a doctrine is highlighted through examples from the Qur'an and relevant stories from the Jewish prophets and Shi'a heroes. At the commencement of the plays, the Angel Jibreel brings Muhammad a key, which the Prophet puts into the hands of his beloved and sinless grandson. The key opens the doors of Paradise. Thus Hussain's martyrdom contains strong overtones of salvation and redemption – a voluntary sacrifice on behalf of true believers to whom he will allow entry to Allah's final resting place for the faithful.

The festival of Muharram has a number of other features which bring Shi'a sensibilities to the surface. In the *Majalis*, assemblies of mourning, of which the passion plays form part, the replica of Hussain's tomb is carried in procession on the ninth day of the festival. The males of the Shi'a communities who participate, including adolescent boys, flagellate themselves with whips and chains, creating an atmosphere of frenzied guilt and mourning, but above all, glorifying the concept of *shahid* (martyrdom). Such processions take place in every village or town where sufficient numbers of Shi'a live and are the major religious event of the Shi'a strongholds of Iran and Southern Iraq, although banned in the latter under the regime of

Saddam Hussein, who feared their ability to mobilise the Shi'a against him. Interestingly, they have been restored since his downfall. The importance of the *Ashura* and its ritual re-enactments, which recreate and maintain the passions aroused by the martyrdom of Hussain, cannot be overestimated in understanding Shi'a sensibilities. It is ingrained in their religion and culture and it dominates their history as the enduring memory, repeated in every act of injustice felt to be perpetuated against them. Those who die in the cause of Shi'a resistance to oppression are assured entry to Paradise but are also held up as followers in the footsteps of the Prophet's blessed grandson, the prince of all martyrs.

The Iranian revolution

The evidence of the above is found in the events of the Iranian revolution in 1978, when the people rose up behind the leadership of Ayatollah Khomeini and overthrew the regime of the Shah. The initial act that sparked the revolution can be traced to the police opening fire on demonstrators in Qum protesting at a visit by President Carter and the continued enforced exile of Ayatollah Khomeini in France. Over seventy students were killed and on the traditional commemoration of their martyrdom, forty days after their deaths, the crowds poured on to the streets. Once again the police responded by shooting, killing another hundred people in Tabriz. Each killing resulted in more demonstrations, and each demonstration resulted in more martyrs.

Thus the nation approached the festival of Muharram at the beginning of December. The protests against the Shah were now religious in nature rather than political, as he had assumed for the Shi'a masses the identity of all the persecutors throughout history: a modern Yazid in whom each young student martyr took on something of the character of Hussain. At the request of the exiled ayatollah, the people came to the streets or to their balconies and shouted *Allah Akbar!* (God is great!). Millions responded to the call, showing the force of the opposition and the support for the revolution. When Muharram began, millions demonstrated each day, government offices were seized, massive strikes closed down the nation. Significantly, the demonstrators dressed in the white garb of martyrs, daring the troops and police to fire upon them. By the end of Muhurram, the Shah's regime was as good as over and in January 1979, he fled the country.

The Shi'a pattern of success and failure

It is not that the Shi'a never achieved moments of success in their troubled history; it is the emphasis that differentiates them from their Sunni compatriots. The Sunnis expected success and were surprised by failure. They reacted with religious revival against any outward manifestations of failure. The Shi'a embraced failure as their proof of being Allah's suffering remnant doomed to maintain the truth against overwhelming injustice until vindicated at the final days. Success was fleeting, evidence of the odds against them, and to be distrusted as they were surrounded by enemies and even apparent friends were waiting to betray them.

The pattern of Shi'a success and failure in history can be shown as the following key stages but it is the theological interpretation of the events that is significant:

1. The pre-Safavid empire marked by failed attempts to carve out a Shi'a state
2. The Safavid Empire – a taste of 'Manifest Success'
3. The collapse of the Safavids
4. Modern Iran – a Shi'a stronghold
5. The Pahlavi dynasty – a godless tyranny
6. The Iranian revolution
7. The Islamic Republic – *Velayat-i Faqih*

The pre-Safavid period

During this period, up until the end of the fifteenth century, the Shi'a had developed their distinctive religious identity based on their own understanding of the events of early Muslim history. However, they were not without a political dimension for their main cause of discontent was rooted in the question of leadership. Yet this question of dissent from the Sunni mainstream was able to harbour a number of other discontented factions. Southern Arabs used the Shi'a identity to provide a vehicle for their need to assert their separation from Northern Arabs. More significantly, the Persians, with their ancient memories of civilisation and empire that pre-dated the Arab conquest, resented the inferiority that was imposed on them because of their non-Arab identity. Culturally and linguistically they were disadvantaged, for the revelation of God had been given to Arabs and in the language of Arabic. Their dissatisfaction was to have a major impact on the success of the Abbasid uprising. The movement of the centre of the Muslim world from Damascus to Baghdad demonstrates the success of the Southern Arabs and the Persians, but it also brought the capital of the empire closer to the Shi'a heartlands. Fazlur Rahman argues that it was at this stage that a political movement was transformed into a unique religious sect, with its fundamental impulse derived from the death of Hussain at Karbala (Rahman, 1979:172).

We have already examined the Abbasid betrayal of their Shi'a supporters and it is during the period of the resulting persecution that the twelfth and final Imam, Muhammad al-Mahdi, disappears into occultation. After this event in 874CE the Shi'a remained in their strongholds of Kufa and Qum, referring to themselves as the *Imamiyya* but called *rafida* (rejectors) by their Sunni opponents. They are branded as *ghulat*, a term of abuse used for those who either believed in prophets after Muhammad or conferred divinity on someone other than Allah. In practice, only a few extreme Shi'a groups regarded Ali or Hussain as manifestations of God, but it is easy to understand how to outside eyes, the emotional veneration of the Prophet's family may have appeared suspect.

In 945CE, Baghdad was seized by the Buyids, who were adherents of Shi'a, and thus the capital of the Abbasid Empire and the home of the Sunni caliph was ruled over, along with territory in central Iraq, until 1055CE when overthrown by the Seljuq Turks. Additionally, another Shi'a dynasty, the Hamdanids, were able to establish control over northern Iraq and Syria in 944CE. These dynasties were to have far-reaching consequences. First, it established the possibility of Shi'a success but it also provided the legitimacy for Shi'a to spread throughout the Middle East. In this period, the Isma'ilis, the other branch of Shi'a, had established the Fatimid state in Egypt and North Africa.

The Shi'a states in Iraq and Syria came to an end with the rise of the Seljuqs, who had adopted a rigid and oppressive Hanifa interpretation of Sunni Islam. The Seljuqs were able to rule over the Shi'a heartlands in Iran and Iraq with little toleration for their Shi'a subjects. The situation remained as the status quo until the invasion of the Mongols in 1220CE. The sacking of the great centres of Muslim civilisation was to be the first major challenge to 'Manifest Success' for the Sunnis. However, the Shi'a seemed to have done better under the rule of the Ilkhanate Mongols than they did under the Seljuqs. For a short while,

Shi'a hopes were resurrected when the Mongol ruler, Oljeitu, who ruled from 1304 to 1316, converted to Shi'a Islam. However, his son, Abu Sa'id, was a deeply committed Sunni and the apparition of a Shi'a state over the conquered Muslim territories dissolved as quickly as it arose. In the second wave of Mongol invasions under Timur, the Shi'a landowners were allowed to retain their property and the Timurid period, although Timur was a Sunni, provided a period of relative calm throughout the fourteenth and fifteenth centuries, in which Shi'a numbers grew rapidly throughout Iran.

The Safavids

The Safavids were originally a Turkish Sufi order who in the fifteenth century converted to Shi'a, taking on a militancy that insisted upon Shi'a supremacy, claiming in the process to be descended from the seventh Imam. Throughout the sixteenth century, they expanded their domain throughout Iran, Iraq, Azerbaijan and the Caucusus, creating the first significant Shi'a empire. For many of the troops fighting under the charismatic leadership of Isma'il, he was the representative of the 'Hidden Imam', perhaps even the Imam himself. By 1512, still only 25 years old, he controlled all of Iran and declared himself the Shah. Shi'a was introduced as the state religion and Sunnis were asked to renounce loyalty to the caliphs and be governed by Shi'a *ulema* in religious matters. However, not all went smoothly, as major conflicts broke out with the Ottomans which went on for the next two centuries, thus continuing the ancient struggles between Sunni and Shi'a. The fortunes of the Safavids rose and fell but certainly reached their apex under the reign of Shah Abbas I (1588–1629), who succeeded in defeating the Ottomans, restoring large amounts of territory previously lost, and also making significant treaties with Europe. It was during Abbas' reign that Isfahan became a centre of arts and culture that rivalled anywhere in the Eastern or European world. After Abbas, the empire slowly declined under the continued opposition from the Ottomans and the Uzbeks in the North.

Modern Iran

After the decline of the Safavids, Iran was conquered by Afghanistan, the Russians invaded from the North and the Ottomans from the South. Any hope of an independent Shi'a state seemed to be at an end.

However, in 1726, Nadir Shah, an Afghan warlord, converted to Shi'a and drove the enemies out. After crowning himself Shah of Iran, however, he converted back to Sunni but his efforts to convert the people failed. After Nadir Shah's assassination in 1747, Iran fell into chaos until the Qajar dynasty was established in 1796. The religious significance of this period lies in the division of power between the Shi'a *ulema* and the court. The Qajars renounced one half of the old Safavid title given to the Shahs, that of 'Shadow of God on Earth and representative of the Hidden Imam'. The *ulema* were declared 'the representative of the Hidden Imam' and remain so to the present day.

In the nineteenth century, Iran attempted to modernise along European lines. Shah Nasiru'd-Din (1848–1896) granted several economic concessions to European powers, but failed to recognise either the strength of nationalism developing amongst the population or the growth of Pan-Islamic movements. He was assassinated in 1896. In the early decades of the twentieth century, a constitutional movement sought to provide a parliamentary democracy similar to that of European nations. The Constitutionalists won, dissolved the monarchy and declared Shi'a as the state religion, but in 1911 the Russians invaded and restored the Shah.

In 1923, Reza Khan, influenced by the new secular republicanism of Turkey, overthrew the Shah but was not able to challenge the considerable authority of the Shi'a clerics who had both the loyalty of the masses and massive wealth, as *zakat*, the obligatory alms offering, was at their disposal. In reality the division of 'Shadow of God on Earth' and 'Representative of the Hidden Imam' had created a situation where Iran was ruled by two powers: the Shah on the one hand, and the *ulema* on the other. Reza Khan bowed to the wishes of the clerics, ceased his efforts to create a secular republic and instead began a new dynasty, with himself crowned as Shah Reza Pahlavi. Throughout the rest of his reign, Reza Pahlavi struggled to decrease the power of the *ulema*, introducing secular legal codes, the European calendar, and banning the wearing of the veil. In addition, he created government colleges that trained new clerics and issued official government certification.

The Shi'a struggle was now not so much with their Sunni counterparts, but with a new enemy, the secular values and modes of government of Europe and North America influencing their rulers. In 1941, Reza Khan was succeeded by his son Muhammad Reza Khan, who remained in power until forced to abdicate in 1979. From 1953, with the help of Britain and the USA, the Shah dismantled all the democratic institutions of the nation. In 1961, he disbanded the National Assembly and suspended elections, going further than his father to establish a government-controlled religion to challenge the historic power of the clerics. In addition, he tried to reclaim the title 'Representative of the Hidden Imam'. In order to enforce conformity to his regime, the Shah created a network of secret police, SAVAK, who engaged in torture and executions. The end result of these attempts to force the Iranian people to bend to his will was an empowerment of the clerics and a hatred for the Shah's regime and his supporters, the United States and Britain.

The Iranian revolution and the creation of the Islamic Republic

The most vocal of the Shah's critics, the Ayatollah Khomeini, had been exiled but had maintained his popularity with the people of Iran through radio broadcasts from neighbouring Iraq. Arguing the illegitimacy of the Shah's regime, he proposed government by Muslim jurisprudence, *velayat-i faqih*, with the *ulema* responsible for all administrative and judicial aspects of running the state apparatus. Legislation would be in the hands of an elected assembly but the *ayatollahs*, the elite of the *ulema*, would form a Guardian Council to watch over the assembly and maintain the purity of Islamic government, with the ultimate power kept to themselves to disband the assembly if it seemed to contradict the laws of Islam.

After the shift of US foreign policy towards a human rights agenda in 1977, Iran's censorship laws were relaxed. The result was the manifestation of people's grievances and a series of demonstrations and strikes. Khomeini's texts were circulated throughout the country in tracts which called for justice and the establishment of an Islamic state. Since the revolution in 1979, Iran has been involved in an experiment to govern itself by the tenets of Islamic jurisprudence as interpreted by the *ulema*. Government is by *velayat-i faqih*, interpreted as rule by *fiqh*, where the most learned of the *ulema* utilise their knowledge of the Qur'an, *Sunna*, and the precedent of the body of law created over time, to respond to new challenges thrown up by modernity. Although the elected government could pass new laws, the Guardian Council decides if they are in accord with Islam by applying the judicial principles of *fiqh*, or traditional Islamic jurisprudence.

Conclusion

It is ironic that the despised Shi'a, who had challenged the historical leadership of the Sunni caliphate unsuccessfully since Muhammad's death, and who had rarely had more than glimpses of the promised success due to the final community of God, should be the first to establish an Islamic state in the post-colonial period. Yet the Shi'a *ulema* were able to draw upon a unique history in which they shared with the people a sense of injustice and persecution, contained within a religious sentiment of suffering and martyrdom and a hope for final vindication as God's true but patient remnant. The Shi'a sense of history and destiny became a powerful weapon against the Shah and his Western allies, aligning the government with the evil forces that had persecuted the faithful as far back as the trials, tribulations and martyrdoms of Ali, Hasan and Hussain. However, the oppressors were no longer the powerful and the proud from amongst the Sunnis but found in the domination of the West, especially the USA and their allies in Muslim nations.

There is a strong passion motive in Shi'a Islam, where emotional sensibilities are keener than amongst their Sunni rivals. The strong opposition and crushing defeats that took place so many times in their history led to a seeking of consolation in religion. The verses on martyrdom in the Qur'an that accompanied the Muslim setback at Uhud would always be of more significance than the optimism of the 'Manifest Success' that appeared after Badr. Martyrdom would have a special place in the Shi'a psyche. The success at Badr may have had its martyrs, but their noble sacrifice was secondary, overlooked in the excitement of victory. It was at Uhud that the dead drew the attention of the Qur'an and its verses proclaimed the fortunes of the martyred as the ultimate witnesses of the faith. In failure, caused by disobedience or error, they paid the ultimate price of faithfulness. For the Shi'a, whose history was marked by injustice and hope of final vindication, martyrdom took on a special significance, enwrapped around the glorious death of Hussain, the ultimate sacrifice.

Shi'a religious sensibilities were built upon a cult of martyrdom and it is interesting to ask the question whether Shi'a patterns of failure, resulting in a grand narrative of suffering, rather than doctrines of 'Manifest Success' usually associated with Sunni Muslims, can throw any light on the contemporary phenomena of 'suicide bombings'. Although such cases need to be examined in the context of local causes, the necessary and concomitant embracing of martyrdom and its celebration after Uhud would seem to offer a way to theorise such sacrifices amongst Sunni movements. Certain situations, such as the lack of success in resolving the Palestinian question, or the more endemic problem of Muslim failure to revive their fortunes in a post-colonial situation, still leaving apparent 'Manifest Success' to the secular or post-Christian West, may lead to the Sunni psyche having more in common with the Shi'a worldview of non-vindicated injustice and a sense of continuing defeat. In such circumstances, some of the faithful may develop a cult of martyrdom closer to the theology of their Shi'a brothers, where Uhud rather than Badr provides the model and the Makkan theology of a longsuffering, despised people of God replaces Medinan triumphalism.

CHAPTER 7

Sufism: an aberration or the voice of traditional Islam?

*In this chapter, difference will continue to be explored by assessing the con-
tribution of Sufism to Islam and examining the claim of contemporary Sufis
that they represent traditional Islam. The contrary views of Muslim movements that criticise Sufis will be briefly considered and will build upon
Chapter 3 and further explore the tensions that exist between a variety of
nineteenth- and twentieth-century revivalist movements and traditional
Islam, especially its manifestations within Sufism. In so doing, attention will
need to be given to the term 'traditional' and 'orthodox' as understood by
Muslims.*

Contemporary studies of Islam often focus on the tensions between
Islam and the West or even conflicts between Islamic movements and
secular regimes in Muslim countries, but they rarely provide any in-
depth study of the sometimes equally vociferous divisions between
neo-orthodoxies and the many Sufi movements that remain across the
Muslim world. These conflicts are also entirely absent from the
Western media. Yet it is true to say that Sufism was regarded as the
traditional enemy of the neo-orthodox movements long before they
perceived the West as a threat. Before the domination of Europe, any
sign of decline in the Muslim community was blamed on inner lapses
within the *umma* and often laid at the door of Sufism by its critics.

With the belief that they were the custodians of the final revelation
for humankind from God, the representatives of Islam zealously
guarded the community from deviation or innovation. Either of
these could lead the community from the straight path and result in a

failure to protect the revelation in the original purity of its genesis. Internal political failure or conquest by non-Muslims were both likely to be interpreted as punishment for failing to maintain pristine Islam. Events such as the invasion of the Mongols, which destroyed the Abbasid Empire, or the rise of European domination from the eighteenth century onwards, drove Muslims in upon themselves to examine their own religious belief and practice. As a consequence a number of neo-orthodox movements were born that puritanically tried to purge the Muslim community of religious and cultural accretions said to be the influence of foreign cultures or other religions. Such movements were highly critical of Sufism and attempted to present it as a corrupted form of Islam influenced by Buddhists, Neo-Platonists, Hindus or Christian mystics, depending on the prevalent traditions within a given geographical region. For the neo-orthodox reformers, Sufism was the cause of Islam's decline.

So what is Sufism and how accurate are the claims of the neo-orthodox movements? To what degree is the Sufi counterclaim, that they are the authentic custodians of the beliefs and practices of traditional Muslims throughout Islamic history, a more accurate portrayal of the situation? Does Sufism remain a significant force within the Muslim world in the contemporary period?

Western scholars have often asserted that Sufism corresponds to Islamic mysticism and that the term derives from *suf*, the Arabic for wool, the material of the traditional Sufi garb. Yet Sufis themselves are more likely to refer to *safa*, meaning purity, or to trace their origins to the *Ahl al-Suffa*, the People of the Bench or Porch, picked out from amongst the original Companions of the Prophet as particularly pious in the Qur'an. It is believed that these poor but very devout Companions were offered a porch and bench in the entrance to Muhammad's quarters in the first mosque built in Medina. From this favoured position they were said to remember Allah day and night, remaining in constant prayer. It is believed by Sufis that the following verse from the Qur'an refers to these Muslims:

> And keep yourselves content with those who call upon their Lord morning and evening, seeking His Face, and let not thine eyes pass beyond them, seeking the pomp and glitter of this life; nor obey any whose heart We have permitted to neglect the remembrance of Us; one who follows his own desires, and his affair has become all excess. (Qur'an 18:28)

This description in the Qur'an of certain Companions of the Prophet who remembered God day and night constitutes the essence of Sufism to the present day. Those who define themselves as Sufis within Islam practise *tasawwuf*, defined as cleansing of the heart or purification of the ego through the constant remembrance of Allah, achieved through inward or spoken repetition of His divine Names. However, the primary reason for the recollection of Allah's names is to maintain God as the primary focus of the individual's life. The term *tasawwuf* is derived from the Arabic word *safa* and hence someone who attempts to purify their inner being by following *ilm al-tasawwuf* (the path of self-purification) is regarded as a Sufi.

Western orientalist scholarship has tended to concentrate its energies on translation and commentary of various Sufi texts written by those who were exceptional mystics and had experienced oneness with God, and has generally ignored the apprehension of Sufism by millions of Muslims worldwide, dismissing their experiences as 'folk' or 'popular' Islam. This has led to the common assumption that Sufism is solely Islamic mysticism, experienced by fortunate elites within the Muslim world.

Most Sufis do not consider themselves to be mystics, although they may aspire to experiences of closeness to God. Nicholson describes Sufism as: 'The transformation of the One transcendent God of Islam into One real Being who dwells and works everywhere, and whose throne is not less, but more, in the human heart than in the heaven of heavens' (Nicholson, 1989:8). However, most contemporary Sufis in my experience describe themselves simply as followers of the inner dimension of Islam, which they insist must accompany the outer practices and rituals of the religion. They would not deny the need for the outer practices nor the requirement for obedience to the *shari'a*, and they would also acknowledge the transcendence of God but, in addition, assert his immanence. Many would not be happy to be defined as Sufis at all, arguing that the necessity of the inner dimension of the faith alongside the outer cultic practices only makes them complete Muslims.

They would not be concerned too much about the etymology of the word 'Sufi' but they would be concerned about any definition of themselves that stated that their religious beliefs and practices were derived from outside the fold of Islam. Most practising Sufis are very keen to identify themselves at the core of Islam and support their beliefs and practices by constant reference to the Qur'an and the

Sunna of the Prophet. They trace their origins back to Muhammad and his Companions, and often even further, to the prophets of Israel and the figure of Jesus who is perceived as an outstanding Sufi. As stated by a contemporary British Sufi of the Naqshbandi order:

> The Sufi path is a path that did not originate from the Prophet Muhammad but it came at the time that Islam came, from Adam. It has always been the essence of Islamic teaching. It is like the soul/body relationship. Islam is the guidance of God for mankind. Sufism is its core, its soul. (quoted from Geaves, 2000:21)

The Sufi belief that their path to intimacy with God pre-dates the final revelation to Muhammad is not in any way unusual for Muslims. On the contrary, it is a central tenet of Islam that the revelation of the Qur'an was only the completion of a succession of contacts between God and human beings since Adam, the first Prophet. Neither would Sufis be too concerned with the criticism that their teachings can be found in the mystical paths of other religions. However, it would be imperative for them to deny that they were influenced by contact with such communities or as a result of syncretist processes. Rather they would argue that the similarities were echoes of the one universal truth revealed by God since the beginning of time to all communities, a doctrine taught in the Qur'an.

Perhaps the best illustration of Sufism's relationship to Islam can be summed up in the following example, often repeated wherever Sufis gather. The story is based on a Hadith narrated by Muslim ibn al-Hajjaj (d.875), whose collection is regarded as the most reliable along with that of Muhammad ibn Ismail Bukhari (d.870), and it speaks of the relationship between *Islam* (perfect submission), *Iman* (perfect faith) and *Ihsan* (perfected character).

> A man came up to the Prophet whilst he was sitting with some of his companions. He was unknown to any of them and wore white clothes. His hair was very black. He sat close to the Prophet and placed his hands on the Prophet's knees. He asked Muhammad, 'Tell me about Islam?' The Prophet replied, 'Islam is to bear witness that there is no god but Allah, and that Muhammad is His Prophet; to perform the prayer; to pay *zakat* (the poor tax); to fast in the month of Ramadan; and to undergo

the Hajj if it is possible.' The man replied, 'Correct, you have spoken the truth.' Then the man asked, 'What is *iman*?' The Prophet replied, '*Iman* is to believe in Allah, His Angels, His Books, His Prophets and in the Day of Judgement; and to believe in what has been ordained whether it is good or evil.' The man responded again, 'Correct, you have spoken the truth.' The man then asked, 'Tell me about *ihsan*?' The Prophet replied, '*Ihsan* is to worship Allah as though you see Him for it is certain that He sees you.' Later the Prophet told Umar that the man was Jibreel (Gabriel) who had come to teach them their religion.

This Hadith is clearly a directive to all Muslims as it includes the compulsory five pillars and the six core beliefs of Islam. But for Sufis it is the third part of the questioning by Jibreel that has become central to their belief and practice and their understanding of Islam. For a Sufi *Islam* and *Iman* must be based in *Ihsan*. In other words, it is essential to perform the rituals of Islam as if in the presence of Allah or, at least, with the awareness that Allah sees and knows not only a Muslim's actions but also his intentions. *Ihsan* thus guards against the danger of the religious practices provided by revelation becoming dry rituals. It also serves to remind the Muslim that the presence of Allah is a reality. Therefore, it is necessary for Muslims to maintain the remembrance and awareness of Allah's presence in their hearts at all times. The ultimate condition of worship would be to recollect Allah at every moment to the complete forgetfulness of the world or self. It is the goal of the Sufi to achieve this by perfecting *ihsan* through modelling themselves on the actions of the Prophet and by practising *tazkiyat al-nafs* to purify the *nafs* of impurities such as anger, greed, jealousy, hatred and lust. The variety of disciplines which allow the Sufi to remember Allah (*dhikr*) are taught in the various *tariqas* and are collectively known as *tasawwuf* (Geaves, 2000:24).

It is believed that all the qualities of *ihsan* or excellence of character were perfected in the Prophet. These would have included virtues such as patience, humility, compassion, generosity, modesty and courage. The Prophet encouraged the development of these character traits in his Companions, who, in turn, observed his behaviour and actions attentively and modelled themselves upon him (*adab*). It is believed that the Companions continued to pass on what they had learned from the Prophet and each gathered to themselves groups of committed students. It is claimed that the most notable among these were the schools of followers that developed around Hazrat Ali and Abu Bakr (Geaves, 2000:24). Most Sufi orders will authenticate their particular disciplines by chains of succession (*silsila*) that lead back to the Prophet through either Ali or Abu Bakr. However, these chains need to be treated with caution with regard to their reliability.

The chains that are used to demonstrate authenticity by contemporary Sufis are part of the apparatus used to legitimise themselves as the upholders of traditional Islam. The belief by Sufis that they represent the 'true' Islam practised by the Prophet and his Companions is found amongst early exponents of Sufism. Al-Hujwiri (d.1089) wrote in his *Kashf al Mahjub* that once Sufism was a reality without a name, but 'now it is in danger of becoming a name without a reality' (Ling, 1995:45). Al-Hujwiri is arguing that the experiential dimension of Sufism was so much a part of the first Muslims' apprehension of Islam that it did not require a separate nomenclature or definition outside of being Muslim, and this would have continued with the first generation after the Prophet. For al-Hujwiri, the term 'Sufi' would only have been necessary when many devout Muslims, horrified by the worldliness of the Umayyad Empire, retreated into isolation, maintaining an austere poverty and unworldliness, based on the life of the Prophet and his early Companions. Yet al-Hujwiri seems to be suggesting that already in his time, Sufism had somehow lost its vital thrust. Other Muslims of the ninth and tenth centuries have defined Sufism as 'abandoning one self to God in accordance with what God wills' (Ruwaym ibn Ahmad); 'Sufism is that you should not possess anything nor should anything possess you' (Samnun); 'Sufism consists of entering every exalted quality and leaving behind every despicable quality' (Abu Muhammad al-Jariri); 'Sufism is that you should be with God without any attachment' (Junayd); 'Sufism is that at each moment the servant should be in accord with what is most appropriate at that moment' (Amr ibn Uthman al-Makki); and finally, 'Sufism consists of extending a spiritual station and being in constant union' (Ali ibn Abd al-Rahim al-Qannad).

Most of the above were exponents of Sufism themselves and their definitions are recorded by al-Sarraj (d.988), who wrote the first comprehensive book on Sufism, the *Kitab al-Luma* (the Book of Flashes). With the exception of the last definition, which refers to stations and unity, none of the attempts to verbalise the mystic's path is at odds in any way with traditional Muslim piety. However, it is the last definition made by al-Qannad that causes difficulties for Sufism within Muslim 'orthodoxies', especially, as we have already seen, the Sufi understandings of union with God and its implications for *tawhid*.

The states and stages

As Sufism formalised itself under the guidance of a number of skilled exponents of its disciplines, a variety of 'maps' appeared that are identified as 'stages' (*maqamat*) and 'states' (*ahwal*) on the progress within the path to self-annihilation in God. Each of these variations on a theme became distinct orders of Sufism, each with a founding master (*shaikh*) and a lineage of masters that succeeded him. These orders are known as *tariqa* and are considered by most Sufis to complement the outer practices of Islam (*shari'a*). Discipleship is therefore central to Sufism, to provide guidance to the *murid* (student) along the way of transformation from a self-centred existence to one which is God-centred.

Three elements are required to complete the fullest transformation possible, sometimes described as the moment when the disciple no longer makes effort to remember God because God constantly remembers him or her. Such human beings are *awliya* (the friends of God), a more accurate terminology than the use of 'saint' often ascribed in English-language texts. The first element required is *maqamat*, the stages of progress. Although these vary from *tariqa* to *tariqa*, the first such 'map' of this kind is outlined in the *Kitab al-Luma* of Abu Nasr al-Sarraj mentioned above. They are as follows:

- Repentance or conversion, a process whereby the seeker recognises that his/her life is not as it should be and turns towards Allah for comfort and release from the illusory and fleeting nature of pursuing contentment in the creation. There is a spiritual awakening in which the seeker asks for the forgiveness and mercy of Allah. At this point the seeker would take the help of a *shaikh* for guidance by formally requesting to become a *murid*. The formal oath by the *murid* and acceptance by the *shaikh* is known as *bai'at*. The *shaikh* then undertakes to direct the *murid* through the stages according to the *murid's* spiritual and psychological capacity.
- Abstinence or fear is where the seeker passes his/her time in prayer and fasting. This is a time of constant vigil where ceaseless watch is kept on the heart in order to purify it and maintain distance from

the corrupting influence of the *nafs*. The seeker should keep thoughts pure and direct them towards Allah. This stage is regarded as the process or preparation for moving towards feeling at ease in the presence of Allah.

- Renunciation or detachment is then cultivated. For the Sufi attachment to the world rather than complete dependence on Allah is regarded as the root of all evil. A distinction is made between inner and outer detachment. At this stage the seeker begins the process of rooting out desire which leads to worldly attachment. Poverty is then developed. This is not poverty in the sense of being materially poor but in the spiritual sense of non-ownership. In this stage the seeker learns to live in the present, accepting each moment for itself. Whatever the moment brings is regarded as the gift of Allah. The Sufi now cultivates the 'vacant heart' which can be filled with Allah's Grace and Mercy.
- Patience, perseverance and steadfastness are next required in order to withstand the trials and hardships of spiritual discipline as the seeker waits for Allah to transform the path into wonder and grace. Trust and self-surrender are next cultivated in order that the seeker may come completely under the control of God. The cultivation of unbroken contentment or satisfaction follows.

Accompanying these stages, but differing from them in that they cannot be achieved by effort but are rather gifts from the divine source, are the states or *ahwal*. The same author cites ten states or gifts from Allah direct to the heart of the Sufi, which are listed as meditation, nearness to God, love, fear, hope, longing, intimacy, tranquillity, contemplation and certainty. *Yaqin*, or certainty, is the highest of all the states. In this condition, the Sufi knows *ma'rifat* (gnosis or experiential awareness of Allah's being) but the final state is *haqiqat*, where knower, knowledge and the Known are one.

This final state, also known as *fana fi l'haqq*, or union with the ultimate reality of being, is *tamkin*, the achievement or arrival at the cessation of self. Al-Qannad's definition of Sufism as 'extending a station' referred to the viability of the experience: the ability to retain the experience beyond a special moment in time so that it becomes a lasting characteristic of the personality. Even *fana*, therefore, is not an end in itself, but the gateway to *baqa*, or existence in God.

Although the states and stages were controversial, as they seemed to establish an alternative paradigm for God-surrender to the outer dictates of Islamic law, the idea of divine union confronted many amongst the *ulema*. Indeed, even Sufis were unsure about the nature of union with God. The transcendental mood of Islam mitigates against such confessions of intimacy and Semitic monotheism has never been happy with the total identification of Self and God found in some forms of Eastern religion. Yet the path of the Sufi is essentially experiential and these lovers of Allah seek deep intimacy and communion with their Lord. Such mystical experiences have always defeated the power of human language to provide descriptions and Sufis found themselves with similar dilemmas. Although their paths rest on the deep conviction that when the individual self is lost Allah remains as the universal Self and the eternal ground of existence, the idea of literal union was difficult to sustain in the Semitic religious imagination. Even though many agreed that once the process of purification is completed, the heart can communicate directly with its creator in a glorious experience of illumination and ecstasy, the nature of the experience was open to interpretation.

Some of the more extravagant utterances of Sufis expressed from within their condition of ecstasy caused some discomfort, not only amongst the opponents of Sufism. Statements such as those attributed to al-Bistami by al-Sarraj:

> God raised me once and placed me before Him and said: 'O Abu Yazid, My creation desires to see you.' So I said: 'Adorn me with Your I-ness and elevate me to Your uniqueness, so that when Your creation sees me, they will say: "We have seen You," and then You will be that and I will not be there.'
>
> (Zaehner, 1994:94)

The even more unacceptable *ana'l haqq* (I am the Truth) that provided the justification for Mansour al-Hallaj's death sentence, was difficult to reconcile with Islam's uncompromising monotheism and the central doctrine of God's uniqueness. Other Sufis softened their language of unity, such as Jalalu'd-Din Rumi's statement that:

> The motion of every atom is towards its origin;
> A man comes to be the thing on which he is bent.
> By the attraction of fondness and yearning,
> The soul and the heart
> Assume the qualities of the Beloved, who is the Soul of souls.

or al-Khurqani:

> I do not say that paradise and hell are non-existent, but I say that they are nothing to me, because God created them both, and there is no room for any created object in the place where I am.

Even al-Bistami seemed to moderate his language of unity in the following saying: 'His love entered and removed all besides Him and left no trace of anything else, so that it remained single, even as He is single.'

Sufi understandings of the experience of unity can be categorised into three broad interpretations. First is *ittihad*, a state of literal oneness or union with God that is difficult to reconcile with Islam's monotheism. Such a description of the loss of self experiences is usually maintained by the more unconventional amongst the Sufis, often those prepared to dispute the need to remain within Islam's orthodox framework. More influential was the doctrine of *wahdat al-wujud*, developed by Ibn Arabi, which remains influential to this day in the subcontinent. To Ibn Arabi, the soul achieves a condition of self-annihilation and is able to perceive visually and experientially the unity of all things, both the Creator and the creation. This is reconciled with orthodox Islamic theology through an emanationist philosophy influenced by neo-Platonism. In essence, then, God reveals Himself in His creation because He wanted to be known. This is summed up in the divine utterance 'I was a hidden treasure, then I wanted to be known.'

For many Sufis, even Ibn Arabi's understanding of divine unity was problematic. In sixteenth-century India, Shaikh Ahmed Sirhindi countered with the doctrine of *wahdat al-shuhud*, in which he asserts that the mystic is so absorbed and overwhelmed by the object of his contemplation that he is no longer aware of himself or his condition. The condition of ecstasy arises from the loss of self that arises from intense prayerfulness rather than an actual oneness with the divinity. In this way, the Sufi may sometimes make ecstatic utterances of oneness which may be considered idolatrous, but he is not blameworthy as his state of consciousness is outside of the functions of normal human faculties.

Ibn Arabi's solution was to make a distinction between 'God-in-Himself', always transcendent and unknowable, unable to be experienced directly and God 'coming down' into the cosmos. Human beings are able to draw near the latter, who has chosen to limit himself in order to be known through his attributes or divine names. The 'Universal Intellect' is one such attribute which is revealed to the Sufi adept and allows their own purified intellect, free from ego, to discern the meaning hidden within every form and to perceive reality. The perfected human being is able to reflect God's own ability to recognise the 'Hidden Treasure', that is God's own presence within themselves. Thus human beings are the crown and final cause of the created order, the first in the process of divine thought, whose essential being is part of the primal intelligence that emanates directly from God. Human beings are therefore a copy – a microcosm made in the image of God and the eye through which God sees His own creation. The person who knows his or her self, knows God. Self-knowledge is therefore an all-pervading sense of unity, a consciousness of the omnipresent where individuality disappears. To be in such a state is the sign of the 'Perfect Man', most fully manifest in the person of Muhammad, who is both the Seal of the Prophets and the embodiment of sainthood.

Thus humanity draws near God through experience of oneness obtained through self-purification, rather than mainstream Islam's emphasis on obedience to the revelation handed down to Muhammad through the Angel Jibreel. There are problems involving authority and authenticity innate to this redefinition of Islam. Although Ibn Arabi, for example, acknowledged the centrality of the Qur'an and the Prophet, he argued that Sufis should concentrate themselves on the *Khayali* Qur'an, that is the primordial text that pre-existed the sending down of the oral and written script to Muhammad. Thus it is possible for Sufis not to require the external Qur'an but to access the spiritual Qur'an through the process of self-purification and self-knowledge.

Although there is no contradiction for Ibn Arabi with conventional Islamic doctrine, as it would not be possible for the man of self-knowledge to contradict the revelation brought to the Messenger of God, such a doctrine is open to abuse by charlatans and religious impostors claiming to be such elevated beings. Indeed, there were Sufis who insisted that they were not required to follow the externals of Islam as their experience of immediacy made redundant the ritual life of the religion or its encompassing framework of laws and ethics. At best, this led to heterodox interpretations of Islam freed from the confines of obedience to the outer disciplines; at worst, it led to sexual impropriety, abuses of power and misappropriation of funds. Although, for most, the inner path complemented the outer, for others the experience of God's presence within supplied an authority that overrode the historical revelation. Some were to claim the elitist position that the revelation and its outer strictures were given to the ordinary masses, whereas the inners truths of the mystical journey were the only guidance required for a spiritual minority.

The development of Sufism

The classic pattern for the evolution of Sufism is the four-stage development as follows below. However, it is one that Sufis them- selves would be ill at ease with since it appears to cast doubt on their own claims to have appeared fully fledged as the Islam practised by Muhammad and his Companions:

1. Asceticism

Appearing as early as the seventh century and argued to be rooted in a sense of fear and awe before Allah and in a desire to escape divine retribution. Some Muslims believed that the creation of an empire and a dynasty had resulted in the loss of the piety and religiosity of the founders. Thus asceticism provided an option to return to the funda- mentals based around the teachings of the Makkan *suras* of the Qur'an. A key figure in such analyses is Hasan al-Basri (d.728).

2. Love

The shift from fear to love is argued to have commenced in the ninth century and is embodied in the life and teachings of figures such as the woman saint, Rabi'a al-Adiwiyah (d.801), together with Dhu'l Nun (d.859) and al-Muhasibi (d.857). Certainly all three use the inti- mate language of love to describe their relationship with Allah. The emphasis on reward and punishment was shifted to the ideal of a loving God and fear was regarded as an unacceptable motive for service and devotion.

3. Unitary and pantheistic mysticism

The focus on love led to the idea of the possibility of union with the divine beloved, achieved through self-purification and self-stripping. Certainly, by the tenth century, Sufis had developed both the doctrine and the methodology for a path to mystical union premised in the doctrine that Allah existed as the sole reality. The spiritual quest became a journey to remove the veils that obscure the reality of Allah's unity. Key figures of this approach are al-Hallaj (d.918) and al-Bistami (d.874) amongst many others.

4. Attempts at resolution
The development of mystical doctrines and practices antagonised those who saw the outer practices of Islam as sufficient, and in the eleventh and twelfth centuries there were attempts to reconcile the inner and outer dimensions of Islam, most notably from al-Ghazali (d.1111).

Yet it could be argued that the chronological transformation from asceticism to unitive mysticism is too neat and like many scholarly models provides a working tool rather than a precise model of reality. Certainly, the characteristics of asceticism and love were not lost in the development of full-blown Sufi doctrines, but rather combined. For this reason Sufis have always honoured the figure of Isa (Jesus), who appeared in their eyes as the ultimate contemplative, bringing together in his person the attributes of ascetic renunciation and love for the divine. Above all, he achieved the Sufi ideal of intimacy, a devotional unity which, as Cragg points out, led Muslims to believe that the early Christians had mistakenly developed into a cult of incarnation (Cragg, 1985:60). It is easy to perceive in Jesus' early life the ideal pattern of a Sufi. His practices of long fasting, his prayer retreats, and his renunciation, manifested in apparent wandering and homelessness, are all aspects to this day of Sufi initiation and practice (Cragg, 1985:60).

The transformation from mysticism to popular religion
The rapid expansion of Sufi teachings infiltrated the Islamic consciousness as the *tariqa* networks spread throughout the Muslim world in a spider web pattern. Although the *silsila* chains functioned to ensure the legitimacy of the individual *shaikh* and the teachings that he promoted, time and distance enabled many teachers to attract followers with less credulous claims of authority linking them back to the eminent *awliya* and eventually the Prophet himself. As thousands of *shaikhs* and *pirs* across the Muslim world taught their individual methods of self-purification they attracted groups of followers of

varying sizes, and it was not surprising that a cult of saints began to develop in the Muslim tradition. This cult of saintship took on several recognisable features that arose out of the organisation of the *tariqas*, the doctrines of Sufism, the credulous imagination of increasing populations of rural followers and even blatant manipulation and false claims on the part of less reputable *shaikhs*.

The loosely organised localised structures of the *tariqas* around an individual *shaikh* and his followers allowed for no central control of either doctrine or practices. Even reputable *shaikhs* had little control over belief and practice outside the inner circle of his followers. The classic pattern of Sufi allegiance which still exists to the present day, consisted of an inner circle of initiates who resided with the *shaikh* and an outer circle who still maintained the *shaikh's* teachings but also had other more worldly priorities. The *shaikh* could exercise a considerable degree of control over these two groups of followers. However, outside of these groups of loyal and committed disciples there was a wider circle that took *bai'at* (initiation) with the *shaikh* as a means of acquiring status and prestige in their social milieu. Over this group the *shaikh* would have little control, either over their behaviour or the way in which they promoted his teachings and spiritual prowess. The more they communicated stories of miraculous powers to the credulous, the more their own reputations soared through vicarious holiness or sanctity. Outside these three groups of followers would have been an even larger group of the general populace who would have used the *shaikh* to resolve a whole range of medical, social and psychological problems through access to his spiritual counsel or belief in his miraculous powers based on his proximity to Allah. Finally, an even more nebulous connection to the *shaikh* existed in the wider population, based on pride or status in having such an elevated figure in their locality.

This situation combined with attempts by eminent Sufis to provide a coherent doctrine of sainthood. Ibn Arabi (1165–1240) made the essential distinction between sainthood and prophethood in which he stated that all the prophets and saints were manifestations of the spirit or reality of Muhammad, which pre-dated creation as the original emanation or Light of Allah (*Nur al-Muhammad-i*). He argued that prophets were also saints but saints were not prophets and some heterodox movements have taken this one step further to affirm the authority of their own founders by suggesting that sainthood replaced prophethood after the death of Muhammad as the means for

Allah to keep his final revelation alive. However, Ibn Arabi's position was that just as the historical Muhammad was the seal and culmination of all the prophets, there was also a seal of the saints who was the perfect manifestation of the primordial spirit of Muhammad (Ling, 1995:101). This complete manifestation or ultimate saint was known as the *Qutb* (axis). Hujwiri (d.1075), a Persian Sufi, defines a saint (*wali*) as one who cannot be known through scholarship, asceticism or good deeds but only through the essential qualification of ecstasy which demonstrated their intimacy with Allah. He goes on to provide a classification of sainthood based on an invisible hierarchy with the *Qutb* at its pinnacle. Below the *Qutb* are a variety of classes based on their piety and sanctity who all work for the *Qutb*. Although they might not appear to know the *Qutb* of the age, they meet with him in a supernatural conference beyond the confines of time and space (Nicholson, 1989:123–124). The saints all share in the mystical awareness of their connection to the *Nur* (Light of Allah), which is also passed down through the *silsila* from master to master, originating in the highest manifestation of this Light, the Prophet himself.

This mystical doctrine of a hierarchy of saints who maintain the spiritual well-being of the world from outside time combined with popular belief and dependence upon living *shaikhs* to create the doctrine of *karamat* or special favour that was bestowed upon the saint to perform miracles and even intercede on behalf of those requiring Allah's mercy and assistance. This belief in miracles caught the imagination of the populace and led to extravagant and fantastic stories of the deeds of Sufis. When the *shaikhs* died the religious piety of their followers turned to the graves which would then develop as important shrine centres and the focus of the continuing development of the *tariqa* as was explored in Chapter 3. It was believed that the power to intercede and perform miracles was contained within the remains of the saint who was in some way still alive awaiting Judgement Day. Similar to the Shi'a belief concerning their Imams, it was also believed that the Sufi's power was retained in his bloodline and it was usually his immediate remaining family who would take over the religious functions and administration of the shrine. The proliferation of shrines of deceased saints brought a new dynamic into Muslim belief and practices as millions of rural adherents of the faith concentrated their devotional practices and petitions around the tombs.

The decline of Sufism

The development of a fully fledged theosophy of sainthood, both living and in the tomb, troubled many orthodox Muslims especially
amongst the ranks of the *ulema*. There was considerable criticism of
the need to submit to the authority of charismatic men who claimed a
special relationship to Allah through ecstasy. Some believed that
Islam was being subverted through vicarious holiness arising out of
dependence on holy men, pilgrimage to their shrines, adoration
of their relics and total commitment of physical and mental resources
to their service (Nicholson, 1989:146). Arberry suggests that the cult of
miracles led to the incredulous masses allowing themselves to be
duped by impostors and that the Sufism represented by illustrious
figures such as Ibn Arabi and Al-Farid fell into decay caused by
superstition and ignorance (Arberry, 1956:119).

The other major criticism of Sufism appeared from both outside
and within its own ranks. As observed above, some Sufis began to
assert that the intimate relationship with Allah which is enjoyed by
the *wali* (friend of God) negates the requirement of obedience to the
outer laws of Islam, ie, the *shari'a*. Some suggested that obedience to
the exoteric laws and requirements of Islam was a duty required only
during the early stages of spiritual development. It was inevitable
that a dichotomy should arise between the experience of those who
claimed direct inner access to the divine and therefore felt themselves
to be completely surrendered to the divine will and those who duti-
fully followed the external requirements of the *shari'a*. As a corollary
of the view that the outer requirements of Islam contained in the
revelation were only for the masses and were not binding on the
spiritually elect, some, like Niffari, claimed that the inner knower of
truth only had to follow the outer requirements of Islam if they were
in accordance with his vision of reality (Nicholson, 1989:72).

If such sentiments are followed through to their ultimate logical
conclusion, Sufism can be completely disconnected from its Islamic
roots and perceived as a form of universal mysticism. Haeri, along
with many other Muslims including those from within the *tariqas*,
finds this view extremely problematic and labels it as 'pseudo-Sufism'
(Haeri, 1995:41ff). It is important to acknowledge that the emphasis
on such extreme viewpoints by Sufis usually originates from members of the Muslim reform and revivalist movements who often blame
Sufism for the decline of the *umma*. However, most Sufis have been

equally critical of those who have departed from obedience to the *shari'a*. The vast majority of the *tariqas* teach that inner development is not possible without the exoteric demands of Islam contained in the final Revelation to humankind from Allah delivered to and fully manifested in the behaviour of Muhammad, the final Prophet of God.

Arberry exemplifies the views of those who believe that Sufism has gone into deep decline. He even affirms that 'Sufism has run its course' (Arberry, 1956:134). Although he acknowledges that new *tariqas* such as the Tijaniya and Sanusiya have appeared in the eighteenth century and that a few isolated individuals have upheld the genius of the original Sufi masters, Arberry argues that Sufism no longer commands the loyalty of the Muslim *umma*. He concedes that the decline varied from country to country but is of the opinion that Sufism only exists as a tradition practised by the ignorant masses and led by *shaikhs* with little knowledge of Islam, many of whom even hold in contempt the ritual obligations of that faith (Arberry, 1956:120ff).

Arberry's analysis would be echoed by many within the Muslim world who feel strong opposition to Sufism; on the other hand, millions would be deeply offended. The difficulty with Arberry's assertion is that it rests on the presumption that Sufism is Islamic mysticism. Even if it is true that the heyday of manifestations of mystical experience has passed, the vast majority of Muslims feeling allegiance to the *tariqas* would never have had ecstatic experiences of unity. Just as today, they would have considered themselves to be deeply pious Muslims attempting to model themselves on the lives of the first generation of Islam.

Sufism in the modern period

Although deep mystical experiences of God remain rare, Sufism continues to produce such personalities. However, the vast majority of Sufis, as in the past, do not claim union with the divine. The key elements of the Sufi path remain as the *shaikh/murid* relationship, belonging to a *tariqa*, practice of *dhikr* (the remembrace of the name(s) of God) and an elevated love of the Prophet. Increasingly Sufis and their supporters are found focusing on *aqida* (correct doctrine) in order to assert that they are the vanguard of traditional Islam as practised by countless Muslims since the time of Muhammad. Certainly, it is true that in some parts of the Muslim world, most notably the subcontinent, Sufism and its influence on ordinary Muslims is normative. In other places, especially Saudi Arabia, it has all but disappeared as the result of being discouraged by a Wahhabi sympathetic regime.

But the Sufi assertion to represent traditional Islam needs to be viewed in the light of transformations taking place in the Muslim world. Tradition is usually used in Islam to signify the historical activity of the *ulema*, operating within the four schools of Islamic law, to codify the accumulated body of law, practices and customs defined as legitimate. Such traditions have found themselves under attack from various individuals and movements founded by them, who insist that the process of codification took the emphasis away from the Qur'an and the Hadith. Such reformers usually insisted upon their own right to go direct to the original sources and reinterpret them without recourse to 'tradition'.

Increasingly, in the twentieth century we find Sufis asserting themselves as champions of tradition as opposed to the reformers who would dismiss or negate it. This strategy has two-fold benefits for Sufis. First, it places them back at the heart of traditional Islam, able to meet their opponents from the centre rather than the fringes, and second, it allows them to develop defences for their own practices and beliefs that are rooted in the traditions, thus turning the tables on their enemies from within the ranks of the reformers, who are then dismissed as innovators.

However, Malise Ruthwen reminds us that tradition also refers to everyday practices and beliefs that 'occur unselfconsciously as part of the natural order of things' (Ruthwen, 2004:16). Ruthwen quotes Martin Marty who stated that 'most people who live in a traditional culture do not know that they are traditionalists' (Marty, 1992:18). This is highly pertinent to contemporary Sufi manifestations, for many of the beliefs and practices that they defend are accused by their enemies from within Islam as being cultural superstitions. Even academics have displaced them to the realm of 'popular' or 'folk' religion. Yet it would seem to me that the Sufi defence of these practices, once unnoticed as part of normative everyday life, indicates that in our modern world all *weltanschauung* or worldviews are noticed and required to be defended.

Certainly, criticism and hostility towards Sufism had always been there in the past but it increased with the advent of the eighteenth century and picked up pace in the nineteenth century. This probably occurred as a reaction to Muslim failure in this period: the loss of territory and power to European nations led to Muslims looking for scapegoats and the blame was placed on the apparent corruption of Islamic practices by Sufis, especially in rural areas. Reform movements, seeking a regeneration of 'scriptural' Islam argued that the common people were failing to achieve 'true Islam' practised in accordance with the Qur'an and Hadith. The reason for this apparent collapse was laid at the door of immoral or corrupt Sufis (especially wonder-working charlatans).

Often Sufism was accused of having foreign religious or cultural influences but the struggle for renewal also came from within the ranks of Sufis themselves, who began to move away from ecstatic and metaphysical aspects of Sufism to Muslim piety and orthodoxy with a re-emphasis on conformity to the *shari'a*. As a part of this process there was a growth of Sufi orders as organised mass movements with more central organisation, most notably the Naqshbandiya. Ironically, attacks on Sufis came not only from the reform and revivalist movements such as the Wahhabis but also from secular forces within the Muslim world who also perceived Sufism as primitive and superstitious.

Yet the ancient respect for the man or woman who gave up everything for the love of Allah remained as strong as in the medieval period. Although, in the present time, one is more likely to come across Sufism in one of the countless tomb-shrines to the pious or mystical figures of Islam's past, the image of the wayfarer, the traveller setting out on a journey in which intimacy with God is the final destination for the pilgrim, rather than the communal benefits of the Hajj, remains the mark of the true *awliya*. Pnina Werbner notes the significance of the renunciatory journey that leads to the discovery of a *shaikh* and initiation into discipleship in her research on Zindapir, a Pakistani Sufi only recently deceased (Werbner, 2003).

As she reports, in fact, Zindapir's journey was not to take him far from his own village, but for his followers, it took on mythic proportions as the sign of the man who gave himself over to total trust in God's mercy, retiring to the wilderness to live in a cave. Werbner notes that neither the *ulema*, the official representatives of mosque-based Islam, nor the *sajjada nashin*, the hereditary custodians of the shrines, could compete with the fame and charisma of the living saint who duplicated the original wayfaring asceticism of the Sufi path. The living saint is replete with *faiz*, the divine light of God which flows through his being to bless all that come into proximity with him and which shines on his countenance. As stated by Werbner, Zindapir was 'a doer, an ascetic, a world renouncer, a man who blessed the crowds and fed the multitudes' (Werbner, 2003:263) but above all he was endowed with *faiz*, able to project it at will, and to 'transfer it at a glance to a trusted *khalifa* (disciple) (Werbner, 2003:251). For millions of Muslims, the *ulema* may have the textual knowledge of Islam gained through their studies, but it remains the pious Sufi who above all others demonstrates the life of the Prophet, leading by his example.

However, the link between charismatic saint and tradition as represented by the *ulema* is further affirmed by Werbner who notes that after the saint's death, the *sajjada nashin* and the *ulema* reclaim the geographical space tamed and sacralised by the presence of the Sufi on behalf of tradition, a process marked by the increased Qur'anic recitals taking place at the tomb-shrine (Werbner, 2003:257).

Nile Green notes that the travelling narratives of Sufis function to link the shrine in the new sacred location with authenticating myths located in the heartlands of Islam (Green, 2003). New territory for the religion is embodied in stone and brick by the saint's presence, but the hagiographies tell of his God-directed travels from *dar al-Islam*, the land of Islam, to the wilderness of *dar al-Harb*, the godless regions that lay beyond Islam's frontiers. Although the shrine centre may well offer succour to the pilgrims outside of the mosque's normative rituals, the saint's origins demonstrate his connection to Islam's classical heartlands and his place in the hierarchy of mystics. Thus 'popular religion' is inextricably linked to the saint's intimacy with God.

Struggle with Wahhabism

Today, a battle continues to rage in many Muslim countries, as Wahhabi and neo-Wahhabi forces criticise both the network of shrines where saint veneration continues unabated and the elevation of the Prophet along neo-Platonic lines as forms of idolatry that risk leading Islam down the same path as Christianity. Added to this is a deep unease with prayers of intercession addressed to either prominent Sufis or the Prophet. Elizabeth Sirreyeh has charted this rejection of Sufism in the Middle East but her claim, that 'the mood of the times is one of gloom' to be blamed on the ignorant masses (Sirreyeh, 1999:4) 'who have failed to live up to the Sufi ideals', seems to offer sympathy to the iconoclastic destruction of shrines and tombs carried out by the Wahhabis in Arabia. In her assertion of a corruption from the mystical ideal to the 'folk' practices of the common people she follows in Arberry's footsteps. However, the premise of the rise and decline of Sufism is flawed. It is likely that the masses always behaved in a similar fashion around the charismatic presence of the living saint: embellishing events, and creating hagiographies and tales of miracles. Yet, the presence of the pious Sufis in their midst has been as much a story of reform, conversion, and, to use that favourite word of the contemporary revivalists, reversion to Islam but without the distraction of the politics of nationhood or the emphasis on *jihad* as holy war.

However, the two decades of the 1980s and 1990s have seen a revival of the *tariqas* as they begin to counter-attack the Wahhabi critique of tradition. The threat of a common enemy has pushed the *tariqas* towards their own reform programme in an attempt to remove any trace of the kind of excesses described by Arberry. This has resulted in a better organisation of the *tariqas* and recently there have been signs of them working more closely with each other to promote a common identity and develop common strategies to present themselves as the heirs of traditional Islam claimed to originate in the time of the Prophet.

The counter-attack consists of reversing the Wahhabi strategy, linking traditional Sufi beliefs and practices to those of traditional Muslims and in turn accusing the revivalists of being the greatest threat to Muslim unity and guilty of destroying Muslim consensus on matters of faith and belief by charging the majority of Muslims with departing from true Islam. Shaikh Kabbani, a Naqshbandi Sufi resident in the USA, cites a typical paragraph of neo-Wahhabi writing to demonstrate this point, which states:

> The majority of Muslims for 600 or 1,000 years ago until today have deviated from the belief of the Pious Predecessors (*Salaf as-Salih*) and the correct doctrine (*aqida*) of the Sunnis by following the ideas of Al-Ashari. They have become like the Jahmiyya, the Khawarij or the Mutazila, falling out of the bounds of correct Islam. (Kabbani, 1998:52)

Certainly, Kabbani is right to point out that Al-Ashari is usually regarded as orthodox and the Ashari school of thought is considered to be doctrinally orthodox among mainstream Sunni Muslims.

Thus the battle lines have been drawn between these two conflicting groups within the world of Sunni Islam. It has been argued that a protestant reformation is taking place in the Muslim world in which the Wahhabis and neo-Wahhabi movements such as the Salafis represent the protestant reform movements and the supporters of Sufism are analogous to the Roman Catholic majority that formerly existed in Europe. In this analogy the Sufis play a similar part to the intercessionary role of saints in Catholicism. The analogy is crude but it does provide some insights into the cleavage. Thus some civil wars taking place in various parts of the Muslim world can be paralleled to the conflicts that tore Europe apart after the Protestant Reformation (Abbasi).

All of this has to be placed in the context of shifts taking place in the wider Muslim world. The Wahhabi teachings were able to move successfully across the globe, meeting local needs for reform partly as a result of the Hajj's ability to bring Muslims to one place where they can discover new trends and movements. In this context, Fuad Nahdi's account of participating in the Hajj in 2004 could be very significant. Fuad Nahdi is Editor-in-Chief of *Q News*, a prominent Muslim magazine read extensively by younger generation Muslims in Britain. The article was first published in the *Guardian* newspaper and was reproduced on the home page of the *Q News* website. Nahdi reports that the atmosphere of the Hajj was more spiritual than in previous years and the pilgrims were less harassed by the Saudi Arabian authorities, previously keen to maintain doctrinal purity along Wahhabi lines. He states:

> Everywhere I find well-produced leaflets focusing on the spiritual aspects of the Hajj. The literature is more inclusive and more tolerant than one used to expect. In the past, this kind of spirituality would have been banned or cursed from the pulpits. The men in uniform are looking for political troublemakers and no longer bother to harass Muslims who have brought with them traditional practices the official royal scholars consider unacceptable such as religious songs and chants. The religious thought-police, once all powerful and perfectly able to administer a caning if they overheard a religious poem they considered improper, seemed subdued and disheartened. Everyone, in consequence, was having a good time, within an atmosphere of prayer and meditation.

Reading between the lines of Fuad Nahdi's carefully crafted words, he is suggesting that the Wahhabi influence, both in Saudi Arabia, as represented by the ineffectualness of the religious police, and in the rest of the Muslim world, represented by the pilgrims, is in decline. Those familiar with the practices of Muslims influenced by the Sufi *tariqas*, would recognise in Nahdi's descriptions the songs and poems that praised the Prophet and aroused the ire of the Wahhabi clerics of Saudi Arabia. The Sufis were always at the Hajj, but it seems that in 2004, in the atmosphere of piety and devotion, they captured the *zeitgeist*. It will take time to discover whether the Sufi revival has been given impetus by the events of 9/11 and its aftermath or if it was already in progress and this year reached a point where it was able for the first time to show itself openly at the Hajj, unafraid of its traditional opponents sensing their unease towards world opinion.

David Singh claims that the epithet 'Sufi' first appeared in Shi'a circles in the eighth century and then became widespread throughout the Muslim world by the tenth century, used to describe any mystical tendencies in Islam (Singh, 2003:95). He argues that from its inception it had its problems with traditional Islam, problems that continue to the present day. However, Sufism came to be accepted throughout the Muslim world and its total rejection in the contemporary period needs to be explored as an aspect of colonial and nationalist struggles. It is possible to argue that the neo-revivalists, with their rhetoric of reform and their iconoclastic version of Islam, as embodied in the various Wahhabi and Salafi tendencies, are the more recent feature, an innovation partly created by the reaction to the success of Western modernity. If this is true, Sufism can claim with some justice to represent traditional Muslims. If it is true that they were influenced by philosophical ideas from outside Islam, such as neo-Platonism, their genius was to thoroughly Islamicise them, something which could not have been achieved without a degree of affinity between such philosophy and the teachings upheld in the Qur'an and Hadith.

The usual categorisation of the essentials of Islam, taught to every schoolchild in Britain, that the religion consists of the five pillars and six beliefs, focuses the attention on the ritual external practices and the doctrines that support them. They tell us little about Islam's spirituality. The definition also helps divorce the exoteric from the esoteric, the inner from the outer, the spirit from the trappings. Perhaps a more useful definition is that the Muslim is a subject of God, in fact His deputy, the message contained in the Qur'an and Hadith., who lives not for himself only but to bring goodness to humanity. The understanding of Islam presented by Dilwar Hussain of the Islamic Foundation, not an institution noted for allegiance to Sufism, that the concepts of *tawhid* (God's unity and uniqueness), *istikhlaf* (viceregence), *dhikr* (remembrance), *taqwa* (God-consciousness) and *rabbaniyah* (relationship with God) form the core of Muslim being and essence (Hussain, 2004:122) supplies us with a comprehension of Islam that brings the fundamentals of the Sufi much closer to Islam's heart.

CHAPTER 8

The Prophet of God: human messenger or a manifestation of divine qualities?

The themes of the previous chapter will be further developed here, but with the focus on Muhammad, the last and final Prophet. Different traditions within Islam vary considerably in their view of the Prophet. Debates over the role of the Prophet, his relationship to Allah, and his primordial as opposed to his human existence dominate contemporary discourse between 'traditional Muslims' and neo-orthodox movements. Thus the relationship between the 'Muhammad of history' and the 'Muhammad of popular piety' will be contrasted. The chapter will pick up the themes of Chapters 2 and 7.

Introduction

There are not so many problems with the historicity of Muhammad as there are with some founders of ancient religions; on the contrary, there is a large amount of material from within the Muslim community, where the Prophet's biographers were detailing his life from within a century of his death. These texts, known as *sira*, were written by Ibn Ishaq (d.767), al-Waqidi (d.823) and Ibn Sa'd (d.845). However, any founder of a religion quickly takes on an existence which is far more than the sum of its biographical parts and goes on to become an expression of an intense religious imagination. So although Muhammad is an historical figure whose life events have been explored by both Western and Muslim sources, we have to also understand that tradition allocates him a special place for Muslims. This expression of Muslim feeling towards the last Prophet of God is felt in the following invocation:

Exalted is Allah who created him, for such as him in all creation I have never seen. The best of all creatures, the apex of Messengers, the treasure of human kind and their guide to integrity! In him I have taken refuge: and perhaps Allah will forgive me.

It is not surprising that feelings for Muhammad run high amongst Muslims for, after all, the two essential articles of Muslim allegiance are expressed in the dual clauses of the *shahada*, that is *La illaha il'Allah, Muhammadun rasul Allah* – there is no god but God and Muhammad is the messenger of God. Belief in the final Prophet of God is an imperative and a defining feature of Muslim identity and it becomes essential for all Muslims to know the nature of the Prophet, his deeds and actions and to feel their allegiance to him. Many will speak of him as if he remains an intimate companion whose stories are told and retold with vitality as if they only happened yesterday. Barnaby Rogerson, in his recent biography of Muhammad, tells of his engagement with the story tellers who keep alive the Prophet's deeds to the crowds who gather around them, even though each individual in the audience already knows each act intimately (Rogerson, 2003:2).

Rogerson reminds us that the story is little known in the Western world, even going so far as to possess a 'negative rating' (Rogerson, 2003:3), but within the Muslim world there is no character who is his equal or so well known, for he possesses all the human values: the mine of all virtues and manners. He is the last of those special beings who have been chosen to bring the word of God to men and women throughout history, but he is also the bridge between the worlds, the intermediary to the divine, the source of ecstatic visions and dreams to his lovers and a source of contention amongst Muslim factions. Rogerson also points out the obvious: that even without the religious sensibilities here is a man who transformed the history of the human race, a founder of one of its greatest empires and civilisations, and the developer of one of the significant world languages and its literature, having taken the Arabic language of the Qur'an from the backwater speech of the desert Arab to a vehicle for a transmission of culture that was known from China to Europe. He remains, to this day, the focus for the spiritual imagination, prayer and petition of the second largest religion in the world, still thriving and growing while others go into decline.

First and foremost, Muhammad is unique because he is the

recipient of the Qur'an, according to Muslims the final and complete revelation of God. He is also the Prophet of God, the last of a long lineage that is believed to extend back through Jesus, to David, Moses, Abraham and finally Adam. The nature of the 'Seal of the Prophets', as he is considered to be, aroused considerable speculation amongst Muslims, although Muslim orthodox views have no doubts about his humanity. What kind of man would Allah choose to be the chosen vehicle for the ultimate revelation? What would be his qualities? In addition, the Prophet was the exemplar for Allah's new community. His actions would be copied by the pious and his words would supplement the Qur'an as a primary source of guidance for all future generations.

For the mystics of Islam, he is perceived as the closest of the 'friends of God', the inspiration and guide for the deepest spiritual aspirations for those who sought unity and intimacy with the divine. However, not everyone was as respectful. Muhammad has also come under close scrutiny from Christian sources, especially in the Middle Ages as we saw in Chapter 2, when Christianity felt the impact of his new religion as a rival, when both their dominion over the world and the claim to be God's chosen vehicle for salvation were threatened. In these criticisms, his life was examined unfavourably with that of Jesus and he was often depicted as an impostor and a sexual dilettante.

To get at the real Muhammad, it is necessary to explore all the avenues, realising that it will be impossible to sift out, this far away from his life, the figure of history from the Muhammad of faith who continues to remain a vital part of the living religious existence of countless men and women throughout the Muslim world. The emotional feeling for the Prophet can be illustrated by my own experience of many years of contact with Muslims from all shades and varieties of religious commitment to Islam. I have observed that one is far more likely to offend sensibilities by making negative criticisms of Muhammad than by challenging the truths of the Qur'an. The latter is likely to lead to an earnest religious debate on belief and unbelief, for Muslims an everyday aspect of missionary engagement with an unbeliever, but the former is seen as a deep insult and provokes an impassioned response which indicates how deeply affection and respect for the Prophet is maintained in the Muslim psyche.

These feelings often border on veneration, but not worship, for that would indeed be a sin, bringing Muhammad to the level of God, for the Muslim the ultimate mistake of all, and the one charged to

Christians who are believed to have elevated their prophet to the status of divinity. Yet sometimes, to the untrained observer, veneration and worship appear to have a very narrow line between them, and some enthusiastic manifestations of veneration of the Prophet have incurred the ire of fellow Muslims.

Zaki Badawi, a prominent British Muslim, an *alim*, and Principal of the Muslim College in Ealing, West London, once stated that there were three Muhammads: the first as described by his enemies; the second as perceived by his followers; and the third, the historical figure of the Prophet which he argued needed to be reclaimed by Muslims around the world. It is not my intention to dwell on the Muhammad of history for it seems to me that it is not too problematic except as an exercise for both Muslim and non-Muslim historians. Religious founders exist both as historical or mythological figures, and also as symbolic beings who represent the hopes and fears of their communities of faith. It is the symbolic representation of Muhammad that is problematic and can divide the Muslim world. It is also the equally symbolic representations of Muhammad, presented by Christians throughout the centuries of rivalry between these two religions and civilisations, that can remain as a thorn in the side preventing mutual discourse when relations between Islam and the West are difficult.

The Muslim biography of Muhammad

Muhammad's life can be constructed around a series of events that become significant in his role as prophet of God. They are as follows:

22 April 571CE	Muhammad's birth
596	His marriage to Khadijah
610	First revelation of the Qur'an
620	The death of Khadijah
621	The *Mi'raj* (the believed ascent to the realms of God that is said to have taken place from Jerusalem)
621	The *Hijra* or migration from Makkah to Medina
627	The Battle of Badr
627	The conquest of Makkah
8 June 632	His final speech and death

Muhammad was born into the family of the respected Banu Hashim of the Quraysh tribe. Although this tribe was the most powerful in the city of Makkah and its surrounds, Muhammad's family was not a part of its influential elites. Sometimes much is made of his harsh childhood after becoming orphaned at a young age but this is not necessarily a true depiction. After the loss of his parents, he was taken under the protection of his uncle and although sent out into the harsh wilderness of Arabia to learn the ways of the desert Arab, this was regarded as normal practice for the young boys of good families raised in the city. The desert was the place where it was considered that the true virtues of manliness such as honour, generosity, hospitality and courage remained. Once inculcated in the desert they could be returned to the city, bridging the manly and virtuous desert lifestyle to the new urban communities. In addition, in the desert one learned about nature and interdependence in order to survive. Muhammad's uncle certainly brought the young boy up with the necessary skills for survival, where even a prophet of God would need to learn martial skills. Even before the responsibilities of his prophethood descended upon him, Muhammad was known to the citizens of Makkah as trustworthy in his business dealings and wise in his decisions.

And it was these qualities that attracted the wealthy widow Khadijah to him, when she first employed him as a leader of her caravans and then proposed marriage. Muhammad was twenty-five and she was a mature woman believed to have been in her forties. It was a love match and survived until her death fourteen years later, but no children were to survive from the union, probably as a result of her age.

Some scholars have speculated on the contact Muhammad may have had with Christian or Jewish teachings as a result of his trading expeditions. Tradition states that he came into contact with a Christian monk who declared the young man to be the last of the prophets of God. However, such stories need to be seen in the context of narratives which authenticate religious truths. Just as the young Jesus is claimed to have visited Egypt, the land having associations at the time as a repository of wisdom, so the young Muhammad similarly is given authenticity by a representative of the established revelation that preceded Islam. However, Muhammad seemed to have been reflective by nature, often going up into the mountains above Makkah for long periods of isolation and retreat in between his caravan journeys. It was on one such occasion, when he was nearing forty years old, that a supernatural being appeared to him and commanded him to 'recite' or 'read'. Tradition states that he was illiterate and the command had to be made three times before the visibly shaken Muhammad was persuaded for the first time to recite from the Book of God, the Qur'an, believed to have been brought to him by Jibreel (Gabriel), the angelic messenger always chosen by Allah as his intermediary to the chosen prophets.

It is said that the terrified Muhammad ran to take shelter under his wife's robes, probably believing that he had been approached by one of the terrible supernatural creatures known as *djinn*, who according to Arab folklore haunted the unwary in the desert. However, when Khadijah heard the story, she recognised the truth, embraced Islam and in the process became the first Muslim, accepted her husband as the Prophet of God and sent him back to the Angel for further guidance. Thus began the process of twenty-two years of revelation that would produce the final Qur'an as it exists until today, and would transform the religious life of the world.

Muhammad began to preach a message of uncompromising monotheism in Makkah, passing on the verses of the Qur'an to his audiences as he received them from the Angel. There was little success to begin with although he attracted some of the younger scions of the Makkan merchant families and other less important members of society. His key support came from his wife, his son-in-law Ali, and Abu Bakr, a doyen of the Quraysh. In addition, he retained the protection of his uncle and it was just as well for his safety was now a concern. The wealthy merchants resented the Qur'an's criticism of wealth that was not underpinned by a social concern for the poor and needy. In addition, the Qur'an's commitment to the exclusive worship of Allah was not likely to endear the powerful of the city to its monotheism as it threatened the income that accrued to the wealthy middlemen of the city who controlled the ancient shrine of the Ka'aba and its plethora of deities. So, too, the Qur'an's view of the afterlife was a new concept for the Arabs, not known in the ancient traditions of the desert tribes.

At first Muhammad and his band of followers were met by ridicule, but on the death of his uncle, and when no longer protected by a powerful ally and patron, the ridicule turned nasty. A female follower was killed, and the new community of worshippers was harassed and suffered minor persecution. Muhammad sent one group of his supporters to the Negus, the Christian king of Ethiopia, where they received sanctuary even though the Makkan powers also sent representatives to Ethiopia demanding that the Muslims be returned as escaped slaves.

In 622, significantly for the fledgling Muslim community and the success of Muhammad's mission, he was invited to leave Makkah and come to the oasis city of Medina as an honoured personage, able to arbitrate and resolve certain tensions in the city resulting from tribal conflicts and the inability of the leaders of Medina to forge a community from its disparate factions. As the situation with the Makkan leaders grew tenser, Muhammad sent his followers ahead of him and then, barely escaping an attempt on his own life, departed in the middle of the night.

The move to Medina was to transform the situation. From a despised religious leader in Makkah, Muhammad came to be a political figure with both temporal and spiritual leadership that provided him with the authority to establish a community that found its unity in God and his revelation and which agreed to guidance under the authority of God's prophet. Although there were factions that undermined and resisted this development, especially amongst the Jewish tribes around and within the city perimeters, Muhammad appears to have welded the people together under a unique and historic document called the Constitution of Medina. Bringing together both the Muslims of Makkah, the new converts in Medina and other tribal allegiances forged into a community that overruled the primacy of blood ties in favour of a supratribal alliance that acknowledged belief in Allah and the leadership of his Prophet was an act of genius. It not only provided legal and political authority to Muhammad but paved the way for the concept of a universal community of believers that would be known as Islam.

From hereon in, faith would become the criterion for community membership, and Muhammad's new-found position as spiritual and temporal authority would provide the rationale for the Muslim political position that there can be no division between 'church' and 'state' but rather both authorities are united under God's sovereignty and Muhammad's office as prophet of God. An examination of the Qur'an's revelations after the *Hijra* (migration) to Medina provides insight into a community that is incorporating God's new law, especially in the realm of personal family law, into an organised political and social life, where the laws and customs of tribal loyalty were carefully negotiated to become a religiously bonded community governed by Allah's ordinances. In Medina, Muhammad finally broke his ties with the older revelations of Judaism and Christianity, defining them as communities that had gone astray and were now superseded. As a part of this process of separation and distinction, the unique religious rituals and observances of Islam were formulated.

The significance to Muslims of the *Hijra* in 622 is marked by the year becoming the first of the Muslim era. But Muhammad's trials were far from over. Even if his fledgling community appeared successful in Medina, the Makkan merchants remained deeply cynical and antagonistic. The skills of warfare taught by his uncle, and his youthful stays with the desert Arabs, were now to be called upon in a series of armed conflicts with the forces of the Makkans. The Battle of Badr in 627 would transform Muhammad's reputation amongst the tribes of Arabia in a way which was as significant as his new role in Medina. The inferior force of the Muslims and their Medinan allies were to engage in battle with a much stronger enemy gathered together by the Makkan confederacy and pull off a victory that was to surprise even the Muslims, confound the Makkans and bring Muhammad increased respect amongst the tribes of Arabia who above all admired strength.

The consequences of the victory had, first and foremost, a considerable impact on the religious sensibilities of the Muslims. Their Prophet had led them to a significant victory over powerful forces, deemed to be the strongest in the land. No longer would a theology carved out of weakness and persecution be considered sufficient. On the contrary the Qur'an was to speak of 'Manifest Success', and Muslims would thereafter, with the noted exception of the Shi'a – as we have already seen – link success in the world with proof of God's favour. If the Makkans were alarmed and more likely to take Muhammad seriously, and the Muslims confirmed in their faith and overjoyed with the positive proof of Allah's beneficence, there were also to be negative effects for the victorious. In future, the Muslims would face the problem of how to integrate into their faith community, the tribes who would come to offer Muhammad their allegiance and seek his protection and patronage, but whose motives would be very different from the original followers. Muhammad was now a substantial presence on the Arabian peninsula, whether people accepted the religious message or not.

The next twelve months of Muhammad's life would revolve

around the quarrel with the Makkans, but so powerful would he become as a result of new allies drawn to him by the Arab tribes, that the Quraysh, even though some of their leaders now hated him intensely, decided to pragmatically negotiate with the Muslims in their new-found position of strength. When Muhammad requested to come on pilgrimage to the Ka'aba, they initially agreed. But when they resisted his terms and reneged on the agreement he brought the weight of his forces to camp outside the city. The city decided to surrender, and in 628 Muhammad entered the precincts of the Ka'aba, destroyed all the idols that were contained within it and announced that forthwith the shrine would only exist for the worship of Allah. Both parties were satisfied and there was no bloodshed. The Muslims of Makkah could return to their family homes and all could take part in the rites and practise their religion, but the merchants of the Quraysh would not lose their traditional income from the shrine as the city was now even more successful as a focus for pilgrims rapidly embracing the religion of the victors.

Four years later, Muhammad died. His faith in Allah had established the new faith on the Arabian peninsula, and his own reputation amongst the Arabs, believers and non-believers, was assured. At his last sermon delivered in Makkah on the occasion of Muhammad's final pilgrimage, we see some of his concerns for his community, and the voice of the Prophet merges with and subsumes the statesman. Although he mentions some of the ethical codes bequeathed to his community concerning the rights of women and the treatment of others, it is the overwhelming simplicity and power of the lines that speak of equality before God that generate something of Muhammad's religious conviction.

> O my people listen to me in earnest, worship God, say your daily prayers, fast during the month of Ramadan, and give alms. Perform the Hajj if you can afford to. All mankind is from Adam and Eve, an Arab has no superiority over a non-Arab nor a non-Arab has any superiority over an Arab: also white man has no superiority over a black nor a black has no superiority over white except by piety and good action. Learn that every Muslim is the brother of another Muslim, and that Muslims constitute one brotherhood. Nothing shall be legitimate to a Muslim which belongs to a fellow Muslim unless it was given freely and willingly. Do not therefore, do injustice to yourselves. Remember, one

day you will appear before God and answer for your deeds. So beware, do not stray from the path of righteousness after I am gone. (Rogerson, 2003:208)

Muhammad was to make his very final words to the gathering, 'Be my witness, O God, that I have conveyed your message to your people.' The answer affirming assent resounded from the hills and valleys of Makkah – *Allahumma na'm*, 'O God, he has!'

The Prophet of faith

It is said that Abu Bakr, Muhammad's trusted Companion, announced on the Prophet's death, 'O people, whosoever has been wont to worship Muhammad – truly Muhammad is dead; and whoever has been wont to worship God – truly God lives and never dies' (Ling, 1983:345). He then recited the verse from the Qur'an delivered after the Battle of Uhud when Muhammad came close to being killed: 'Muhammad is only a messenger and messengers have died before him. If he dies or is slain, will you turn back upon your heels?' (Ling, 1983:346).

Yet in spite of the acknowledgement of the mortality of Muhammad, a prophet is regarded by Muslims as an extraordinary personality, and already in the process of gathering the material for his life story, his biographers felt the need to go further back into the past than the Prophet's arrival in the world. Just as Islam itself is perceived as predating Muhammad, part of the ancient story of humanity's struggle with the forces of good and evil and God's eventual victory, so the final Prophet becomes inextricably linked with a long history of the Arab world to overcome idolatry and establish the worship of the One God in the region. The religious imagination is already at work, authenticating the Prophet's birth and pre-empting his arrival in the generations that preceded him.

The pre-history of Muhammad

We have already seen that the roots of Islam are believed to lie with the story of Ibrahim's (Abraham) birth of a son from his handmaid Hajjar (Hagar). It is stated in the Qur'an that Ibrahim visited the estranged mother and child in Makkah where they had come to rest after the miraculous discovery of a spring named Zamzam. The water had sprung up out of the desert at Ismael's feet when the family were dying of thirst and had called upon God for succour. It was Ibrahim, according to the Qur'an, who had on one of these visits built a sanctuary for the worship of God with the help of his son. Some versions of the story claim that the shrine had been built by Adam (see Chapter 10). The sanctuary had been named the Ka'aba, and it is said that God instructed his prophet to establish a pilgrimage there.

Thus it is believed by Muslims that Makkah became a place of pilgrimage to the one God, with its rites established by Ibrahim and Ismael. However, it is believed that over the course of time, the shrine fell into disuse and became a centre of idol worship. The well of Zamzam was filled in by the Jurhamites, invaders from South Arabia, who had been driven out but decided that no other people should benefit from possessing the oasis. It is said that a powerful tribe of Abrahamic descent known as the Quraysh settled in the area, and it was one of them named Qusayy who ordered his people to build houses around the shrine rather than inhabit tents. Thus the settlement of Makkah came into existence. The story tells us that Qusayy gave the right to be the keeper of the keys of the shrine to his son Abd al-Dar and his descendants, whereas Hashim, his first-born son, and his descendants were granted the privilege of providing food and shelter for the pilgrims.

The story goes on that Hashim had a son, from a woman of Medina, thus connecting the two cities, who was brought to Makkah by Hashim's brother who did not consider his own sons fit to succeed him at the task. The young boy inherited the right to feed the pilgrims and loved to sleep in the sacred confines of the Ka'aba. One night in a vision, he heard the voice of a supernatural being commanding him to dig. After some days of disbelief, he finally rediscovered the spring of Zamzam and his clan were given charge over it to assist in the feeding of the pilgrims.

Muttalib, the son of Hashim, is reputed to have never prayed before idols but only to have offered worship to Allah. It is believed that there were a number of significant individuals among the Quraysh who remembered the old religion of Ibrahim and remained true to its monotheism. Although they maintained the custom of welcoming the tribes to Makkah they considered the worship of the stone and wooden gods to be an innovation. These proto-monotheists were known as Hanifa, neither Christian nor Jew, but worshippers of the same God nevertheless. Famous amongst the ranks of the Hanifa was Waraqah, who had converted to Christianity and prophesised the coming of a new messenger from amongst the Arab people.

Muttalib had nine sons of whom the best loved and youngest was named Abd Allah. In a parallel story to the famous sacrifice attributed to Ibrahim, Muttalib had made a vow to sacrifice one son if God blessed him with many. The drawing of lots selected Abd Allah but the women of his clan prevented the sacrifice and camels were slaughtered in his stead. Abd Allah died whilst trading in modern-day Syria or Palestine, leaving behind a pregnant wife named Aminah. It is stated by tradition that on the day of the birth of her son a voice spoke saying: 'Thou carriest in thy womb, the lord of this people, and when he is born say: I place him beneath the protection of the One, from the evil of every envier; then name him Muhammad' (Ling, 1983:21).

In this story of the Prophet's forerunners we see elements that begin to lay the foundations for the Muhammad who grips the religious imagination of the Muslims down through the generations. As with the Christian version of Jewish history, the story of Muhammad's antecedents establishes the logic of inevitability, a need for a prophet who would come as the culmination of the struggle to overcome idolatry and bring victory for the primordial worship of the one God. Just as Jesus is linked to the family of David in some of the Gospels, so Muhammad is born to a lineage associated with the sacred shrine of the Ka'aba, never losing the true faith and never accepting the idols as did the original inhabitants. The unfulfilled sacrifice of a son, Muhammad's own father, reminds us of a primordial monotheism where a patriarch was prepared to kill a child for God. The stories of each generation's service to the Ka'aba stone are embellished with stories of divine intervention to save the shrine from oblivion. In all this, we can see the creation of an alternative location to Jerusalem which has an equally authentic pedigree of worship to the One God. In addition, the story provides the Arabs with an ancient lineage of worship that can rival that of the Jews. Muhammad's birth itself is prophesied and announced by heavenly visitation and tradition tells us that his mother felt herself surrounded by light throughout her pregnancy. When the orphan child stayed in the desert after the death of his mother, it is said that two men dressed in white apparel came and laid him down, opened his breast and stirred his heart (Ling, 1983:26).

The Night Journey

There is one other element of Muhammad's life, so far not mentioned, that requires examination. In the history of key events provided earlier, I have mentioned the *Mi'raj* that took place in 621. For Muslims, this miraculous experience, which falls somewhere between vision and mystical epiphany, marks Muhammad as the closest of all the prophets to Allah and the beloved friend of God. It compares with Moses' encounter with the Burning Bush or Jesus' transfiguration on the mountain top. It happens when Muslim fortunes are at their lowest, a year before the *Hijra*. However, the tale of Muhammad's divine encounter has some unusual features, in that it is believed by many that it did not happen to him in spirit but rather took place literally in the flesh.

The *Mi'raj* or Night Journey is significant enough an event in Muhammad's life for it to appear in the Qur'an itself: 'Most High praise to Him who carried His servant by night from the sacred mosque (Makkah) to the farthest sanctuary (Mosque Al-Aqsa)' (Qur'an 17:1). Not only does the Night Journey experience establish Muhammad amongst those who have directly been in close contact with the divine reality, but it also has the effect of linking the Ka'aba in Makkah, a remote outpost in the Arabian desert, with the spiritual capital of monotheism, the city of David, always associated with the prophets of Bani Israel and with Isa, the messiah of the Christians.

The 'farthest mosque' is believed to refer to Jerusalem, and to this day the mosque on the Temple Mount is named Masjid al-Aqsa, and forever associated with the mystical ascension of Muhammad in the flesh to the highest realms of God. Ibn Ishaq, the oldest of the Prophet's biographers, tells the story as follows: that the Angel Jibreel lifted Muhammad from his prayer vigil onto a heavenly creature named Buraq, from where he is transported to Jerusalem and meets with former prophets and leads them in prayer. From the site of the 'farthest mosque' he is taken up a heavenly ladder (*mi'raj*) with the encouragement of Jibreel. On the way, he passes through a number of stages guarded by significant figures at different levels. For example, Isma'il, the son of Ibrahim asks if he is a messenger of God at the Gate of the Guard. Other stages are the places of abode for significant figures in the hierarchies of prophets, such as Adam, who guards the lowest spiritual realms and where he oversees the punishments of sinners. Isa (Jesus) is seen at the fourth heaven and Ibrahim at the seventh. Finally Muhammad is brought before the presence of God.

According to tradition, Muhammad negotiates with Allah in regard to the number of prayers his people should utter in God's praise, finally settling at five. Other traditions state that it was here that Muhammad gained the right to be an intercessor on behalf of Muslims.

Throughout history Muslim theologians have debated the significance and the nature of this mystical encounter. Some have declared it to be physical, others that it was Muhammad's spirit that was taken up. There is also intense speculation concerning how close Muhammad came to the divine presence. The significant *sura* of the Quran is 53, where it speaks of 'two bows or closer' as the distance that Muhammad stood from the divine presence. Verse 17 affirms the status of Muhammad and his attainment, in that his eye did not flinch from the countenance of God. 'The eye did not rove' became the epitome of one-pointed longing for intimacy by the countless mystics of Islam, and an example of the purity of Muhammad's heart.

The Night Journey was to fascinate the faithful; the mystics and the pious saw in it the possibility of closeness to the divine being, writing poems and songs which elaborated on the extraordinary nature of the Prophet in the world of spiritual hierarchies, where even Jibreel, the great archangel, was further from the presence of God than Muhammad. The songs reached out to the Muslim masses and were sung in praise of God's beloved and brought them closer to the Prophet who now stood as their saviour, in the sense that someone so intimate with Allah could speak on their behalf before the throne of judgement. In addition, the story of the Night Journey elevates the final Prophet of God above his predecessors.

Many songs and poems exist to compare Muhammad with Moses, that other great recipient of divine law, who had swooned when near the divine presence and had not been permitted to see the face of God when confronted by the Burning Bush. The Qur'an confirms this in Sura 7:139 when it states of Moses 'You will never behold Me!' The Indo-Persian poet Jamali Kanboh, in a couplet typical of this genre, wrote the following: 'Moses went out of his mind by a single revelation of the Attributes – You see the Essence of the Essence, and still smile' (Schimmel, 1985:163).

Muhammad in Muslim prayer life

In her excellent study of Muslim prayer manuals, Constance Padwick quotes a nineteenth-century Indian source who suggests that the second clause of the *shahada*, the testimony of faith that asserts *'Muhammadu rasulu 'llah'* is the primary defence against elevating Muhammad to divinity. His reasoning is that as Muslims all over the world repeat every day 'Muhammad is the Apostle of God' (Padwick, 1996:138) they are unlikely to attribute divine status to the Prophet. In the Qur'an, at the most sublime moment of his prophetic career, when about to step on the heavenly ladder, Muhammad is described as *'abd'*, one who is in a condition of servitude, a creature who is only fit to be in a state of worship, even if at its most elevated. Yet it is also immediately after the incident that propelled him amongst the ranks of God's closest, that Muhammad is reputed to have stated: 'I was a Prophet when Adam was yet between water and clay.' Although this can be interpreted as a statement of Muhammad's realisation that in the deepest level of his own innermost reality he was immortal and timeless spirit, to the simple pious it could so easily become an understanding of Muhammad as the primordial Prophet, something akin to the Greek idea of Logos, that had already so significantly impacted on Christian understandings of Jesus.

Padwick notes a variety of ways in which Muhammad is used in popular piety, including the use of his epithets or names, descriptions of his qualities that are strung together in litanies. Disturbingly for those who would keep Muhammad clearly apart from God's divinity, some of these names echo the ninety-nine names of God described in the Qur'an, which list Allah's attributes (Padwick, 1996:138–140). The mystics of Islam meditated upon Muhammad at prayer, at vigil, whilst fasting, and recreated their lives on his model as the ideal pattern of spiritual attainment. Above all, it was the deep mystery of the Night Journey that fascinated them. In this manifestation, it is not Muhammad the law-revealer or the statesman of Medina that is significant but rather the spiritual leader, the innermost heart of Islam, one who achieved intimacy way beyond any other religious figure, even surpassing Jesus, that other magnificent intimate of God. It is thus that he maintains the predominant place as a bridge between a transcendent deity and his people.

For the pious, especially the burgeoning mystical orders of the early medieval period, Muhammad is approached with awe and is present spiritually at both *salat* (ritual prayer) and *dhikr* (the remembrance of Allah's names). Kenneth Cragg reminds us that in all three Semitic faiths, God works in history and it is in the development of human civilisation and culture that the clues to divine nature and providence can be found. Above all, of course, for all three religions it is revelation, given at a transcendent moment in time but worked out through human progress and conflict over the millennia to arrive at the final justification of divine mercy and justice at the end-time. However, for Muslims, it is Muhammad, through his prophethood, that embodies the point of association 'between God and the human world, the context in which men experience God's ways and God's mercy'. Cragg reminds us that Sura 3:31 established the relations between Allah, the faithful and the final Prophet. 'Say: "If you love God, follow me; God will love you and forgive you your evil doings. For God is forgiving and Merciful"'(Cragg, 1999:190).

For millions, to follow the Prophet is to go beyond his exemplary and ethical role, and to love him intensely. But religious love often leads to magnification and many of the countless prayer manuals written by devout Muslims exalt the Prophet of Islam beyond all other living creatures. Constance Padwick quotes As-Suyuti's *al-Hirzu 'l-mani,* typical of the genre: 'Then he said, "it is our duty to love him and render him honour and magnify him more abundantly than the honour of every slave to his master or every son to his father"' (Padwick, 1996:143).

Most prayers concerning the Prophet, calling down blessings on him and his family, are known as *tasliya,* and remain common throughout the Muslim world. Such invocations are added to the prayer-call and even included in the obligatory *salat* where the devout simply say, 'May God call down blessing on our Lord Muhammad and on the family of our Lord Muhammad and greet them with peace.' However, it is but a short step from this to addressing prayer to Muhammad himself. Although Muhammad cannot be the final goal or recipient of the prayer, intercessory prayer is common throughout the Muslim world and is authorised by many Hadith and confirmed by traditional practice. Padwick records from the prayer manual, *Wirdun sa'diyya mukhtasar, Majmu'atu 'l-ahzab,* the following supplication:

> O Thou who are transfigured in radiance, have mercy on my abasement. O Thou who art exalted, set to rights my state. O Apostle of God, help! And supply of succour! O Beloved of God, on thee is reliance. O Prophet of God, be to us a mediator. Thou, by God art an intercessor who meets with no refusal O my Lord, O Apostle of God, O my support, my refuge, my Apostle, thou

suffices me. I have placed in the praise of the Apostle of God my
confidence, for he, when I seek for sufficiency, suffices me.
(Padwick, 1995:144)

Muhammad's role as the intercessor for his community began in the
early days of Islam. The Qur'an states that no one can act as an intercessor before God 'except with His permission' (Qur'an 2:256). The
meaning is ambiguous and allows for different interpretations. In the
case of Muhammad's role as intercessor for his community, both in
day-to-day supplication and as a special interlocutor on the Day of
Judgement, the verse is understood to mean that the final Prophet
has such assent, but to the revivalist movements the same verse is
translated to mean that no one has such permission.

Annemarie Schimmel records an early and well-known Hadith
concerning the Prophet's special role at the Day of Judgement. All the
prophets are approached, from Adam through to Isa (Jesus), before
the multitudes of human beings gathered on a hill to await God's
judgement. The atmosphere is charged with fear and grief. First
Adam, the father of the human race, is requested to plead for God's
mercy. But he replies that he cannot because he also fears judgement
for his disobedience at the beginning of creation. All the prophets
recall an act of sin or disobedience with the noted exception of Isa but
even he says that he has to fear the Day of Judgement. Finally
Muhammad is called and begged to intercede. He replied:

> Thus I shall go and come before the Throne. He reveals Himself
> to me and inspires in me such a glorification and praise as He has
> never inspired in anyone before that. Then He says: 'O
> Muhammad, lift your head, ask, and you will be given; intercede,
> and you will be granted!' (Schimmel, 1985:84,85)

The Prophet's intercession is of two kinds: *shafa'a* and *tawassul*, also
known as *istighatha*. *Shafa'a* refers to intercession provided for peti-
tionary prayer, which is also attributed to angels and sometimes to
the Qur'an itself. *Tawassul* refers to any means that a human being can
use to come closer to Allah and help them surrender to the divine
will. *Tawassul* is ultimately pragmatic, and based on the idea of what
works rather than what is doctrinally correct. If a time-honoured
practice has brought Muslims closer to a state of humility and gratitude, then it should be acknowledged. *Shafa'a* comes in the category

of *tawassul* but *istighatha*, which refers to the practice of requesting specific intercession of the Prophet, is regarded by millions of traditional Muslims, and certainly by the Sufis, as the most beneficial form of *tawassul* (Geaves, 2000:31).

The vast body of popular poetry and songs that praise the Prophet of Islam, calling down blessings upon him and his family, combine with his role as intercessor for his people to produce a strong tradition of love and veneration for Muhammad that goes far beyond his role as exemplar and embodiment of Islam's ethical codes. The Muslim world is sanctified not only by its mosques and the shrines of the *awliya*, but also by a network of relics of Muhammad. The faithful gather in awe on special occasions to see a hair from his beard or a piece of leather reputed to be from his sandals.

However, the two most significant occasions for understanding the popular piety to the Prophet can be found in the *Maulid*, the celebration of his birthday that takes place throughout the Muslim world (with the noted exception of Saudi Arabia) and, second, the sacred expressions of emotion that occur at Muhammad's tomb in Medina. But the development of a spiritualised Muhammad, surrounded by miracle stories and able to appear in dreams and visions to those in need of guidance, was not without its problems and exerted tensions on the centrality of the doctrine of Muhammad's humanity. Padwick states that: 'Islam of today must be ever on her guard against what may be a tacit, though never explicit, deifying of the Prophet, whose position in these prayers is so immeasurably beyond that of humanity' (Padwick, 1996:138).

The cosmic Muhammad

However, if the above special role in Muslim devotions was to outrage some conservative Muslims, it palls in comparison with the idea of the pre-existent Muhammad. The stories of the Prophet's role at the Day of Judgement already indicate that in some way the final Messenger of God has escaped the shackles of ordinary mortality. So too does his role as intercessor for his people on a day-to-day basis. For those Muslims who offer to him prayers of supplication or who call down blessings upon his name, or are blessed by his presence in dream or vision, Muhammad remains alive, an intense spiritual presence, rather than an historic figure who lived and died in Makkah in the sixth and seventh centuries. Even in his tomb, a living proof of his humanity, Muslims speak to him as if alive, recording countless incidents that offer evidence to each other of his living presence. They sometimes claim to have mystical intercourse with him or, more matter of fact, to have had their prayers personally answered by him.

The issue of whether Muhammad is alive or dead separates Muslims to this day. In Britain, mosques are divided between those who place '*Ya Rasul Allah*' and '*Ya Allah*' behind the *minbar* (pulpit), to the left and right of the *qiblah* (the niche in the wall that marks out the direction of prayer) and those who are horrified by the deification implied. The two exclamations of praise to God and His Prophet are controversial because they are in the present tense and indicate that Muhammad remains alive beyond the grave, *hazir u nazir*, 'present and watching'. Recently I spoke with a Malaysian Muslim who teaches in Britain. He told me of divisions that took place in a mosque in Oxford when he was a student at the university. He said that the problem arose when subcontinent Muslims began to use the mosque and sent their prayers of supplication to the Prophet, addressing him as standing alive before them. Then he said they began to petition for '*Ya Rasul Muhammad*' to be written in Arabic on the wall of the mosque. The students who prayed in the mosque were from the Middle East and could not accept the idea of a living Prophet. The Prophet was dead and buried in his grave as far as they were concerned. The suggestion of a living Prophet was too close to Christian doctrines of an eternal Christ who is also God.

Even more problematic for some Muslim sensibilities, trying to maintain a slippery foothold on the idea of Islam as a rational religion, is the belief in the primordial Muhammad. If Muhammad transcends the grave by living in the present, and in the future where he holds the hopes of Muslims everywhere to soften the divine wrath on the Day of Judgement, then it is but a short leap for the religious imagination to cast his living presence back to the time of the original act of creation itself.

The claim to be a prophet before the existence of Adam has already been noted, but the doctrine of the pre-existent Muhammad is related to the Hadith that states that the Prophet appeared to his mother as light prior to his birth. This idea of Muhammad existing as an emanation of Allah's light is found in a number of Hadith. Typical of the genre is the Hadith in which Jabir ibn Abd Allah asked the Prophet a question concerning the first creation of Allah. The Prophet replied:

O Jabir, the first thing that Allah created was the light of your
Prophet from His light, and that light remained in the midst of
His Power for as long as He wished, and there was not, at that
time, a Tablet or a Pen or a Paradise or a Fire or an angel or a
heaven or an earth. And when Allah wished to create creation,
He divided that light into four parts and from the first made the
Pen, from the second the Tablet, from the third the Throne, and
from the fourth everything else.

Annemarie Schimmel describes the theosophy of a primordial light of
Muhammad as 'mystical prophetology' (Schimmel, 1985:123) and
dates its origins, or at least its prominence to the ninth century
(Schimmel, 1985:125). The light is described in texts of this period as
a solidification of the eternal light (*Nur*) of God at its centre. This
transparent column went on to become the primordial Muhammad
(Schimmel, 1985:125). So my own Sufi informants, who claim that
God is everywhere but in the centre of God is Muhammad surrounded
by God in all directions, are supported by classical early sources
(Geaves, 2000:30).

It is said that because Muhammad's light is primordial and of the
same substance as Allah, it predates the fires of Hell which were a
later creation. Thus the true believers who purify their being in the
light of Muhammad will escape the hellfire, for Hell will say to them,
'the light of Muhammad has extinguished my fire' (Schimmel,
1985:129). Later mystics in Islam were not above actually claiming
that Muhammad was created because Allah in His eternal loneliness
wished to be loved and known and created the Prophet as the
Beloved, the first of the *awliya*, the friends of God, and the model for
all aspiring mystics. Pure of heart, the Prophet is a cosmic mirror in
which Allah can look at Himself and see the fullness of divine
love. On the other hand, Muhammad gazes on the divine face full of
adoration and servitude.

The mystical tradition of Islam generated a fully developed theosophy of Muhammad, the primordial prophet, which certainly seems to
bear resemblance to the Christian doctrine of the Logos as expressed
in the Gospel of John. Through the generations, musicians, poets and
mystical utterances would fuel popular piety to the degree that
some or all of the above beliefs in a 'cosmic' Muhammad were incorporated into traditional Muslim practice. Unless purged by reformers,
such as the Wahhabi movement in eighteenth-century Arabia or the

Deobandis in nineteenth-century India, the Muslim masses have retained their passion and veneration for the last Prophet of God. Today such beliefs tend to exist in their more extreme manifestations in the perimeters of the Muslim world rather than the Arab heartlands. India, Pakistan, Bangladesh, Indonesia, North and sub-Saharan Africa are the strongholds, places where Sufism remains dominant. In the Arab heartlands, Syria remains a centre of such traditions, and in the Ottoman Empire they were part and parcel of everyday life, until banned by Ataturk in his successful attempt to carve out a modern nation in Turkey, or suppressed by the Wahhabi movements.

Conclusion

The dangers of deifying the Prophet are there, and Annemarie Schimmel mentions that Muslim theologians have discussed the issue of Muhammad's primordial existence for centuries, and although some were opposed, many were in favour, citing a range of authorities from both classical and postclassical sources (Schimmel, 1985:87). The debates continue in the contemporary period and Schimmel quotes a *fatwa* (legal or theological decision) made in South Africa as recently as 1982 which declared it confirmed by tradition to address praise to a living Muhammad and call on his intercession (Schimmel, 1985:87).

Many opponents would like to blame this adoration of the Prophet on subcontinent Islam, where the influence of Sufism is very pronounced, but the traditional sources predate the advent of Islam in that region. Recently, Shaykh Kabbani, a Muslim leader of Syrian origin, has written a seven-volume *Encyclopedia of Islamic Doctrine* in which the fourth volume is solely on the topic of intercession. The third volume is on the role of Muhammad and quotes innumerable classical sources to authenticate the Prophet's continuing role as spiritual master of all Muslims.

Not all agree, and there are vociferous counterclaims accusing those who hold the Prophet to be more than his mortal manifestation guilty of *bida* (innovation) and *shirk* (raising others to the status of God). For such critics, the advent of the Qur'an was sufficient for all human beings to receive divine guidance. Although there are many millions of Muslims who do not hold to the idea of a prophet who has transcended the grave, most of the real criticism comes from the Wahhabis and Salafis. On the other hand, millions also venerate a prophet who has certainly become far more than his human lifespan, and most devout amongst these are those pious Muslims known as the Sufis.

The criticism of *bida*, or innovation, is one that needs to be taken seriously by Muslims, for it suggests a watering-down or contamination of God's final revelation, exactly the criticism which the Qur'an itself makes against Christianity and Judaism. Yet all religions operate in a cultural context where they interact with and are influenced by the world around them. Islam came into contact with Christianity very early on, even at the time of Muhammad, but later, as the Arabs became a people of substance, there was considerable interaction between the two empires of Islam and Byzantine Christianity. It would only be natural if in the environment of intense competition, some of the qualities that pious Christians attributed to Jesus should have been taken on by equally pious Muslims, for surely the final prophet could not be less than the penultimate, and his community could not be less committed in veneration.

On the other hand, all three of the Semitic-origin monotheistic religions were heavily influenced by neo-Platonic ideas of heavenly hierarchies and emanation theories of creation, where the substance of God gradually descends to matter from the divine essence. Muslim scholars themselves were amongst the first to reclaim the works of the Greek philosophers, translating them into Arabic and sending them back into the Christian world to be translated into Latin.

The neo-Platonic influence provided a massive impetus for mysticism in all three religions, not least to the medieval Sufis, who dominated the world of Islam in this period. The idea of the primordial Muhammad, created from the Light of God, certainly suggests a neo-Platonic influence that rivals in its theosophy the Logos theory of early Christianity, itself influenced by the Greek world. For those Muslims who perceive the outside influences, the accusations of *bida* and *shirk* will rumble on, but there is enough evidence to be drawn from the Qur'an and Hadith to justify such veneration and millions of Muslims will continue to draw upon Muslim tradition as authority for their love and devotion to Muhammad.

To this day, the accusation of not 'respecting the Prophet' made by one Muslim group to another signifies that the accusers maintain allegiance to a human being endowed with divine qualities, and firmly places the Muslims who makes the accusation within the fold of a Sufi-influenced tradition. Those against whom the accusation is levelled defend themselves by asserting that they do respect the prophets of God but that they were only human beings, dead and gone, but examples for all good Muslims to follow. The revelation is the Qur'an, and the Prophet only lived by its tenets, as all Muslims should.

CHAPTER 9

Jihad: Islamic warfare or spiritual effort?

The following chapter will explore the controversial concept of jihad *and how it came to mean 'holy war' in certain Islamic movements and in the Western media. The idea of religious war and its justification will be assessed in the classical sources. Throughout, the chapter will argue that warfare is a very narrow definition of* jihad *even amongst contemporary Islamic movements as it is also used for* da'wa *activities to promote Islam both to Muslims and non-Muslims. In addition, the idea of the greater* jihad, *the struggle to overcome the negative aspects of the self, will be presented as more significant than military struggles in the everyday life of Muslims. The ideas of Ayatollah Khomeini on* jihad *will be explored in order to understand contemporary political understandings of* jihad.

Introduction

Jihad has certainly become both the most misunderstood and disturbing aspect of Islam, now inextricably associated with the catastrophic events on 9 September 2001 (commonly known as 9/11), suicide bombers in Palestine and Iraq, and all other acts of violence performed with a religious or political motive in any part of the Muslim world. It has been linked with an ongoing campaign by certain segments of the Muslim world to declare war on Western lifestyle in general, especially where secularisation and consumer capitalism impact on Muslim societies through globalisation. This has led to a 'clash of civilisations' thesis where the Islamic world replaces communism as the enemy of 'enlightened' and liberal democratic values. Muhammad Sirozi, picking up on this limited understanding of *jihad*, cites some Western critics of Islam, for example Daniel Pipes, as interpreting *jihad* as a 'holy war', 'to extend sovereign Muslim power' (Pipes, 2002). He goes on to accuse the Western media of being guilty of referring to *jihad* only in the context of 'terrorist attacks organized by so-called militant fundamentalist Muslims' (Sirozi, 2004).

On the other hand, many devout Muslims have claimed that *jihad* has been misrepresented not only by the Western media but also by a minority of Muslims who interpret it only in the narrow sense of religious war. However, it is necessary to remind ourselves once again that the Muslim world is represented by a wide range of political and religious expressions, each of whom may place a very different emphasis on the significance of *jihad*. This chapter intends to explore some of these positions and also to assess the Qur'anic revelations concerning *jihad* and how these have been interpreted by classical scholars of Islam, both in the medieval and modern period.

The origins of *jihad*

The historic roots of *jihad* are located in the events that took place in the birth of Islam, first at Muhammad's reception in Makkah and then in Medina. Initially despised by the wealthy merchants of his home city for his uncompromising monotheism and claim to be receiving revelations from Allah, Muhammad struggled to gain a foothold. As we have seen, his followers met resistance and some degree of persecution. The Qur'an's early revelations attack both idolatry and the self-reliance of men of wealth. Both messages struck at the vested interests of the merchants who also controlled the city's traditional location as a pilgrimage centre for the surrounding Arab tribes. Muhammad's responses to persecution and ridicule from his detractors were straightforward: either *Hijra* (flight or migration) or *jihad* (sacred struggle).

In the event, *jihad* was not considered as an option. The Muslims were too weak and the Qur'an's messages instead justified the despised position of Muhammad as evidence of his calling as a prophet of God. Instead, Muhammad sent some of his followers to seek shelter with the Christian ruler of Ethiopia. However, the far more significant *Hijra* from Makkah to Medina in 622CE transformed the fortunes of Muhammad and the fledgling Muslim community. Invited to Medina, on the basis of his reputation for judgement and integrity, which was required to resolve tribal divisions in the town,

Muhammad was effectively transformed from a ridiculed founder of a new religious sect to a respected leader. In Medina the *umma* developed into a body of people which incorporated an organised political life in which a society previously centred on tribal loyalty, laws and customs was replaced by a religiously bonded community governed by God's law.

In Makkah Muhammad's followers had already forsaken kith and kin out of loyalty to Islam and its Prophet, but the *Hijra* further fractured blood ties as it removed the Muslims physically from their kinfolk. The increasing faith in the oneness of God and the prophethood of Muhammad came into conflict with old tribal loyalties and kinship networks as a result of their opposition to the new faith. It is possible to argue that the opposition to the new religious community would have helped create the sense of separation from their fellow Arabs. In an earlier book I have suggested that it was this persecution and animosity that helped form a bond of unity, a common faith and a shared moral outlook (Geaves, 1996:14).

In Medina, Muhammad was able to consolidate his position and insist that Islam must take precedence over all other loyalties to kith and kin. Muhammad, in turn, was to be recognised as deriving both his new political authority and his religious power from his office as Prophet of Allah. No longer the despised irritator of the Makkan merchants, he was now accepted by most in Medina as an honoured statesman and the messenger of God, the recipient of the Qur'an.

Once Islam began to grow in strength, the key division in Arab society became that of believer and unbeliever rather than the old inter-tribal conflicts. In fact, the Islamic scholar and historian, Montgomery Watt, suggests that Muhammad's genius was to transform the old tribal practice of *razi'a*, the looting of each other's caravans for spoils, into the performance of *jihad*, or holy war (Watt, 1972). However, this claim needs to be carefully assessed, for as we will see the Qur'an frames its monotheistic message against a backdrop of a titanic struggle between good and evil that goes far beyond the simple transformation of tribal conflicts.

It is suggested by Muslims that the various struggles that took place between Muhammad's opponents in Makkah and the new Muslim community in Medina, consisting now of the original followers who shared in the *Hijra* and new converts in Medina, together with various other kin networks and tribal alliances, took place because of the aggressive stance taken up by the Makkans. Western orientalist scholars, however, have stated that the Medinans were the first to take up arms when they raided a Makkan caravan that passed nearby. As we are reminded by John Esposito, the world of the desert tribes of Arabia and the developing city states was one where conflict was considered the norm (Esposito, 2002:29). Daily life was punctuated by tribal raids and vendettas of vengeance, which affected extended kinship networks. The two surrounding empires of the Byzantines and the Persians were locked in a long struggle for supremacy and had fought each other on several occasions. Violence was never far away.

It is unlikely that Muhammad would have given up on the idea of reclaiming Makkah for the worship of Allah. The revelation of the Qur'an began in the city; the Makkan merchants had declared themselves the enemies of God through their insistence on rejecting the revelation and continuing to worship the city's idols; victory over them would be a triumph for God, the establishing of the new message and vindication of Muhammad's prophethood. Regardless of who caused the initial act of aggression, the Makkan merchants and their allies confronted the fledgling Muslim community with an overwhelming force at Badr and were defeated. Later, at the Battle of Uhud, they regained some pride but were still unable to achieve a complete victory. Finally, Muhammad re-entered the city of Makkah in triumph without a battle taking place, destroying the city's idols and turning the Ka'aba, the ancient place of pilgrimage, into a site of worship for the One God. It is during this period of conflict the Qur'an says most about both *jihad* and its consequences of martyrdom.

Jihad and the Qur'an

The Qur'an in Sura 22:39–40 refers to the expulsion of the Muslims from Makkah and gives them permission to take up arms against aggressors, remarking in verse 41 that if the Muslims were 'given power in the land' then they would establish regular prayer and charity. The verses are significant in that along with 2:190 they provide the justification for 'defensive *jihad*'. However, there is a suggestion in the above verse 41 that power should be actively sought in order to establish true religion in the land. The verses justifying a defensive *jihad* are as follows:

To those against whom war is made, permission is given to fight, because they are wronged – and verily, Allah is Most Powerful for their aid. They are those who have been expelled from their homes in defiance of right – for no cause except that they did say, 'Our Lord is Allah.' (Qur'an 22:39–40)

It is in this same chapter that the rewards for martyrdom are mentioned. 'Those who leave their home in the cause of Allah, and are then slain or die – on them will Allah bestow, verily, a goodly provision' (Qur'an 22:58). In 2:190 and the following verses, defensive war is once again permitted where there is oppression and 'tumult' but there are restrictions and limitations. These limits on taking up arms are later developed into a charter for legitimate *jihad* by Muslim jurists. 'Fight in the cause of Allah those who fight you. But do not transgress limits for Allah loveth not transgressors' (Qur'an 2:190).

After Muhammad

As with most religions, the death of the founder was to have serious implications for how the new faith developed and structured itself. Muhammad had succeeded in welding together many of the Arabian tribes into a social organisation united by religion, but there were problems that arose from the rapid success of the new community. In the beginning, both individuals and groups of people came to join Muhammad, embracing Islam with conviction, but the military and political victories would have influenced their motivation for conversion. But as we have seen already in Chapter 5 it was normal in Arab society for weak tribes to seek patronage from stronger ones for protection. Certainly several tribes now joined for reasons of expediency and convenience and the problem is recognised in the Qur'an's verses by references to hypocrites. As the Arab empire spread after Muhammad's death this problem became more acute, with conquered nations and empires having to be incorporated into the Muslim fold as well as simply Arabian tribes.

In addition, we know that the issue of succession was not clear-cut. There were those who disputed Abu Bakr's right to lead the Muslims. Dabashi argues that the issue of the leadership after Muhammad's death had been left to the community. He considers that the appointment of Abu Bakr, although a trusted and devout Companion, was a successful attempt by the Quraysh, the dominant tribe, to reaffirm

their traditional status amongst the Arabs, after being amongst
Muhammad's most vociferous opponents (Dabashi, 1984:124). Other
Muslims felt that the succession should be kept within the bloodline
of the Prophet. The issue of the leadership was to lead to the main
division within the Muslim ranks, developing into the formation of
Sunni and Shi'a as the two main branches of the religion.

Although rapid expansion of the Arab tribes, involving conquest of
both Byzantine and Persian territory, took place under the first four
caliphs, and there were also a number of civil wars pitting Muslim
against Muslim, it was the beginnings of the Umayyad dynasty under
Mu'awiyya that would have the most significant impact on the development of *jihad*. Mu'awiyya, a senior member of the Quraysh tribe,
was governor of Damascus under Ali. Mu'awiyya had been a late
convert to Islam, after Muhammad's victorious entry to Makkah. His
family background connected him to opponents of Islam. Gaining the
position of caliph after Ali's assassination, Mu'awiyya moved the
capital of the Arab empire from Medina to Damascus and thus began
a dynastic line that would see the Arabs extend their territories from
Europe to India.

However, there were a number of Muslims who felt uneasy concerning the wealth and decadence of Mu'awiya's court and wondered
how it compared with the ascetic simplicity of Muhammad and his
Companions. Many of the surviving Companions established their
base in Medina, concentrating on religious piety and remaining outside the world of status and prestige available though positions in the
empire. The development of an ascetic pious attitude, focusing on the
fear of Allah and His wrath in the afterlife, provided the impetus for
a mystical, inward-focused tradition, later known as Sufism, and with
a very distinctive emphasis on *jihad* as internal purification.

Of greater significance to militant *jihad* were the opposition groups
known collectively as Kharijites. It is believed that Muhammad's concern in his latter days was for the unity of his community, reflected in
the words of his farewell speech before his death (see Chapter 8).
Muhammad's concern for brotherly relations between fellow
Muslims made it difficult for them to justify violence against each
other, but the already recognised problem of lack of religious motivation among many who were joining the ranks of the Muslims, had
given rise to a debate over who was deemed a 'hypocrite'. The
Kharijite movements, numbering around twenty, were the first to
decide that the hypocrites could be defined as non-Muslims and

therefore it was permissible to declare *jihad* against them. Their justification for the *jihad* to be deemed defensive arose from the argument that the 'hypocrites' had threatened the integrity of Islam.

The Kharijite solution was to withdraw themselves physically from the growing empire, disagreeing with both the Sunni and Shi'a understanding of leadership. They neither accepted the appointment of hereditary caliphs as rulers, nor did they accept that anyone was divinely ordained to lead. On the contrary, they insisted that authority was invested in the *umma* itself, and thus their leaders were appointed by the majority and could be removed in similar fashion. The essential requirement for leadership was piety and an acceptance of equality. Dabashi remarks that they challenged both the Umayyads and the Shi'a by declaring that they would create a society in which 'even a black slave could become the leader of the *umma* through popular consent' (Dabashi, 1989:124).

The insistence upon equality and piety would have struck a chord with both the desert Arabs and devout Muslims seeking a return to the pristine days of the Prophet, especially as the Kharijites made the decision that their secessionist communities should be regulated strictly according to the Qur'an. In addition, some other Kharijite groups went further and condemned even Muslims who stayed at home and refused to join their ranks. They were regarded as complicit in the lifestyles of the non-religious Muslims and therefore guilty of disbelief by association and eligible for the punishment of death (Watt, 1961:100). Practising a radical puritanism and seceding from the majority of Muslims, the Kharijites justified their position by referring to a significant verse in the Qur'an which appears to define the *umma* not as the totality of Muslims, but rather as a righteous group within the whole. 'Let there arise out of you a band of people inviting to all that is good, enjoining what is right and forbidding what is wrong. They are the ones to attain felicity' (Qur'an 3:104).

Thus this verse seems to justify the right of a self-defined righteous group to declare themselves as the true Muslim *umma* and brand others as either non-Muslims or hypocrites. Certainly the Kharijite movements permitted assassination for religious reasons and they declared *jihad* to be the sixth pillar of Islam (Lambton, 1989:24). Hitti states that 'in endeavouring to maintain the primitive charismatic principles of Islam, the puritanical Kharijites caused rivers of blood to flow in the first three Muslim centuries (Hitti, 1970:247). Dabashi states that the Kharijites considered their own communities as *dar al-Islam* (the territory of Islam) and everyone else as *dar-al-Harb* (the territory of war) and permitted the use of *jihad* against everyone that had not made a *hijra* into *dar al-Islam* (Dabashi, 1989:131), defining it as defensive by their criteria.

The Kharijite groups were not to survive, probably because they were prone to division within their ranks over leadership, and because the majority of Muslims accepted their circumstances within the various empires that arose and fell within the Islamic world. These dynasties developed political frameworks and legal systems that pragmatically worked more or less in conjunction with the Qur'an and the *Sunna* of the Prophet and satisfied the requirements of most of their citizens. However, the Kharijites left a lasting legacy of a particular relationship between *jihad* and *umma*, which was to be picked up by the Jamaat revivalist movements in the twentieth century.

The cosmology of *jihad*

Jihad literally means to 'struggle' or to 'strive' and at first glance there appears to be a contradiction between this injunction to fight and the meaning of Islam itself, usually understood by Muslims to signify 'peace'. Peace is commonly understood as the cessation of struggle, but not in the context of Muslim understanding of the relationship with God, either at an individual or the collective level. Instead 'peace' is synonymous with obedience, an act of surrender to Allah's will, a process which requires effort to maintain throughout life to the final moment. Although not often mentioned in the context of understanding the significance of *jihad*, the primordial religion of God begins with an act of cosmic disobedience that results in the human race becoming a battleground for a titanic struggle between Allah and Shaitan (Satan).

The Qur'an speaks of three kinds of being each created from a different element: the angels from light, the *djinn* from smokeless fire and human beings from clay. All were created to worship God but both *djinn* and human beings have free will in which they must choose to do so whereas angels can only follow the divine command and have no free will. The Qur'an tells us, 'They (the angels) do not rebel in what Allah has commanded them, and do what they are commanded' (Qur'an 66:6).

When Allah created the first man and woman (Adam and Eve) out of clay he requested the angels to bow before them. Iblis, a powerful *djinn*, was so elevated amongst all beings because of his knowledge and love of Allah. The Qur'an informs us that he kept the company of the angels for his piety and love of God. Yet he baulked at the idea of humbling himself before the newly created human pair. Addressing his Lord, he complained: 'You created me from fire and you created him (Adam) from clay' (Qur'an 7:12). This original act of disobedience took place from one who was free to choose. 'Iblis was one of the *djinn* and deviated from the command of his Lord' (Qur'an 18:50).

Muslims believe that Iblis was the first being to look at his self and make a comparison with another, in which he judged himself to be superior. In his pride he refused to prostrate along with all the angels. However, the angels themselves would have had no choice in their actions. But Iblis could choose to be an unbeliever, however elevated amongst the ranks of God. 'When We said to the angels, "Prostrate to Adam," they prostrated except for Iblis. He refused and was arrogant and was one of the unbelievers' (Qur'an 2:34). Of interest here is that the Qur'an does not define unbelief as a lack of faith in God, but rather an act of disobedience. The Muslim struggle is to obey God; atheism does not appear as an option.

The full story of the disobedience of Iblis is told in Sura 7 of the Qur'an, clearly showing the connection between Iblis and Satan, the tempter of humankind in both Judaism and Christianity. It is worth quoting the full text in order to fully comprehend the role of Iblis/Shaitan in the subsequent cosmic battle between good and evil, which will only cease when evil is finally defeated in the last days and the human race will submit to the worship of God.

He said, 'What kept you from prostrating when I commanded you?' He said, 'I am better than him. You created me from fire and You created him from clay.' He said, 'Get down out of it. It is not for you to become haughty here, so get out. You are among the humbled.' He (Iblis) said, 'Respite me until the day that they (Adam and Eve) will be raised.' He said (Allah) 'You are among those who are respited.' He said, 'Now, because You have sent me astray, I shall surely sit in ambush for them on Your straight path, then I shall come on them from before them and from behind them, from their right hands and their left hands. You will not find most of them thankful.'

He said (Allah) ' Go out of it, despised and banished. Those of them that follow you – I shall surely fill Jahannam with all of them.'

'O Adam, inherit, you and your wife, the Garden, and eat wherever you wish, but do not come near this tree, lest you be one of the wrongdoers.'

Then Shaitan whispered to them to reveal to them that which was hidden from them of their private parts. He said, 'Your Lord has only prohibited you from this tree lest you become angels or lest you become immortals.' And then he swore to them, 'Truly, I am a sincere advisor for you.'

So he led them on by delusion, and when they tasted of the tree, their private parts were revealed to them, so they took to stitching upon themselves leaves of the Garden. And their Lord called to them, 'Did I not forbid you this tree and say to you, "Shaitan is a clear enemy for you."'

They said, 'Lord, we have wronged ourselves, and if you do not forgive us and have mercy on us, we shall surely be amongst the lost.' He said, 'Get down, each of you an enemy to one another. In the earth you shall have rest and enjoyment for a time.' (Qur'an 7:11–24)

In Islamic belief, it is Iblis who achieves the first victory in the titanic struggle for the allegiance of the human being. His motivation is twofold: first, he desires revenge for their part in his own downfall and second, he wishes to justify his act of defiance by demonstrating to Allah that human beings were not worthy of divine trust. Iblis determines that the best course of action is to guide all future human beings into disbelief and disobedience to God and thus deny them re-entry to Paradise and condemn them to the punishment of the hellfire. Most significantly, Iblis decides to subvert the human being by leading them to neglect of God's worship and remembrance.

Medieval Muslim accounts indicate that Adam and Eve were initially separated from each other after their expulsion from Paradise. Eve, the mother of the human race, wandered in the desert, coming to a halt in the vicinity of Makkah. Adam was allowed a glimpse of the true worship of God when he was permitted to see the host of angels circumambulating the divine throne. After successfully pleading for forgiveness they are reconciled with each other in Makkah. Adam is asked to establish a place of worship that will imitate the actions of the angels that he had been permitted to witness. It is this myth which explains the origins of the act of circumambulation at the Ka'aba. However, it is Iblis, now known as Shaitan, who again and again distracts the Arabs from the worship of God and the Ka'aba becomes a place of idol worship. It is restored again by Ibrahim and finally by Muhammad. To the present time, when Muslims gather in prayer throughout the world, facing towards the Ka'aba and circumambulating it on the great pilgrimage of the Hajj, they believe themselves to be performing the eternal rite of prostration and worship performed by the heavenly hosts. Final victory over Shaitan will come when all human beings join in true obeisance to the creator by circumambulation of the Ka'aba in the final days.

Thus a cosmic struggle ensued: a fight for the heart of the human being. On one side, there is the 'respited' Iblis, freed from the confines of death, allowed to retain his great power and ability until the battle is ended. On the other side, there is Allah, who in his mercy sends assistance to human beings through revelation; a clear reminder of the 'straight path' that leads back to him. The messengers and the book used to convey revelation are also powerful allies against Shaitan's machinations. Also, all around there are clear signs in the creation for the discerning, which will warn them of the right and the wrong way, bringing inspiration and wisdom.

The idea of *jihad* then is built into the Muslim conception of the origins of humankind, and will be finally vindicated at the end time when Allah will be ultimately victorious. From this perspective, *jihad* is inextricably part and parcel of the Last Judgement when all human beings will receive divine justice according to their deeds. If the origin of the religion is believed to be in a struggle which is to be continued through to the end of history, then the present life of the believer is where *jihad* is played out. There can be a number of differing emphases in the everyday application of *jihad*: the general attempt to live a moral life according to the principles of the final revelation; the struggle to achieve a more just society based on God's precepts; utilising one's time and energy in preaching or teaching in order to establish Islam in the world; inner transformation of the self; and finally armed conflict in defence of Allah's last revelation which might lead the believer to the blessed goal of martyrdom.

Muslim jurisprudence echoes this multiple applicability of *jihad* by declaring that it can be performed by the heart, by the tongue, by the hands and by the sword. Each of these requires exploration in order to amplify our understanding of *jihad*, but what remains beyond doubt is the struggle against evil, whether personified as Shaitan attempting to turn the world away from God or as the corrupting whisperer in the depths of the human being leading the human being away from constant remembrance of Allah. Both the external and internal dimensions of *jihad* impact on the individual and the community. There is both a process of internal purification and self-discipline, which is combined with an imperative to bring all humankind to Allah's will. As stated by John Esposito: 'The Quranic notion of *jihad*, striving or self-exertion in the path of God, was of central significance to Muslim self-understanding and mobilization' (Esposito, 1999:30).

As we have already seen, Islam is a religion with both an external and esoteric dimension and *jihad* impacts on both. It takes place at an individual level in a struggle to purify the heart and avoid wrongdoing whilst living by the tenets of God's revelation. It is also performed at a communal level, where Muslims support each other in promoting and maintaining God's religion (*din al-Islam*). On the other hand, it can be literally the defence of the faith: an armed struggle against those who threaten Islam's existence or prevent a Muslim from worshipping God in the prescribed way. Most Muslim scholars would agree that there are two categories of *jihad*. The first, the greater *jihad* (*jihad akbar*) concerns the inner struggle. Philip Herbst defines it as: 'the inner struggle for one's own soul against the flesh and for righteousness against the forbidden' (Herbst, 2003:145).

Within these two categories of *jihad* will also be included the struggle for justice and compassion, but it is here that the borders between the two types of *jihad* can get blurred. The struggle for justice can be against tyrants, embodied in the Qur'an in figures such as Pharaoh, and will mobilise sectors of the Muslim community, but individual Muslims must guard themselves from Pharoah's error of being self-reliant, in no need of God. Where armed struggle takes place, the lesser *jihad* (*jihad asghar*) is invoked against those who threaten the community. However, this is a far different understanding of holy war than that of drawing the sword against non-believers or to convert others to Islam, both of which are not permitted in the Qur'an.

For the majority of Muslims, *jihad akbar* is of far more significance in their lives than *jihad asghar*. Most would pass their lives without being involved in a 'holy war' to defend Islam and even if unfortunate enough to find themselves in a conflict zone, the war rarely meets the stringent requirements to be defined as *jihad* even though sometimes the name of *jihad* is invoked to summon support for the conflict. For the pious, *jihad* 'simply refers to a spiritual striving to attain nearness to Allah' (Malek, 2001:121). We will see that this particular interpretation of *jihad* has special significance for Sufis.

The call to *jihad*, to participate in a cosmic struggle against evil, involves everyone, Muslim or non-Muslim, but for the believer it goes beyond the confines of only individual transformation. The Qur'an frequently calls upon Muslims to 'enjoin what is right and forbid what is wrong' (3:110) and Islam demands an active participation to forbid evil in the world, especially placed upon the hearts, minds and actions of Muslims, who as the recipients of final revelation, are the 'best of peoples, evolved for mankind' (3:110). This understanding of *jihad* is invoked by the Qur'an in the verse that states: 'Those who believe fight in the cause of Allah, and those who reject faith fight in the cause of Evil. So fight against the friends of Satan: feeble indeed is the cunning of Satan' (Qur'an 4:76).

Thus at the most inclusive definition of *jihad*, most Muslims would agree that it is 'the use of the powers, talents, and other resources of believers to live in this world in accordance with God's plan as known through the Islamic Scriptures' (Mir, 1987:112). In this understanding, it can include social action, financial support, or private endeavours to live as a good Muslim and will utilise spiritual, physical, moral and mental resources. In the widest sense, any endeavour that contributes towards the eradication of evil and promotes the good, but carried out in the cause of God, can be defined as *jihad*.

Generic *jihad*

At the most basic level, then, all Muslims are called to make their own individual effort to struggle for the victory of good over evil. This goes beyond a simple moral imperative, something common to all religions, to a specifically Islamic method derived from the Qur'an and the exemplary behaviour of Muhammad. As we saw in Chapter 3, at the heart of Islam is the awareness that God is one and unique, without any partners. The most terrible of sins for Muslims is to associate any created being with Him. Each individual Muslim is a witness to this unity of God and affirms through the *shahada* that 'there is no god but God, and Muhammad is His Messenger'. To defend God's unity with everything at his/her disposal is an act of witnessing (*shahad*) and to die defending Islam (*shahid*) is the highest form of witness to God and one's faith, guaranteed immediate arrival in Paradise without waiting for the arrival of the Day of Judgement. The link between martyrdom and witnessing to one's faith is demonstrated by the common origin of both words in the Arabic (*Shahid* – martyr and *Shahada* – the statement of witness to the faith).

In the relationship with the One God, the Sovereign Lord, the Lawgiver, the Creator, Sustainer and Final Judge of all beings, human beings are entrusted with the privilege of being God's trustee on earth (*Khalifa*). However, human beings are both weak and forgetful, as indicated by the Arabic term for human being, '*insan*' meaning the 'one that forgets'. At the same time, the human being is called upon to remember God at all times (*dhikr*) and remain conscious of dependence upon him (*taqwa*). At the minimum, this would require allegiance to the five pillars of Islam and the six core beliefs. But Muslims believe Islam touches every dimension of life, with no division between the sacred and the secular dimensions of existence. Thus the revelation provides the means to maintain obedience to God in every aspect of human existence.

The promotion of Islam

It is the mission of the Muslim community, as the trustees of Allah on earth, to promote his final revelation to all human beings, and in the act of doing so, to defend the territory that has been reclaimed for God. Islam is more than individual piety; it has strong community awareness, an imperative from God to be His last community, a sacred people. As we saw in Chapter 5, the Qur'an develops a full understanding of the term *umma*, beginning with the idea of totalities of people who have been chosen to receive God's message, such as the 'People of the Book', the *ahl-i kitab*, referring primarily to Christians and Jews and finally arriving at the fully formed idea of the Muslim community as the last recipients of revelation (Qur'an 3:110). Those who follow the Qur'an's message, carry out its commandments and worship according to the prescribed rites, live by its code of life and obey the last and final Prophet of God are constituted as a model *umma* (*Umma Muslimah* or *Umma Wusta*) (Geaves, 1996:13). This community of God is defined as a model for all humanity and is a witness to all human beings just as Muhammad was a witness to the Muslims themselves of God's manifest will (Qur'an 2:143). Thus the Muslims replace all the *ummat* which preceded them and exist not only as a moral community which upholds and enforces God's laws but is also entrusted to enlarge itself to eventually include all the peoples of the world.

Millions of Muslims and even some well-known scholars of Islam portray the *umma* as a single transnational entity that transcends ethnic, racial, linguistic and national identities. For example, Hamilton Gibb wrote:

> It consists of the totality of individuals bound to one another by ties, not of kinship or race, but of religion in that all its members profess their belief in one God, and in the mission of the Prophet Muhammad. Before God and in their relation to Him, all are equal, without distinction of rank, class or race. (Gibb, 1963:173)

Yet the ideal of the *umma* remains a potent symbol for those who pursue *jihad* both in political and religious terms. However, the reality of Muslim life is marked by considerable diversity of religious positions all distributed among a number of nationalities and ethnic groups, who do not always co-exist harmoniously.

Continuing in the context of the Muslim community as the last people of God, allied to *jihad* is the idea of *da'wa*, literally 'to call', or 'to invite'; in other words, the promotion of Islam to both non-Muslims and Muslims. Since the Qur'an enjoins Muslims that 'there is no compulsion in religion', *da'wa* activities to non-Muslims take place mostly through preaching activities. However, it must be stated that in most parts of the world, with the exception of Africa, *da'wa* activities are directed at fellow-Muslims in order to bring them back into the practice of the faith. Thus the word 'revert' rather than 'convert' is more often heard in Muslim circles. It also has the connotation that all human beings are originally 'Muslim' in the sense of being surrendered to God on their birth, but are then taken away by social upbringing and forgetfulness of their original divine destiny. The archetypal form of *da'wa* belongs to God, and involves his prophets and messengers communicating his revelation to believing people. This activity is then picked up by the conscientious believers in imitation of God's messengers. Muhammad Sirozi defines *da'wa* as 'a call or invitation to an individual, family, and others to take Islam as a way of life, to live in accordance with Allah's will, with wisdom and consciousness, nourished by His blessings' (Sirozi, 2004:174).

There are a number of *da'wa* organisations around the world, some of them like 'Tabligh-i Jamaat', which although originating in Saharanpur in North India has become truly international. The 'Tabligh-i Jamaat', a non-political organisation, uses a tried and tested formula of sending out groups of volunteers on preaching tours. They base themselves in local mosques from where they conduct a campaign to bring Muslims back to communal prayer, going out from the mosques to knock on doors of households, in non-Muslim nations utilising the local resources of the local mosque officials. Other organisations may fulfil *da'wa* activities through preaching at university Islamic societies, setting out street stalls in city centres, or promoting their tracts and leaflets utilising the mosques as outlets. However, it needs to be noted that such organisations may also possess a political agenda and will usually represent their own strand of Islam even though calling upon the rhetoric of a 'universal Islam'.

For radical Islamic movements, *da'wa* is very often framed within a particular context in which Muslims are seen as having fallen away from the ideal practice of their religion and are called back to a purer form, supposedly practised by Muhammad and the early Muslim community. Radical leaders, who have called for a purification of the community from un-Islamic influences, see the promotion of Islam at the individual, family and political levels as the means to provide Muslims with the renewed power of God that they need to take over leadership of the world once again, which rightfully belongs to the people true to revelation.

In Muslim countries, *da'wa* activities, especially by such organisations and individuals, calling for the creation of an Islamic state, are more likely to include very successful social welfare programmes. It would be hard to ascertain the impact of such organisations in the recent Islamicisation of the Muslim world. The return of countless Muslims throughout the world to the practice of their faith is a complex phenomenon, with local variants added to its causes. However, while not all Islamicisation has a political dimension, there can be no doubt that the activities of the *da'wa* movements have been part of the process of the return to faith.

Political Islam

We have already seen that movements like the Kharijites were able to influence a succession of revivalists and reformers throughout Muslim history who considered that the wider community of Muslims and its various temporal leaderships had departed from the ideal of God. Thus a dichotomy was set up which pitched ideal and reality against each other in both oppositional and creative ways. Creatively, Muslims were able to live in the space between the ideal of the Prophet and the message of the Qur'an and the reality of their everyday life, defining *jihad* as the means by which they variously struggled to get closer to the ideal.

However, the secessionist groups like the Kharijites had provided another model for acting upon the difference between the ideal of God and the reality of the *umma*, wherein direct action to transform the wider Muslim world was considered obligatory for the individual and participation in *jihad* necessary as part of Islam's religious obligations. In fact, the Kharijites went so far as to assert *jihad* as the sixth pillar of Islam and this has been picked up by some contemporary movements and used in a justification for armed struggle. Sometimes, the gulf between ideal and reality was expressed in the everyday life of the Muslim world contrasted with a utopian vision of religious life under the Prophet in Medina continuing through to either the period of the first four caliphs or the first three generations of Muslims (*Salafa*). Thus those Muslims who strived to replicate the ideal past and destroy the corrupted or innovatory (*bida*) Muslim life of the present were considered true and faithful to the revelation. Throughout Muslim history various individuals and movements have arisen with such a framework for direct action and transformation and have seen this activity as *jihad*. A more detailed analysis of these movements will be presented in the following Chapter 10 under an exploration of fundamentalism.

Colonialism in the eighteenth and nineteenth centuries fundamentally altered the Muslim relationship with Europe and set the stage for considerable self-scrutiny. Basic to the process of internal reform and the revival of Islam was the doubt created by the inability of the Muslim world to deal with Western superiority in education, science and technology and the question as to why Allah would allow His final community to decline and be defeated by the ancient rival of Christian Europe. Those who had called various populations of

Muslims to rise up in *jihad* over the invaders or colonisers had seen their uprisings fail, for example, the self-styled Mahdi in Sudan or the Muslim involvement in the 1857 disturbances in India. Some turned to non-co-operation, others to isolation and renewed piety.

Muslim ideologues, such as Hasan al-Banna, Sayyid Qutb and Maulana Mawdudi, tired of Muslim apologists for Islam, called for the creation of an Islamic state, the eradication of Western legal systems and the imposition of Islamic law in the face of the Westernisation of Muslim society and economic decline. Ironically, the call for such revolutions in Muslim society only occurred after independence had been granted, usually after World War II when the European powers were too exhausted and depleted to deal with national uprisings springing up simultaneously throughout the world.

Muhammad al-Farag, an Egyptian member of 'Jamaat al-Jihad' (Organisation of Holy War), argued that the decline of Muslim nations had been made possible by the lulling of the people into a state where they no longer knew that violent *jihad* was permissible against injustice and tyranny. He wrote the influential *The Neglected Obligation* in which he claimed that *jihad* was the forgotten sixth pillar of Islam and armed struggle was the duty of every Muslim against a decadent or corrupt society.

Mawdudi, al-Banna and Qutb blamed the failure of the newly established Muslim nations to thrive and once again rival the West on the fact that their governments had not established Islamic systems but rather aped the ways of either Western capitalism or socialism. Branding the corruption and social injustice they perceived in their societies as a result of Western influence and neo-colonialism, as a new *jahiliyya*, they called for *jihad* to overthrow corrupt regimes and impose Islamic societies. Sayyid Qutb, highly influenced by Mawdudi, perceived the world, but primarily Muslim societies, in the dichotomous and conflictual duality of the party of God and the party of Shaitan and resurrected the old Kharijite argument of the need to create a movement that could be a vanguard of true Muslims. He was the first to suggest the idea that contemporary Muslim governments were a later reproduction of pre-Islamic pagan society because they had replaced the sovereignty of God by human laws based on the sovereignty of the people, and were therefore a modern form of *jahiliyya* or pagan ignorance. This theme was to be picked up by most contemporary *jihad* movements.

Thus the modernist distinction between the secular and the sacred which demoted religious life to the private sphere became even more of a threat to God's role in human history than the old enemy of Christianity which was at least a former revelation. However, the new revivalist movements with their anti-West rhetoric rarely distinguish Western secularism from Christianity and they tend to argue that the modernist separation of religious and secular life is rooted in the Christian doctrine of 'rendering unto Caesar that which is Caesar's'.

Thus the idea of an Islamic Movement came about: a righteous minority afloat in a sea of godlessness with an imperative to create Islamic government; islands of refuge that would exist as examples of Islam in practice and resistance against modernism and its concomitant secularism. *Jihad* was the only way to destroy authoritarian regimes and reform the Muslim world in a last battle against the forces that denied God's role as law-giver and sovereign. Initially, the West itself was not the target, but Muslim society. Those Muslims who refused to co-operate were also infidels as in the old Kharijite vision. The front line of *jihad* is against corrupt Muslim leaders, replacing them with an Islamic order, either by evolution or revolution. However, the various Islamic movements that sprang up throughout the Muslim world were not able to undermine the nationalist ideal. Thus as we have seen in Chapter 5, the new Muslim nations had succeeded by drawing upon existing loyalties to a motherland (*watan*) or developing a sense of patriotism to a new entity. However much the Islamic movements of the twentieth century called for a restored caliphate, reasserting an ideal of a united *umma* that displaced the new Western concept of nation, they had to bow to the success of nationalism and call instead for reformed Muslim nations that revived Islam at the level of public life as well as private piety.

Violent *jihad*

The idea of a 'holy war' is not exactly a Muslim concept but rather a very loose translation of *jihad*, borrowing on the Christian concept of 'crusade' used to refer to the act of liberating the Holy Land from Muslim possession and originating in Medieval Europe. Muslims, however, as we have seen, can legitimately turn to violent struggle for the defence of religion or even move on the offensive in certain circumstances when the onslaught of their enemies is perceived to be imminent – a type of pre-emptive strike. Only these circumstances make war morally justifiable. The war must be fought under the following conditions according to the *shari'a*:

1. It cannot be fought for material gain or possession
2. Non-combatant rights must be protected (lives, property and freedom)
3. No devastation of crops
4. Old people, women, children and invalids cannot be harmed
5. No place of worship can be demolished, nor priests of any religion be killed
6. Prisoners of war must not be tortured or punished
7. The war can only be fought for the defence of the faith.

In 1979, the Western world was shocked as the people of Iran rose up under the guidance and leadership of Ayatollah Khomeini and over-threw the powerful and autocratic regime of the Shah of Iran. Khomeini had already demonstrated both his own authority and the power of Islam on 10 and 11 December 1978, when he called from exile for popular protests on the two most sacred days of the Shi'a Muslim calendar. Hundreds of thousands disobeyed the Shah's cur-few, risked retaliation and shouted *Allah Akbar* (God is Great) from the rooftops and terraces of the capital of Tehran (Kepel, 2002:112).

Ayatollah Khomeini's justification for Islamic revolution and the overthrow of corrupt or tyrannical regimes is framed within a series of writings and speeches that outline the case for legitimate use of *jihad*. First and foremost, Khomeini did not see the mobilisation of the people in the name of Islam as an offensive but rather as a defence against oppression and tyranny, particularly manifesting itself through the exploitation of Iran's resources by the West.

> This misappropriation of wealth goes on and on: in our foreign trade and in the contracts made for the exploitation of our min-eral wealth, the utilisation of our forests and other natural resources, construction work, road building, and the purchase of arms from the imperialists, both Western and communist.
>
> (Khomeini, 1985:132)

In calling for *jihad*, Khomeini does not lessen the resolve of the Muslim people to pursue all the means for establishing Islam, such as the promotion of Islamic social, economic, moral and spiritual values, but he indicated that it is legitimate for devout Muslims to remove oppressive regimes. Citing various Hadith, for example, 'a word of truth spoken in the presence of an unjust ruler is a meritorious form of *jihad*' or 'there is no obeying the one who disobeys God', Khomeini calls for a select band to withstand injustice and then to ignite the Muslim masses. 'Address the people bravely; tell the truth about our situation to the masses in simple language . . . The entire population will become *mujahids*' (those who engage in *jihad*) (Khomeini, 1985:132).

In addition, Khomeini phrased his call for a struggle against tyranny, associated in his mind particularly with US imperialism, in a unique language designed to capture the emotions of the Shi'a population. Referring to the history of Shi'a persecution and the resilience of their religious leaders, he stated:

> The Imams (upon whom be peace) not only fought against tyrannical rulers, oppressive governments, and corrupt courts themselves; they also summoned the Muslims to wage *jihad* against those enemies . . . In short the Imams have given orders that all relations with such rulers be severed and that no one collaborate with them in any way. (Khomeini, 1985:148)

The method of *jihad* is twofold: first that the people should turn against oppression and then that they should be led to a true Islamic society by a righteous minority 'who are just and ascetic and who fight in God's way to implement the laws of Islam and establish its social system' (Khomeini, 1985:149). The solution is the establishment of an Islamic government: 'A government whose form, administrative system, and laws have been laid down by Islam. It is our duty now to implement and put into practice the plan of government established by Islam' (Khomeini, 1985:149). Such a state will not only provide protection for Muslims against the 'tyrannical regimes that imperialism has imposed' upon the Muslim people (Khomeini, 1985:132), it will also provide the example that will stir popular revolutions throughout the Muslim world (Khomeini, 1985:149).

As a Shi'a leader, Khomeini drew upon ancient storehouses of emotion contained in the psyche of the masses that refer back to the origins of the tradition and are associated with the sufferings of the Prophet's bloodline or family in fighting the oppression and tyranny of the first Sunni empire. However, he is careful to authenticate his passionate pleas within the authority of Shi'a Hadith associated with either Ali or his son Hussain, the grandson of Muhammad. For example, he cites a tradition that quotes from a speech delivered by Hussain in Mina in which he puts forward his reasons for *jihad* against the Umayyads, the first Muslim dynasty. By a process of analogy, he compares Hussain's struggle to the contemporary one. It is worth quoting in full.

> The second part is the speech of the Lord of the Martyrs concerning the governance of the *faqih* and duties which are incumbent upon the *fuqaha*, such as the struggle against oppressors and tyrannical governments in order to establish an Islamic government and implement the ordinances of Islam. In this speech delivered at Mina, he set forth the reasons for his own *jihad* against the tyrannical Umayyad state. The *fuqaha* by means of *jihad* must expose and overthrow tyrannical rulers and rouse the people so that the universal movement of all alert Muslims can establish Islamic government in place of tyrannical regimes.
>
> (Khomeini, 1985:108)

In spite of the specific Shi'a emphasis, there is nothing in Khomeini's call for the establishment for an Islamic state (the demand for a righteous exemplary remnant; the justification for the overthrow of corrupt regimes; and the use of *jihad* against nominal Muslims) that cannot be found amongst the ideologues of the Sunni tradition such as Sayyid Qutb or Maulana Mawdudi. The main difference is that Khomeini succeeded in mobilising the Shi'a masses whereas that has never taken place for those who would rally Sunnis to *jihad* as armed struggle against secular Muslim regimes.

Spiritual *jihad*

An interesting feature of Khomeini's discourse on *jihad* is his awareness of the priority for a spiritual struggle against the forces of ego, defined as a preoccupation with our own selves and our own desires. Citing the well-known Hadith, attributed to Muhammad on his return from the Battle of Uhud, 'you have now returned from the lesser *jihad*; the greater *jihad* still remains as a duty for you', Khomeini argues that the lesser *jihad* (armed struggle) is not only of no avail but is actually satanic unless the greater *jihad* has been fulfilled.

Creatively he links *jihad* to *Hijra* by arguing the greater *jihad* is a migration from egoism to self-effacement in God. Thus the struggle to create an Islamic state begins with the destruction of the government of Satan that lies within the unredeemed soul (Khomeini, 1985:384–385). He states:

> Some will even succeed, while still in this world, in reaching a stage that is now beyond our imagination – that of non-being, of being effaced in God. We must desire to make this migration from egoism, and be prepared to struggle in order to migrate.
>
> (Khomeini, 1985:385)

In this kind of discourse, Khomeini shows the influence of Sufism on his thinking, and his knowledge of *tasawwuf* (cleansing of the heart). We have already seen in Chapter 7 that the teachings of the *awliya*, the 'friends of God' as they are known in Islam, renowned for their peity and closeness to Allah, have influenced at some level the majority of Muslims. Thus it is important for us to remind ourselves that those who think first of *jihad* as a political or violent act are the minority in the world of Islam. There are many who would consider that the Sufi alternative of focusing on the inner struggle to purify the ego, to bring about an inner state where the desire to engage in the self-obsessed pursuit of gratification is overcome by the longing to be in communion with the divine, is closer to the spirit of Islam than the political struggle to overcome oppression, although social justice is also at the heart of the Qur'an's message.

After all, it was ego that began the conflict between the forces of good and evil in the original act of Iblis's refusal to bow at Allah's command. It is the presence of the devil within that needs to be juxtapositioned with the Qur'an's affirmation that Allah is also closer to the human being than the jugular vein. For millions of Muslims, although they might not experience the mystical awareness of God of the *awliya*, *jihad* remains the battle within, where both God and Shaitan remain locked in the original struggle to demonstrate to each other the respective value of the human being. Thus the path of *ilm al-tasawwuf* (the path of self-purification) remains influential and is perceived as the greater *jihad*. Perhaps Khomeini's genius was to draw upon the piety of the Shi'a masses by combining the greater and lesser *jihad*, whereas the Sunni *jihad* movements have tended to neglect or even to be critical of the spiritual in favour of the political. Although they may engage the minds of the educated elites, they have not been able to mobilise the masses.

Conclusion

There are those who argue that the term 'holy war' is inadequate to describe the reality of *jihad*, many Muslims preferring to link the concept of religious wars with the Crusades (Malek, 2001). Certainly, where armed conflict does take place, the rules of engagement are defined in Muslim law. Usually such calls to the lesser *jihad* are made in the defence of territory perceived as under threat from non-Muslim aggressors, such as the armed struggle of Hamas to re-establish Palestine as liberated territory from Israeli occupation. This justification for *jihad* is repeated in Kashmir and Chechnya. These are primarily nationalist struggles concerned with perceived occupation by an outside power but given religious credibility by the old concept of *dar al-Islam* (territory of Islam) and *dar al-harb* (territory of war).

The Jihadist groups, such as 'The International Islamic Front for the Jihad Against Jews and Crusaders' led by Osama bin Laden, 'Laskar Jihad' led by Ja'far Umar Thalib in Indonesia, 'Harakat ul-Jihad-i-Islami' in Kashmir, 'Palestinian Islamic Jihad', 'Egyptian Islamic Jihad', and 'Yemeni Islamic Jihad' are different in that they wage war to protect a particular vision of Islam, according to their understanding of the original vision of the Qur'an and *Sunna*. They see this 'pristine' Islam of the Prophet under threat from 'corrupt' or 'tyrannical' Muslim regimes which are aided by the West. They fight either against those regimes in a particular locality or internationalise their campaigns by including the West, especially the USA, as part of a Judeo-Christian conspiracy against Islam.

It might be difficult for the Western world to understand the violence that can erupt explosively from some of these groups, especially since the enormity of the events at 9/11, or to understand how such groups within Islam can justify their actions as defensive. However, the *jihad* movements still operate in their terms within the paradigm of a defensive war. Ba'asyir, the Indonesian ideologue for the Islamic Movements, recently jailed for four years after the Bali bombing, insists that these were appropriate self-defensive actions in response to the violence of the United States against the entire Islamic world (Behrend, 2003:8).

None of these justifications of the so-called lesser *jihad* adequately describes the concept of *jihad*, which remains so much more to all Muslims, even for the Jihadist groups. Western writers such as Bruce Lawrence, who claims that *jihad* is 'being a better student, a better colleague, a better business partner' (Pipes, 2002) or Karen Armstrong who describes *jihad* as 'the effort or struggle to achieve [a just] world where you learn to lay aside your own selfishness and recognize the needs of the poor, elderly and sick' (Armstrong, 2001:12) are partly right in that they move the emphasis away from violence in defining the phenomenon, but they fail to recognise the uniquely Muslim understanding of *jihad*, instead providing a humanistic or Christian understanding of the term. For a Muslim, *jihad* is central to the victory of God over Satan, good over evil, in which every individual and every human society, past, present and future plays a part. Thus Ibrahim Abu-Rabi states that *jihad* is an 'effort against evil in the self and every manifestation of evil in society' (Pipes, 2002) but, above all only Allah's final people of revelation are uniquely qualified to carry out the task.

CHAPTER 10

Muslim fundamentalism: a misnomer or the heart of the faith?

This penultimate chapter will continue on from the previous chapter's themes, explicitly developing an analysis of the movements that advocate Islamic revolution or revival. In particular, it will ask the question whether it is useful to label such movements as fundamentalist. In addition, it will assess whether the category of fundamentalism is useful in any sense within the context of Islam. In questioning the application of the label fundamentalism, it will be necessary to ascertain to what degree so-called Muslim fundamentalism is unique to the religion or part of a universal religious response to the globalisation of secularisation and corporate consumer capitalism.

Defining fundamentalism

Any informed discussion of 'fundamentalism' in the context of Islam, or for that matter any other religious tradition, must endeavour to go beyond both the popular usage of the term by the public and the closely connected media depictions of certain typologies of religion which are seen as anti-modern, traditionalist, intolerant and re-actionary. In addition, there are academic divisions amongst scholars in regard to whether it is more useful to speak of 'fundamentalism' or 'fundamentalisms'. The former would define certain types of Islamic reaction to modernity as part of a religious phenomenon across tradi-tions, where a 'family likeness' of common features can be defined as 'fundamentalism'. The latter would suggest that we need to look more closely at the unique features of Islam which mark it out as different from any other religious tradition.

Underlying this difference of opinion are two quite different perspectives. In the first, perhaps most clearly represented by the ambitious 'Fundamentalism Project' edited by Marty and Appleby (1994–6) is an application of the term as an umbrella appellation describing a common phenomenon that is manifest in a number of different religious traditions. This approach leads to an analysis that seeks to uncover global causes that create the same religious reaction worldwide. The approach, unfortunately, also suffers from a Christocentric analysis that seeks to impose, upon all religions, a model for the development of 'fundamentalism' and its causes that imitate certain developments in Protestant Christianity. Even as far back as 1987, Lionel Caplan was criticising such an approach as 'glib use of concepts whose roots lie in Western tradition' (Caplan, 1987).

On the other hand, Partridge takes the view that 'fundamentalism' does not do justice to the diversity of religious traditions and their own unique historical development, practices and beliefs and although he acknowledges enough common features to identify similar patterns, he prefers to speak of a family of correspondences, but with unique aspects, that is better understood by the term 'fundamentalisms' than the singular 'fundamentalism' (Partridge, 2001). This approach avoids the inherent dangers of simplification and imposing upon other religions a term whose roots lie in a particular historical and theological development in contemporary North American Christianity.

Muslims are rightly suspicious of the term, arguing that it imposes upon their religion a Christian terminology that is laden with theological baggage that cannot be successfully transferred to Islam. On the other hand, they argue that it is implicit within devout or 'correct' Muslim practice to refer back to the Qur'an for understanding and direction. The dependence upon scriptural revelation is the norm of Islam, and thus any Muslim who chooses to take his or her faith seriously is likely to be branded as 'fundamentalist'. This critique has been taken up seriously by a number of scholars who study contemporary Islam and its manifestations, and alternative terminology has been utilised to describe the phenomena of a number of *jamaats* or movements that have arisen around the Muslim world with certain common features that have been compared with fundamentalism. Rather than use the term 'fundamentalist' they have chosen to speak of revivalists (Esposito, 1988), reformists, jihadists, (Chouaeri, 1997), Islamists (Huband, 1995; Kepel, 2002) and Islamic militants (Hiro, 1989). Since the events of 9/11, the vocabulary of the media and politics has added the new and even more pejorative and perfunctory term of 'terrorist'.

There are those who have attempted to define 'fundamentalism' more precisely than the popular usages of the term. These scholars tend to take two approaches. They either attempt to identify a more penetrative understanding of the phenomenon by seeking to define it or, alternatively, they provide lists of its common features. Thus Hadden and Schupe, two sociologists of religion, in 1989 provided us with the definition of fundamentalism as follows: 'A pattern of many contemporary socio-political movements that share certain character-istics in their responses to a common globalisation process which can be described as secularisation' (Hadden and Schupe, 1989).

Hadden and Schupe go on to list the common characteristics as:

1. Resistance to secularisation.
2. Denial of religious forms which have developed by compromising with modernity.
3. A coherent ideology which seeks to bring religion back to the centre stage of public life as well as private life.
4. Fundamentalists claim authority over a scriptural tradition which is reinstated as the antidote for a society that has strayed.
5. They accept the benefits of modernity, particularly technology, whilst rejecting modernism (defined as subordinating traditions to harmonize with modern thought and an ideology that emphasises materialism as a way of life) as an ideological framework.
6. Fundamentalism is a modern phenomenon which attacks the ideology of modernism and very often traditional religious forms. (Hadden and Schupe, 1989)

Thus Hadden and Schupe choose to provide both a definition and a list of common characteristics in order to assist us in identifying reli-gious fundamentalism. A more recent 'list' approach to fundamental-ism is found in Harriet Harris's article, written over ten years later in 2001. Her list contains some of the characteristics found in common with Hadden and Schupe's but with additions.

1. Reactive to the marginalisation of religion – especially secularisation.

2. Selectivity – selecting particular aspects of their religion to emphasise in opposition to particular aspects of modernity.
3. Moral dualism – the world divided into good and evil, light and dark.
4. Absolutism and inerrancy – absolute validity of the fundamentals of the faith – sacred texts are inerrant.
5. Millennialism and messianism – victory to the believer at the end of history.
6. Elect membership – the faithful remnant.
7. Sharp boundaries – the saved from the unsaved.
8. Authoritarian organisation – charismatic leadership with no possibility of dissent.
9. Behavioural requirements – members expected to participate fully. (Harris, 2001:10)

There are methodological question marks over both approaches and certainly both lists of characteristics are open to critique. Some of the characteristics cited by Harris seem to be more attributable to the kind of sectarian organisation equally mislabelled by the media as 'cult' rather than the phenomenon of 'fundamentalism'. Not all of the latter types of religious organisation see the world through the lens of moral dualism, millennialism and messianism, or organise themselves along the lines of charismatic leadership. Even where charismatic leadership is found in Islam, for example, the idea of 'no dissent' has to be examined very carefully. The problem is that both lists of characteristics continue to take their 'ideal-type' of fundamentalism from varieties of Protestant Christianity. Muslim critics of the label 'fundamentalist' might argue that this is the correct approach as that is where the term originated and belongs.

On the other hand, Hadden and Schupe provide us with the useful analytical boundary of 'political' to describe fundamentalism. Therefore any religious movement cannot be called 'fundamentalist' unless there is a 'coherent ideology which seeks to bring religion back to the centre stage of public life as well as private life' (Hadden and Schupe, 1989). However, this may or may not be in response to secularisation. The secularisation thesis has come under criticism even in the West but it is certainly not the necessary pattern of response to modernisation throughout the world. Moreover, neither Hadden and Schupe nor Harris mention the link between fundamentalism, nationalism and the tensions that can exist between loyalty to nation and loyalty to God or the 'unholy' alliances that can be created between the two, as in India or Sri Lanka.

Also implicit in both attempts to identify 'fundamentalism' is a horizontal approach to the investigation of religious phenomena that looks for common elements across the globe but ignores a vertical investigation that looks back into the history of the particular religion to acknowledge unique features that would predispose it to take particular forms and patterns of development. Any examination of the location of fundamentalism in Islam would need to explore both vertical and horizontal formations before answering the Muslim criticism that the label is inappropriate to them. Both the historical context and contemporary social and cultural forces need to be explored.

Vertical approaches: the historical context

The historical development of a religion and its development of unique patterns of behaviour arising from both interpretation of its sacred texts and the formation of tradition cannot be viewed as the sole causes of religious fundamentalism in the twentieth and twenty-first centuries. However, once certain social and cultural forces impact on societies with a strong religious allegiance, then the shape of the religious response will be dictated by the unique past of the faith tradition. In this respect, any observers of Muslim fundamentalism need to be aware of the following factors, some of which have been covered in more detail in the previous chapters:

   i)   Cosmic conflict scenario
   ii) The concept of *jahiliyya*
   iii) The doctrine of 'Manifest Success'
   iv) The Qur'an's justification of *jihad*
   v)   The Kharijites
   vi) The repeated pattern of revival and reform
   vii) Crisis – the Mongol invasion and Ibn Taymiyya (1268–1328)
   viii) The decline of Islam (Muhammad ibn Abd al-Wahhab, d.1792)
   ix) Crisis – the rise of Europe

i) Cosmic conflict scenario

As explored in more detail in Chapter 9, the Qur'an describes history as a linear struggle between titanic forces of good and evil that originated with the creation of human beings. The battle is fought out between the forces of Shaitan (Satan) and Allah for the hearts and minds of human beings. The example of the prophets of God and successive divine revelations become the main vehicles to maintain human beings on the 'Straight Path' that leads to surrender and servitude to the divine being. In this cosmic battle, there is no plane of existence that is not effectively involved in the struggle for obedience to the divine will. Shaitan's divine imperative to be the tempter of men and women manifests both within the human personality and in the various social, political and economic activities of human societies. Muslims perceive Islam as the last and final revelation, the vanguard of the cosmic struggle, to be maintained in its purity and totality, in order for it to provide the means for human victory over evil and the vehicle for God's final vindication at the last days.

ii) *The concept of* jahiliyya

Although initially applied to the pre-Islamic world of the Arabs, the concept of *jahiliyya*, signifying a condition of idolatry, godlessness, social injustices, immorality and a dependence on the self as opposed to obedience to the divine will, can be applied to all societies throughout history who have failed to obey the messengers of God and the message, or, alternatively, appear not to have received any such guidance. Past examples of this mentioned in the Qur'an would be Sodom and Gomorrah and Egypt under the pharaohs. The condition of ignorance exemplified in the term *jahaliyya* offers the opportunity for some Muslims thinkers and activists, since first articulated by Sayyid Qutb, to find a framework to criticise Western society and the condition of contemporary Muslim societies.

iii) *The doctrine of 'Manifest Success'*

As described in Chapter 6, the doctrine of 'Manifest Success', in which the signifier of God's covenant with his chosen people is demonstrated by worldly achievements, contains within it a pattern of religious revival and reform. Any major worldly failure is likely to be perceived as a sign of divine displeasure and a marker to Muslims that they have left the 'Straight Path', not so much as individuals, who may have maintained their own state of piety, but as the final religious community entrusted with revelation. Thus a pattern of religious revival as a response to political or social decline is established.

iv) *The Qur'an's justification of* jihad

As clarified in Chapter 9, *jihad* is about far more than holy war. However, war is permitted to Muslims in certain circumstances. In a wider sense, *jihad* is the response to the cosmic conflict scenario and the immediate struggle to overcome *jahiliyya*. It is more likely to be called for at all levels, both individually and collectively, when political or social decline is identified. If the political decline is perceived to be influenced by outside forces, the emergence of powerful enemies from outside the world of Islam, it is likely to provoke calls for military struggle as a defence against their oppression. Thus religious revivals call for a return to personal piety, the reform of Muslim society and possibly violent struggles against perceived external oppressors, all of which are likely to appear simultaneously when Islam is perceived to be in danger.

v) *The Kharijites*

As described in Chapter 5, the various Kharijite movements that formed after the death of Muhammad provide a number of significant features that supply a model for those who would struggle against perceived injustices and political corruption of the Muslim *umma* in the contemporary period. Although the Kharijites were ultimately unsuccessful in their struggles to establish leadership based on personal piety rather than hereditary dynasties, and eventually disappeared from the spectrum of sects in the Muslim world, the Kharijite critique of nominal allegiance to religion remains as a powerful symbol of resistance. In particular, their redefinition of who is included within the Muslim fold to exclude those who are only nominal Muslims becomes a potent justification for modern revivalist movements to categorise as non-Muslims those who submit to governments perceived as secular or oppressive. In addition, the Kharijite understanding of the Muslim *umma* as a righteous and active remnant, rather than the totality of all Muslims, gives the impetus for *jamaat*-style movements to revive Islam and ferment revolutionary change within Muslim nations.

vi) *The repeated pattern of revival and reform*

As we have seen the doctrine of 'Manifest Success' leads to a pattern of religious revival as a response to external crises. In addition, the Muslim worldview of Islam as the final revelation gives an urgent need to protect the 'purity' of God's revealed practices and beliefs.

Unlike in Judaism and Christianity, for Muslims there can be no replacement of their revelation, as they believe happened to Judaism and Christianity (the revelations that were given before the advent of Muhammad and the Qur'an), for it is believed that Muhammad was the 'seal of the Prophets' and the Qur'an is the co-eternal Word of God in its entirety. Thus it has come to be a part of traditional Muslim belief that Allah sends a reformer every hundred years to maintain the revelation and destroy any innovatory departure from it. Any movement with a new charismatic leader endowed with personal piety and the energy to impact on the world around him can claim that their leader is the *mujaddid*. A special *mujaddid* is also believed to appear every thousand years.

vii) Crisis – the Mongol invasion and Ibn Taymiyya (1268–1328)

The invasion of the Mongols and the subsequent sacking of Muslim centres of culture, political administration and religion led to considerable self-questioning, in fact, a perfect example of the conditions that lead to Muslims seeking to reform and renew their covenant with Allah. Ibn Taymiyya lived through the traumatic period after the Mongol sacking of Baghdad in 1258 and the fall of the Abbasid Empire and he sought to discover reasons for the inconceivable: the defeat of the Islamic world by apparently barbaric and polytheistic infidels. As a learned scholar of the Hanbali school of law, the most conservative of the four schools of law, he called for a literalist interpretation of the Qur'an and *Sunna* and the observation of Islam based on the period of the Prophet in Medina and continuing through to the end of the first four caliphs who had been Companions of the Prophet. Thus the first generations of Muslims are promoted as the ideal for Islamic belief and practice. In addition, Ibn Taymiyya, although a practitioner of *tassawuf*, the Sufi disciplines of inner transformation, perceived the folk and traditional activities of popular Sufism as a corruption of the teachings of the Medinan Muslims and blamed such practices for the downfall of Islam. Linking religion to statecraft, he called for a return to the values of Medinan Islam, the first Islamic state, rather than the later Islamic empires centred on Damascus or Baghdad. Finally and significantly, noting the failure of the Mongol converts to Islam to leave the legal codes created by Ghengis Khan and embrace the *shari'a*, he followed the Kharijite precedent and branded them as non-Muslims (*kafir*), no better than the polytheists of the pre-Muslim Arab *jahiliyya* (Esposito, 2002:45–46).

Ibn Taymiyya takes on a special significance in the contemporary period as the foremost inspiration for all of the revivalist movements and their founders, from the Wahhabis to the Salafis, from Sayyid Qutb to Osama bin Laden. All of the above features of his critique of thirteenth-century Muslim life are reproduced by nineteenth- and twentieth-century Islamic idealogues and his solutions remain their model of renewal and revolution. Emmanuel Siven describes him as 'the model for revivalists and vigilantes, for fundamentalist reformers' (Siven, 1985:96).

viii) The decline of Islam (Muhammad ibn Abd al-Wahhab, d.1791)

The eighteenth century was marked by the acceleration of European expansion and colonialism begun in the seventeenth century and although it reached its zenith in the nineteenth century, the Muslim world began to feel a distinct sense of unease at its own decline and the emergence of the European powers. This time it appeared that divine providence had rewarded the older people of God – the Christians – with 'Manifest Success', resulting in a number of European victories over Muslim forces and the subjugation of Muslim nations.

Whereas in previous eras, the revival and reform of Islam were to appear in localised contexts, responding to local crises, the eighteenth century witnessed Muslim revivals along similar lines across the gamut of the Muslim world. From South-East Asia, Arabia to Africa, significant Muslim figures created movements to reform Islam. Out of these simultaneous revolutionary responses, perhaps influencing each other through significant meetings at the Hajj, the most important has to be the radical attempt to reform the original heartlands of Islam – Arabia – by Muhammad ibn Abd al-Wahhab. The successful cleansing of Arabia of its countless shrines, tombs and sacred objects associated with popular Sufism was linked to the Prophet's cleansing of the pagan gods from the Ka'aba and was achieved by joining the religious zeal of Muhammad Wahhab with the temporal power of Muhammad ibn Saud, a local tribal chieftain. The combination was to create the first Islamic state, to be henceforth known as Saudi Arabia, but more significantly a global religious movement that to this day remains influential as it promotes the ideals of its founder throughout the Muslim world as the 'authentic' and 'pure' version of Islam. This movement was to become known as Wahhabism, but is more often invoked by the enemies of such revivalists, extending it beyond the

actual heirs of Muhammad ibn Abd al-Wahhab to include any movement or ideologue that espouses similar ideas or promotes renewal
and reform.

ix) Crisis – the creation of Muslim nations

Although the *jihad* (in this case literally meaning armed struggle)
movements that appeared in the various parts of the Muslim world
during the eighteenth and nineteenth centuries generally disappeared
as a viable response to colonisation because of the superior firepower
of the various European forces, the ideal of reform and renewal based
on the ideal of a return to Islam's pristine past did not. Invariably the
eighteenth-century movements turned to education of their own local
Muslim populations, attempting to safeguard them from popular Sufi
practices and contamination from Western culture and ideas. Even the
Wahhabi regime of Saudi Arabia saw more mileage in spending
its new-found oil wealth on education of Muslims worldwide than
promoting revolution through armed struggle.

Consequently they lost their radical edge and became neo-
conservative forces within the world of Islam by the time of the
creation of newly independent Muslim states in the twentieth century. It was left to others to create new movements that responded
to the post-colonial situation. However, the twentieth century
ideologues such as Mawlana Mawdudi or Sayyid Qutb did not stray
far from the historical roots of reform and renewal. Only the political
situation was different. Yet there were to be significant differences
as well as key similarities between the twentieth-century and
eighteenth/nineteenth-century callers for renewal and reform.

The call for renewal (*tajdid*) and reform (*islah*) is central to both
nineteenth- and twentieth-century revivalist movements. *Islah* calls
for Muslims to realign their lives on the fundamental tenets of Islam
based on the contents of the Qur'an and the *Sunna* of the Prophet.
Tajdid seeks renewal for all contemporary Muslims, drawn from
the exemplary behaviour of the first Muslim community established
at Medina at the time of the Prophet. John Esposito provides a
comprehensive list of the common features of Islamic revival.

Nineteenth century and earlier

i)   The process of renewal required a re-enactment of the first and
     paradigmatic Islamic revolution or reformation carried out by
     Muhammad.

ii)   Religion is integral to state and society.
iii) Departure from the norm leads to fragmentation and a decline in Muslim fortunes.
iv)   Return to the straight path of Islam is required and that necessitates a purging of all behaviour deemed to be *bida* (innovation) arising from contact with non-Muslim cultures and religions. Life has to be governed by the *shari'a* implemented in its entirety. Only thus can the Muslim community be restored to its rightful place of ascendancy and authority.
v)   The major causes of Muslim decline are blamed on popular Sufism and an uncritical acceptance of a path of imitation initiated by the *ulema*.
vi)   True Muslims may need to separate themselves from nominal Muslims in order to preserve the revelation and form brotherhoods of righteous elites.
vii) Muslims who resist change and renewal can be regarded as non-Muslims and in certain circumstances included in the enemies of Allah. (Esposito, 1988:126–127)

The twentieth-century revivalist movements pick up on all the features of the preceding list but their identifiable features are much more explicitly political. Although earlier reformers, for example Ibn Taymiyya and Muhammad ibn Abd al-Wahhab, had called for a symbiotic relationship between religion and politics based on the paradigm of the first Muslim community in Medina and the early caliphate, they were not so explicit in their challenge to Muslim governments nor did they regard the West as complicit in maintaining such regimes, for quite simply they both predated the colonial era. Certainly the connection between religion and governance is promoted by Ibn Taymiyya, who asserted that government is one of the most essential requirements for Islam as he considered that the ongoing struggle and obligation to 'command the right and forbid the wrong cannot be achieved without power and authority' (Llewellyn, 2003:221). The parallels with the earlier period and renewed emphases can be clearly distinguished in Esposito's features of twentieth-century movements.

Twentieth-century movements
i)   The West is perceived as having a crusader mentality, which has placed its power, allied with aggressive Zionism, against the Muslim world. Muslims must respond by fighting against this Western neo-colonialism.

ii) An Islamic government that fully implements the *shari'a* is not an alternative, but an imperative based on the Qur'an's call to live only in obedience to God.

iii) Muslims who fail to implement an Islamic state governed by God's law can be regarded as non-Muslims and legitimately opposed even by the use of force if necessary.

iv) The struggle against Muslim governments who do not implement the *shari'a* in its entirety can be extended to state-sponsored members of the *ulema* and state-supported mosques.

v) *Jihad* against such regimes is a religious duty. Such struggles should be extended to Western powers who politically, economically or militarily support such governments. The radical movements engaged in such struggles demand total commitment and obedience. They see themselves as the vanguard of the forces of Allah locked in holy war with the supporters of Shaitan.

vi) Christians and Jews no longer receive the traditional protection as 'People of the Book' but are seen as partners in a Judeo-Christian conspiracy against Islam and the Muslim world. (Esposito, 1988:170–172)

In order to explore how the general features of pre-twentieth-century renewal and reform became more focused on opposition to the West and Muslim nation states, it is necessary to move away from a vertical view of the Muslim world and explore contemporary challenges focused around colonial and post-colonial forces in the origins and evolution of the Muslim nation states, especially in the second half of the twentieth century.

Horizontal approaches: the social and political context

Any discussion of Islam and fundamentalism will also need to take account of the wider political, social, economic and cultural contexts framed within the context of both recent and more distant history. Thus it is necessary to examine a number of issues such as secularisation; the rise of modernity and modernism since the Enlightenment and industrialisation of the West; the alternative worldview of scientific discovery and its implications for religion; the rise of the nation state as normative for the political organisation of human society; globalisation of consumer capitalism and the continuing post-colonial dominance of the West, increasingly transferred from old European colonial powers to the new dominance of the USA.

The relationship between these factors is complex. Very often modernisation arrives in the Muslim world dressed up in the clothes of secularisation (defined here as the separation of religion into the private sphere of life and its removal from the public domain) and Westernisation, thus marginalising Islam from the processes of state and society in both the colonial and post-colonial periods. Many Muslims have rightly insisted that this is imposing a Christian model on Muslims (render unto Caesar that which is Caesar's) and ignoring the unique nature of Islam's revelation, where governance and God are interwoven through *shari'a* and the fundamental issue of Allah's sovereignty and humankind's response of submission. Thus many Muslim thinkers have called for modernisation to be sifted out from Western models of secularisation and given a uniquely Islamic mode of expression and development. However, such a project becomes increasingly difficult as the world becomes smaller and more interconnected through technological advances, and corporate capitalism with its emphasis on consumerism takes hold everywhere.

The Iranian revolution in 1978 first shattered the composure of those with faith in the paradigm of modernisation being linked to the secular nation state, and since then the world has seen a revival of religious alternatives entering the political international arena. John Esposito points this out succinctly:

> Religious nationalisms (Hindu, Muslim, Buddhist, Serbian Russian Orthodox) demonstrate the variety of ways in which religion has been used to reinforce national identities, to legitimate governments, to mobilise popular support and even to justify actions that have led to ethnic cleansing. (Esposito, 2002:1)

Esposito goes on to say that 'the discrediting and, in some cases, dethronement of secular paradigms has been particularly vivid in the Islamic world' (Esposito, 2002:1). To further explore these phenomena, it is my contention that in the case of Islam it is necessary to explore and understand the relationship of religion in the role of nation-building in the post-colonial era and to place 'Islamic fundamentalism' within the framework of liberation movements. In addition it is important not to over-simplify Muslim reactions by focusing only on high-profile *jihad* movements.

The significance of these movements goes far beyond high-profile and notorious acts of violence undertaken against the Western world.

The recent attacks on the West, exemplified by the iconic but terrible success of the events of 9/11, are significant in that they appear to demonstrate a move away from the pattern of national resistance movements seeking to find local solutions to the perceived crises and to a concerted internationalisation or globalisation of the conflict.

The degree to which this is true can be measured by Huband's organisation of his book, *Warriors of the Prophet* written in 1995 compared with Esposito's *Unholy War*, published in 2002 after the events of 9/11. Huband's book provides chapter-by-chapter case studies of revivalist movements in the Muslim world located within their unique local situations (Huband, 1995). On the other hand, Esposito focuses on the 'Muslim world' and why it hates 'the West'. In it, Osama bin Laden is described as a 'global terrorist' (p.3). Esposito states that:

> The twenty-first century will be dominated by the global encounter of two major and rapidly growing world religions, Christianity and Islam, and by the forces of globalisation that will strain relations between the West and the rest. (Esposito, 2002:x)

There are a number of problems with this approach, not least the superficial juxtapositioning of Islam and Christianity as adversaries. Certain kinds of Christianity, most commonly those found in the Southern USA, do seem to be at odds with the Muslim world, especially over the issue of Israel/Palestine where Muslims are being demonised as the army of Satan prior to Armageddon. These are paralleled in the Muslim world where there are also some imminent millennarian expectations. Ironically, however, these are not a significant aspect of the political Islamic revivalist movements but are more often found amongst some Sufi organisations.

Certainly 9/11 and other incidents alert us to the globalisation of the conflict and a paradigm shift away from national struggles. This has been accelerated in the meetings of various Islamic movements in Afghanistan where individuals from around the world fought alongside each other against the Russian occupiers and then dispersed to various more localised struggles. However, their new-found camaraderie with each other gave them an international dimension. Thus volunteers from various radical Islamic movements could be found in Bosnia, Palestine, Chechnya and Iraq.

In addition, a number of movements have begun to challenge the focus of the Islamic movements that insist upon creating Islamic states out of existing secular Muslim nations. They argue that the idea of a nation state, even one founded on Islamic principles, is not Islamic. Instead, Muslim activists should be struggling for a universal caliphate that would represent and embody the ideal of the *umma*.

Politically, a number of world events in the years since the collapse of the Soviet Union – namely the failure to resolve the Palestinian issue, the apparent lack of support by the West for Chechnya's struggle for independence, the ethnic cleansing of Muslims in the Balkans, the invasion of Iraq and Afghanistan and the presence of American troops in Saudi Arabia – have reinforced conspiracy theories and the view that the USA and its allies have declared war on Islam itself.

However, in spite of the media's focus on global terrorism and the supposed ability of al-Qa'eda to strike anywhere around the globe or recruit others locally to the same end, the significant impetus of the conflicts still remains local, continuing various national struggles around the world to either establish Islamic states or to give Muslim communities in multi-cultural environments such as Indonesia, Malaysia or the Philippines more authority in the legal frameworks of the nation or autonomous control over territory. Thus the relationship between fundamentalism and nationhood remains an essential aspect of any attempt to understand the former.

Fundamentalism and nationhood

In a scathing article, John Shepherd does not spare the scriptures of the three 'Abrahamic' religions and demonstrates that any literal approach to their content will justify the use of violence, in spite of the attempts by liberals and modernists in each of them to issue sets of apologetics which rationalise violent incidents or teachings in the face of contemporary criticism and human rights discourse (Shepherd, 2004). However, more significantly Shepherd points us to the linkage of a religious people chosen by God and a 'promised land'. The origins of such a phenomenon, of course, lie in the promise of Israel to the ancient tribes of Israel. He writes:

> Thus the Jewish tradition celebrates, as in good measure founda-
> tional, what is euphemistically termed the 'entry into the prom-
> ised land' – an event that in practical terms is described as a
> bloody conquest with periodic divinely sanctioned massacres

and would-be genocide, inaugurating a history of intolerance and persecution of idolaters and deviants. (Shepherd, 2004:31)

Shepherd provides us with an analysis of Jewish fundamentalism that links certain forms of contemporary Jewish orthodoxy with the campaign to re-establish a Jewish state consistent with biblical borders and governed by the implementation of the *Halachah* (Jewish Talmudic law based on the Torah), a religiously inspired legal system that governs every aspect of life according to God's revelation to the Jews. Shepherd points out that certain forms of Christianity have also possessed self-perceptions of themselves as the new Chosen People with rights to a new Promised Land. He cites the examples of the Afrikaner state of South Africa and the 'Calvinist emphasis on "the elect" fused with inspiration drawn from the Hebrew scriptures to engender a sense among the Scots settlers in Northern Ireland that they too were a chosen people sent to redeem the land from idolaters' (2004:37). He makes the link to the original Puritan settlers to America who also perceived themselves as a chosen people with a new promised land and equally had no regard for the non-Christian original occupants. He argues that to this day the USA retains a strong sense of identity based on a sacralised 'manifest destiny' as 'God's own country'. Although generally benign, the linkage between the Protestant right, dominant in the Bible belts of the South, to exert pressure and make alliances with conservative Republicans also reasserts the promise of the Puritans and a role for a cleansed America in the final days and the struggle with Satan.

This link between nationhood, identity and religion can also be found in the Eastern forms of religious fundamentalism, albeit with very different political and religious histories to those influenced by the old Jewish paradigm of a holy land and a chosen people. However, sacred soil is not a foreign concept to the populations of India and a variety of communal movements have organised themselves around religious identity and the recovery of a 'sacred territory'. Thus the Sikhs struggled in the Punjab throughout the 1980s to create a separate state of Khalistan where the ideals of the Khalsa, the Sikh religious brotherhood founded by Gobind Singh, the last of the human Gurus, would rule.

More significantly in terms of contemporary Indian politics is the concept of Hindutva which has not only created the idea of Hindu India as opposed to the Nehru/Gandhi vision of a secular multireligious state but has been a key element of successful election campaigns resulting in successive governments for the BJP political party. The twin concepts of Hindurashtra and Hindutva, respectively deal with the notion of the subcontinent as the motherland of the Hindu people and linked to it a national culture which includes those deemed to be part of an historical Hindu worldview, that is Hindus, Jains, Sikhs and Indian Buddhists. Thus a new definition of Hindu has been forged which includes all who regard the land of Bharatvarsha (India) as a motherland and a holy land. In this process, religious festivals and mythology are used as nationalist symbols and used to promote national consciousness.

Islam and nationalism

Certainly an early form of globalisation significant in the Muslim context was the transformation of 'Christendom' into a collection of more or less secular nation states. Although the religions of the world had struggled with each other for the hearts and souls of human beings, sometimes spilling over into violence, especially when linked to imperial powers, it was nothing compared to the threat offered to their hold on human loyalties provided by the new allegiance to nation. Fazlun Khalid acknowledges this when he says that the secular nation states 'succeeded in persuading or coercing the rest of the human community to organize their lives in a like manner' (Khalid, 2003:300). We have already examined in Chapter 5 how the rise of nationhood and developing allegiance and emotional attachment to *watan* provoked a crisis in regard to the central Islamic concept of *umma*. Khalid argues that the resolution made by the League of Nations in 1920, asserting that the nation state was the only legitimate form of government recognised in the world, directly contradicted the Qur'an's perception that humans were organised into large religious collectives whose ultimate aim was to transform and even encapsulate the entire world (Khalid, 2003:308). If Khalid is correct, the Muslim world cannot help but be dismayed by the proliferation of nation states and the loyalty which their citizens can display towards them.

The nation state needs to be seen in the context of a particular ideology that had become increasingly identified with the Western world since the Enlightenment. As such it was not a neutral phenomenon but part of a highly successful new paradigm where societies,

governments and nations centred themselves on rational organisational structures and developed a philosophy of endless progress
through the fruits of scientific discovery. In other words the 'modernity' project of industrialisation, secular education, the privatisation
of religion and technical innovation took place alongside the ever-
increasing numbers of the new nation states, each competing with the
other.

But there were two major issues for Muslims in this new paradigm
for the organisation of human society. First, not all the new states
were able to compete on a level platform with each other. Many of the
new states were disadvantaged by recent histories of colonial domination, and many Muslim nations fitted this category. The odds
seemed to be stacked towards the old colonial powers of the West
maintaining a relationship of dominance through economic and military superiority. Secondly, the Muslim nations were uncomfortable
with the new paradigm on religious grounds. The humanist project
which underlay the new secularism put humanity at the centre of the
world rather than God. Human rights discourse replaced revelation
as the new moral and ethical high ground. The rationalism and
humanism that was to become dominant after the Renaissance
gradually desacralised the cosmos.

The success of the European nations in the colonial projects they
pursued resulted in what Zygmunt Bauman described as a climate of
superiority where the rest of the world was perceived to be in a state
of arrested development (Bauman, 1993). This appeared to apply particularly to Muslim nations, which were not only often poor, but also
attached to tradition and religiously conservative when it came to
innovation. Khalid states that the same movement that developed the
modernist project also 'ushered in the age of the nation-states,
deployed nationalism in the service of state authority, and promoted
national interests as the criteria of state policy' (Khalid, 2003:307).

He also points out that Muslim elites produced by the modernising
project came to desire what the West had achieved (Khalid, 2003:300).
A new middle class began to develop for those who had taken advantage of the education facilities on offer by the colonial powers.
Generally, the opportunities were provided in order to train a middle-
level administration that could work under the new authorities in
ruling colonised territory. Some of the most successful of these new
elites were educated in the universities of the Western coloniser's
home nations and came to be firm believers in the educational, legal

and political structures they observed in Europe. However, their education did not convince them that their colonisation was just and it
also provided them with the resources to campaign for freedom.

Ironically, it was those trained in Western values who led the way
to independence, often at the helm of resistance movements. Once
freedom from the colonial power was achieved they became the new
rulers of the new nation which they determined should follow the
modernist paradigm, competing with others in a global market and
politically structured on either socialist or capitalist models borrowed
from the influence of non-Muslim nations. However, as it has been
pointed out, these new Muslim nation states were rarely on level
terms with their Western counterparts and often could not succeed in
a world where the rich and powerful were determined to maintain
and increase their prominence. Where economic success was achieved
it was often with the loss of local culture, benefited only the new elites
and failed to carry either the religious elites or the common people
along with its goals. Resistance or non-cooperation with the regime
was often greeted by repressive measures. Corruption became rife as
wealth was gathered into the hands of the Western-trained elites and
increasingly there were those who came to believe that the modern
secular nation state had failed as a project in the Muslim world.

However, the first attempts to seek an Islamic solution for the
Muslim world instead of the imported Western systems of social and
political organisation, did not seriously consider an alternative to the
nation state. Rather the newly formed Islamic movements, influenced
by the ideas of Mawdudi or Qutb, attempted to establish within their
respective nations an Islamic solution based on the imperative to
restore Islamic law in its entirety. A number of options were used to
reach out and gain support from the people. These involved preaching, printing tracts, education, political activism, social welfare, and
armed struggle where governments were intransigent or repressive.

Thus within a few decades of the second half of the twentieth century, many Muslim nations were involved in a prolonged struggle
concerning how they should be structured and the debate was framed
within concerns as to whether the state should be secular or religious.
However, the criteria of success and competition as the goals of the
state were rarely challenged. To the revivalist or *jihad* movements, this
success would come as a result of submission to God not by turning
to the essentially godless humanism embraced by the West since the
Enlightenment.

Islam and fundamentalism

Any analysis of fundamentalism within Islam has to take into account both of these vertical and horizontal approaches to the study of the Muslim world. Factors in the historical development of Islam will influence the shape of Muslim response and reaction to certain political events in the present moment and the recent past, especially where Islam is perceived to be threatened by either internal or external forces or a combination of both. The most significant factor in the history of Islam that is likely to shape contemporary Muslim responses is the identified pattern of reform and renewal (*islah* and *tajdid*) that is seen to periodically occur whenever Muslim society or civilisation is under attack or in decline.

A number of postures and attitudes towards the West have developed in response to Western hegemony, and, from a Muslim point of view, the domination of the world by the wrong authority. Since most of the Muslim world remains part of the poorest sectors on earth, Muslims are also drawn towards Islamic rhetoric borrowing from the Qur'an's powerful voice concerning social injustice and divine retribution for the offenders. For the last hundred and fifty years the Muslim world has been overly concerned with how to react to Western domination; its economic, military, technical, scientific and educational superiority, continuing from the colonial to the post-colonial eras. As succinctly stated by Nomanhul S. Haqq 'the control of the world fell into the wrong hands' (Haqq, 2003:123). The responses range from Muslim apologetics, sometimes very crudely expressed, through to bitter and violent antagonism towards anything perceived as Western. However, a whole range of revivalist and reformist responses are not so lethal to Western interests, nor do they consider violent overthrow of their respective regimes but seek more peaceful methods of transformation.

Yet the most common reaction by most Muslim nations to the domination of the West has been to duplicate as effectively as possible the Western paradigm for material success. It is in the reaction to this imitation by the rulers and governing elites of Muslim nations that we find the more radical responses. Robert Pope has written, 'politics is the place where fundamentalism becomes public' (Pope, 2001:183) but I would go further and argue that it is the combination of certain religious responses to political situations that actually defines fundamentalism as opposed to merely taking one's religion seriously or its sacred texts literally. As stated by Hadden and Schupe,

> The phenomenon of fundamentalism indicates that religion can
> be the corporate public action of religiously motivated individu-
> als to change the social system on behalf of what they perceive to
> be their deepest spiritual loyalties. (Hadden and Schupe, 1989)

However, caution has to be exercised when attributing the causes of
Muslim revivalism in the twentieth and twenty-first centuries to
'common globalisation processes that can be attributed to secularisation' as quoted from Hadden and Schupe at the beginning of this
chapter. The shortcomings of any such attempts to provide a universal causal analysis of 'fundamentalism' is that they do not acknowledge sufficiently the unique features or characteristics of religious
beliefs and practices within a particular 'faith' community. As we
have seen, a kind of secularisation, as defined by models of nationhood that separated religion and governance, entered the Muslim
world as their nation states proliferated in the twentieth century.
However, the claim by Muslim revivalists that Islam and politics were
always inseparable is disputable. Even before the influence of the
Western world, most Muslim rulers had made compromises with
the *ulema* regarding the implementation of *shari'a*, often employing it
no further than the laws concerning worship and private family law.
Generally speaking, with the exception of certain jurists such as Ibn
Taymiyya, this had been accepted pragmatically by the vast majority
of Muslims.

Thus any attempts to analyse the causes of Muslim revivalism,
especially when linked to the ideology and pursuit of Islamic states,
must be rooted in an anti-colonial and post-colonial discourse, combined with attempts to redefine nationhood in uniquely Islamic
terms. Thus new narratives that interpreted original sources, namely
the Qur'an and *Sunna*, were required and a new generation of Muslim
ideologues such as Mawlana Maududi and Sayyid Qutb responded to
the *zeitgeist*, creating both new frameworks of understanding and
activist movements.

In spite of the growth of organisations that are prepared to use violence against their own regime's accommodation with the West or to
strike at Western interests or even attack Western nations, it would be
too narrow a focus to describe only such organisations as 'fundamentalist'. In addition, it would not be helpful for the analysis of such
movements because organisations such as the Taleban in Afghanistan
and al-Qa'eda, although linked with each other for mutual benefit,

and seen by the Western media and the British and US governments as virtually identical 'terrorists', are very different phenomena and deserve to be treated as such if we are really going to understand their origins and objectives. On the other hand, to label any Muslim as fundamentalist who takes his or her religion seriously, adhering to the *shari'a* where possible and living by the words of God as transcribed in the Qur'an and the Prophet's example, is ludicrous and provides support to the views of Muslim critics of the term who argue that it cannot be transferred from Protestant Christianity to Islam.

A more useful exercise might be to ignore the 'definition' approach to fundamentalism and see if certain forms of Islamic understanding meet the 'lists' approach which outlines certain characteristics advocated by scholars such as Harris or Hadden and Schupe. Both sets of characteristics define fundamentalism as resistance to secularisation or the marginalisation of religion. Contemporary revivalist movements in the Muslim world have certainly sought to advocate or create social and political changes based on scriptural authority, in fact it could be argued that they over-emphasised socio-political and cultural issues to the neglect of other aspects of religiosity in their interpretation of the Qur'an. In this respect they could be accused of selectivity in opposing certain aspects of modernity. Indeed, they have also opposed the vast majority of Muslims, perceiving their position as a compromise with modernity. Certainly, they claim that their interpretation of the scriptures is the authentic one, using it to develop a consistent ideology to bring religion back to the centre of public life. However, this chapter has argued that such reactions must take account of Muslim responses to the creation of nation states even if one acknowledges that this in itself is an early manifestation of the globalisation of Western values and domination.

With regard to Harriet Harris' assertion that fundamentalist movements are characterised by charismatic leadership that brooks no dissent, I am not convinced. Certainly, key players have appeared throughout Muslim history to inspire reform and renewal, some of whom have been regarded as *mujaddids*, but they have rarely demanded or received total obedience. Islam's insistence on a non-hierarchical relationship to God advocates against such kinds of authoritarian leadership and Islamic 'fundamentalism' has always had a range of degrees of participation from sympathisers to activists. It is also problematic to define Islamic fundamentalism as a modern phenomenon as it has been shown that certain patterns of behaviour have occurred as a response to socio-political conditions since the first centuries of Islam, where traditional or nominal allegiance to the religion has always been condemned by the advocates of reform and renewal. In addition, the characteristic looking back to an ideal past to be reconstituted in the future, often discovered in fundamentalisms, would seem to be logical behaviour for Muslims, in view of the religious core beliefs. Once one accepts that the present is imperfect, then it is beholden for the devout to remain loyal to the religion's original truth claims, where the past is seen to hold perfection. The hope then is that the past ideal can be resurrected in the future by either piety or activism.

I am not convinced by Harriet Harris' remaining characteristics, in that they would appear to define attitudes that can be found amongst millions of devout Muslims who do not have political aspirations. Moral dualism is inherent to the Qur'an's view of God, humanity and the world and so is victory to the believer at the end of history. Muslims in themselves constitute an elect membership, at least as far as they are recipients of a final revelation, and even if they do not establish sharp boundaries between the saved and the unsaved – after all, how could they know the inscrutable will of Allah – the Almighty will do so at the Day of Judgement. And yes, it is true, the majority of Muslims will assert the validity of the fundamentals of their faith – the Qur'an by definition is inerrant as it is the eternal word of God.

Conclusion

Any assessment of whether the term 'fundamentalism' is useful to describe certain forms of Islam will need to restrict the usage of the label to make it meaningful to both Muslims and those who wish to possess a more informed understanding of contemporary events in the Muslim world. In order to achieve this level of understanding, we have argued that both a horizontal and vertical approach to the study of Islamic revivalism will be required. In addition, 'definitional' or 'listing of characteristics' approaches often adopted by social scientists are inadequate in themselves as they fail to acknowledge the unique history of particular religions. At least John Esposito's list of nineteenth- and twentieth-century revivalism helps us to understand the unique formation and development of Islamic movements that advocate reform and renewal.

However, care needs to be taken with this analysis also; as pointed out by Abdul Said and Nathan Funk there are at least four paradigms for understanding the complexity of the contemporary Muslim world. They list these as:

   i)   the power political paradigm
   ii) the reformist paradigm
   iii) the renewalist paradigm
   iv) mystical Islam. (Said and Funk, 2003:167–174)

The first paradigm describes the present condition of most Muslim nations, arguably borrowed from the Western conception of the nation state but with an historical heritage of triumphalism left over from the old Muslim empires. In this chapter I have argued that it is this paradigm that provides the well-spring of contemporary Muslim revival in all its forms.

For the Muslim governments of contemporary nation states, law and order, stability and power are the priorities, but their respective failure to succeed in competition with Western nations and their lack of enthusiasm for the implementation of Islamic codes in public life, have led to the call for revival of religion as a solution to crisis. But those who pursue revival and criticise the power political paradigm need not be militant. The reformist paradigm seeks to re-establish Islamic values through the twin processes of seeking the essentials of Islam and transforming social practices and belief in accordance with the spirit of the religion, a process that requires sifting out non-Islamic accretions to the religion through the process of individual re-interpretation of the Qur'an and *Sunna*. Although critical of the contemporary Muslim political situation, the reformist paradigm may well harmonise with Western human rights discourse, issues of social justice, rights of women and ecological concerns.

The renewalist paradigm, however, tends to reject the idea that anything good can be found in the West in favour of Islamic solutions discovered by a return to an ideal primordial Islam found not only in the Qur'an and the *Sunna*, but also in the earliest Muslim communities. Only by a return to a pristine Islam and a rejection of the materialist, consumer-societies of the West can Muslim fortunes be restored. It might be tempting to call these movements 'fundamentalists' but Said and Funk disagree, preferring to locate the phenomenon within groups that react militantly to external threats rather than those that seek internal transformation (Said and Funk, 2003:171). However, this would seem to be a differentiation based on degree rather than qualitative distinction. It is further complicated by the very recent globalisation of Islamic movements, where national 'liberation' movements concerned with radical transformation by the creation of Islamic states are intertwined with newer movements that see the conflict in terms of a universal *umma* struggling against a worldwide conspiracy to destroy Islam.

Lastly, Said and Funk mention mystical Islam, commonly referred to as Sufism, which advocates spirituality as the way to transformation, both individually and socially. However, the focus on Islam as an internal process and state of being in relation to God does not lessen the importance of the message of the Qur'an, and will further encourage the insistence upon a life of religious piety and rejection of materialism.

All of the above, except for the power political paradigm, might be labelled fundamentalism by the secular or non-religious, but it is the popular press and, since the invasion of Iraq, the government of the USA, that have conflated both the power political paradigm and the militant variations of the renewalists or revivalists to present a negative image of the Muslim world, even though the two groups are often bitter opponents to each other. It is certainly true that the more radical revivalists have come to dominate Islamic discourse in the last fifty years but there are signs of a revival of Islamic spirituality taking place. Certainly any analysis of the contemporary Muslim world would need to consider that millions in the Muslim world are in some way considering the possibility of religious solutions to questions of identity and purpose, and as dissent to the problems aggravated by industrialisation and globalisation of consumer culture.

To do so will require a renewed understanding of the Qur'an, for it is axiomatic that Muslims will need to work within a worldview that takes scripture as both guide and authority. The Qur'an itself asserts that: 'That is the Book; there is no doubt. It is its guidance for the God-fearing, those who believe in the Unseen and establish the prayer and spend out of what We have provided them with' (Qur'an 2:1–2). But even so the Qur'an remains as not so much an elaborate and consistent set of doctrines but as a 'rich and subtle stimulus to the religious imagination' (Hourani, 1985:86). As pointed out by Haqq, no reconstruction can claim 'epistemological finality on the part of the reader' (Haqq, 2003:125) even though most Islamic movements will claim the privilege, not only amongst the revivalists but also the more esoteric mystical movements.

Whilst Islamic politics may claim to possess the authentic interpretation of the sacred texts, it does so for expediency, a way of resistance against perceived Western hegemony set within a context of post-colonial power relations, globalisation of consumer capitalism, fear of the success of secular values, but above all the context of discovering how to be Muslim within the competing arenas of ethnic and national identity. However, in the process of discovering how to have an Islamic renaissance in the twenty-first century, Muslims will need to remember, and millions of them already have, that the Qur'an is above all else a text to be used for guidance on submission to, and intimacy with God. The central purpose of the *shari'a* in all its manifestations is to foster piety and godly living, not to create governments and nations.

Muslims are called by their religion to activism. As Yasin Dutton reminds us the Qur'an's imperative voice insists that they should 'actively establish justice and combat injustice wherever and whenever possible' (Dutton, 2003:323). It would be too easy to place such a struggle into a dualistic framework which pits two worldviews against each other. Again as expressed by Dutton:

> We have thus, two world views: one that, in putting scriptural authority uppermost, declares its allegiance to a God-centred view of the world; and one that, in putting human authority of scientific discovery uppermost, declares its allegiance to a human-centred view of the world. (Dutton, 2003:325)

It needn't be so polarised, for not everything in the West is bad, neither can everything that has been perceived as corrupt in the Muslim world be attributed to Western influences. That is too facile. However, I agree with Muslims that fundamentalism as broadly defined cannot be a useful category for Islam, for there are characteristics that lie at the heart of their religion that are being located within a fundamentalist outlook, all too often used negatively to denote bigotry, irrationality, militancy and a pre-modern worldview. However, the analysis provided by sociologists such as Hadden and Schupe can provide us with a more narrowly defined usage of fundamentalism that does appear to describe certain kinds of Muslim revivalism manifesting since the second half of the twentieth century with definite political aims. However, even though such movements are relatively small in membership, there are countless more who consider a shift of allegiance back from 'man' to God only of benefit to humankind.

There are two religious revivals happening across the Muslim world, one that my Muslim friends label 'political Islam', which could accurately and usefully be defined as 'fundamentalism'. The other, they call 'faith-based Islam'. The causes of each phenomenon may be entwined with each other, but those who are returning in such large numbers to the latter desire, above all, a concrete living experience of God. It does not help us to define them as fundamentalists, although they may seek fundamentals, nor does it help us to understand the recent rise of politicised religion that may more accurately be called 'fundamentalisms'.

CHAPTER 11

Muslim Women: Islam's oppressed or victims of patriarchy?

This chapter will provide an overview of the situation of Muslim women, looking at Western stereotypes and the views of various female perspectives from within Islam. The focus of the chapter will be on the uniqueness of Muslim women's claims to be able to liberate themselves from patriarchy through the application of a correct understanding of the Qur'an and Hadith rather than the secular feminism of the West.

Introduction

Any discussion of the position of Muslim women and their status within Islam has to be undertaken in the awareness that here lies one of the deepest divides between Muslim opinion and Western conceptions. It is reasonably safe to assert that Islam receives more negative criticism concerning the role of women than any other religious tradition. Muslims are suspicious that outsiders maintain uninformed views, influenced by the prejudices of the popular media, which stereotype Muslim women as victims of male oppression: veiled, passive and invisible.

The Western media has focused on *hijab* (veiling), *purdah* (female segregation) and non-Islamic cultural practices such as 'honour killings', often isolating the attitudes of individual movements such as the Taleban in Afghanistan as typical of Muslim female experience. On the other hand, many Muslim women argue that their religion safeguards women, and that the Qur'an provided rights to seventh-century Arabian women that were not given to British women until the nineteenth century. The debate both within and without the Muslim communities is intense. Western feminists tend to regard Islam as hopelessly misogynist and perceive Muslim women to be oppressed by surviving patriarchal cultures that need to be over-hauled and brought in line with modernist or post-modernist Western cultures. Many Muslim women would regard their Western 'sisters' as corrupted by secular materialism, unprotected by the laws of God, seeking freedoms that are not permitted by God's revelation and hor-ribly exploited by sex industries and consumer advertising that uses women to sell products.

Herbert Bodman points out that the literature on gender issues in Islam, although improving, is dominated by the preoccupation with the Arab hinterlands of the Middle East, which, though they contain only a quarter of the Muslim population, are seen as the 'Muslim world par excellence' (Bodman, 1998:2). He also asserts that fieldwork re-mains comparatively rare. Even though the relatively new academic discipline of Women's Studies has begun to turn its attention to the Muslim world, producing a new crop of literature on the subject, the focus on the Middle East and the lack of sufficient fieldwork together produce a distorted view. Moreover, and arguably more significant, he suggests that:

> more sensational material relating to 'Muslim women' has emanated from the Middle-East in the form of newspaper accounts, television broadcasts, and film documentaries exploit-ing the widespread pejorative image of Islam, especially its presumed dictates on women. (Bodman, 1998:2)

These have now been supplemented by considerable media coverage arising from the presence of significant Muslim populations in the West, which originated in the global movements of population for either economic or political reasons. Many of these articles must be read in the context of right-wing political views on migration and racist polemical discourse.

Western conceptions are not only likely to be stereotypical but to essentialise, failing to recognise the significant diversity of women's experiences across the Muslim world or, for that matter, across the social structures of a single society where class, religious allegiance, education, wealth, and the personal familial environment can all be factors. As stated by Kandiyoti:

Women in the Middle East must be studied not in terms of an undifferentiated 'Islam' or Islamic culture but rather through the differing political projects of nation-states, with their distinct histories, relationships to colonialism and the West, class politics, ideological uses of an Islamic idiom, and struggles over the role of Islamic law in state legal apparatuses.

(Kandiyoti, 1992:246)

Many case studies written on Muslim gender issues do take into account the vast range of cultural factors that impact on Islamic values within the variety of nations that belong to the Muslim world. This is crucial, as the experiences of a Muslim woman in urban India, for example, are unlikely to be the same as her counterpart in a Turkish village. Increasingly, studies of Muslim gender experience explore within one cultural milieu rather than generalising. However, in spite of that rich heritage of cultural difference, the teachings of the Qur'an and Hadith concerning women's roles and her rights and responsibilities are shared by all. Yet the interaction between religion, culture and the hermeneutical process applied to sacred texts does produce a significant variety of conclusions. In spite of all this, as pointed out by Herbert Bodman, the half-a-billion Muslim women in the world can be described as 'a worldwide gender community' (Bodman, 1998:1).

Certainly, since the beginning of the twentieth century, women's issues and gender relations within Islam have generated a vast literature in which religion is presented as both the cause of female subjugation and the solution to all her problems. Ziba Mir-Hosseini makes the point that 'the whole literature has been ideologically charged, and has become an arena for polemics masquerading as scholarly debate' (Mir-Hosseini, 1997:7). Attempts to classify the body of literature written on or by women in the Muslim world are provided by Mai Yamani writing a year earlier in 1996 and are further developed by Mir-Hosseini.

Between them the two writers have identified a number of genres, as follows, from amongst the books which attempt to defend Islam against a perceived attack by the West, and by Western feminists in particular, yet defend the right of Muslim women to full participation and equality within Muslim society. However, these are not always written from the same perspective and can be divided into:

i)   those that locate their feminism in Islam and seek new meaning in the sacred texts; and

ii) those that distance themselves from any Islamic association and expose the patriarchal bias of Islamic texts. (Mir-Hosseini, 1997:5)

Mai Yamani, defining Islamic feminism as 'empowerment of gender within a rethought Islam' (Yamani, 1996:1) provides further insight into category i. These can be categorised as women who:

a)   explore religious texts and Islamic jurisprudence seeking evidence for equality in areas of family law and civil rights, recognising that there is no uniformity of Islamic law across Muslim countries;

b)   those who attempt to provide new Islamic discourses that challenge the domination of male interpretation of the Qur'an (Yamani, 1996:2); and

c)   those who study Muslim history, rereading Islamic religious texts with attention given to the female figures of the formative years of Islam. (Yamani, 1996:5)

The common argument of all the above positions is that women have been discriminated against by social practices and economic realities rather than by Islamic principles which in themselves functioned as tools for emancipation. The conclusion reached is that Muslims need to be made aware of the position of women by an exploration of patriarchy which has circumscribed or restricted the Islamic rights of women (Yamani, 1996:5).

   However, these, too, need to be categorised separately, dividing those which are works of Muslim academics such as Leila Ahmed and Fatima Mernissi from the Muslim apologetics which typically provide traditional arguments illustrating the pitiful conditions of women in various ancient cultures and then providing an analysis of the superiority of the Qur'an's rights and obligations. This approach is typified by authors such as Fatima Naseef (1999).

The historical context

In the context of the criticism aimed at Humayun Ansari by the representative of Jamait al-Nissa Women's Group, that his book entitled *The Infidel Within*, describing the history of Muslims in Britain, had relegated women to one discrete chapter, it should be noted that the Qur'an itself follows a similar pattern, providing a single chapter dedicated to women in Sura 4 entitled *al-Nisa* (Women). However, it is this very chapter that is affirmed by the emic voice of young activist Muslim women who argue that the Qur'an not only has a complete chapter devoted to women, unlike other sacred texts, but that it also asserts her complete equality with men. However, she operates in a complementary but different arena of life with her own qualities suited to that sphere, whereas men are suited to operate in the public realm.

An analysis of the Qur'an's contribution to women's equality will come later in the chapter but for now I would like to assert the proposition that Islam's focus on women as a separate category needs to be understood in the context of the first Muslims' appraisal and critique of the attitudes and values of the non-Muslim cultures that it found itself surrounded by and in competition with. It was this factor of the rival attitudes to women that focused the early Muslims rather than a direct concern with the universal rights of women. This proposition provides the possibility of a chronological analysis of the various historical attitudes towards women in the Muslim world. In other words, we need always to assess Muslim interaction or intermingling with other cultures and their attitudes to women.

Thus it can be argued that the Qur'an's focus on women needs to be appraised within the context of the surrounding and prevailing cultural mores of the desert Arab, values that would have been held by the first male converts. The chapter on women may have been revealed to provide guidance to Muslim males on how to treat their wives and daughters as opposed to being written for a female readership or audience. If this assertion is true, then analysis of the Qur'an's injunctions must be undertaken in the context of patriarchal tribal values of honour. This is not to deny the significant reforms that embryonic Islam brought to the Arab world, so proudly proclaimed by both male and female Muslim authors of contemporary apologetics, but it may transform the way in which those reforms are assessed.

However, the critical gaze of the first Muslims on the apparent unjust treatment of women by the 'pagan' Arabs would have been very different to the influence on later generations of Muslims. These were part of a wealthy and successful empire beginning the process of creating a civilisation, faced with the rich variety of women's experience in already established cultures of the Byzantine Christians, the ancient civilisations of Persia, India and China and the Mediterranean worlds influenced by Greece, Rome and Egypt.

Thus the early and late medieval periods can be assessed by the various interactions with more or less sophisticated cultures where Muslim conquest was indigenised, creating a dynamic tension between assimilation of local customs and the requirement to maintain 'pure' Islamic values. But it would have been Muslims who set the agenda and the parameters of assimilation of values towards women arising out of contact with other cultural customs. After all they were the victors, the colonising power, and there were advantages for the conquered in adopting both the religion and the cultural mores of their rulers. On the other hand, the older cultures may have looked impressive to the desert Arabs, influencing in turn the new invaders.

For example, Leila Ahmed argues that the adoption of the veil by wealthy Muslim women was part of the assimilation of 'the mores of the conquered people', pointing to its usage in the Christian Middle East and the Mediterranean region (Ahmed, 1992:4), themselves influenced by the older female dress customs of the ancient Babylonian, Mesopotamian and Egyptian cultures. Similar arguments of acculturation can also be put forward for the practices of *purdah* and the harems of the ruling classes.

This two-way process of acculturation is summed up by Ahmed:

> Once Islam had conquered the adjacent territories, the assimilation of the scriptural and social traditions of their Christian and Jewish populations into the corpus of Islamic life and thought occurred easily and seamlessly. Converts brought traditions of thought and custom with them. (Ahmed, 1992:4)

A similar chronological focus is provided by Barbara Stowasser, who also notes transformations in the attitudes to women in various historical periods. She argues that medieval Muslim society was far more patriarchal than the early communities established in Makkah and Medina, those who first received the Qur'an's revelation and followed the Prophet of God. Stowasser appears to agree with the assertions of many Muslims, both male and female, that the original equality was lost as Muslims conquered territories inhabited by earlier religions such as Zoroastrianism or Orthodox Christianity and consequently came under their more sophisticated cultural influence. Stowasser states:

Mediaeval Islamic exegesis, however, viewing women's innate nature as weak but also dangerous to the established moral order, largely excluded the Qur'anic theme of female spiritual freedom and moral responsibility in favour of the exegetic maxim that woman is (ie. should be) man's follower in all things.

(Stowasser, 1994:21)

Ahmed agrees, arguing that the Qur'an provides no account of the creation of the first human pair that favours one over another, in spite of its incorporation of so many Jewish biblical stories. As with Stowasser, she asserts that the story of the creation of Eve from Adam's rib only occurs in Muslim traditional literature in the period following the Muslim conquests (Ahmed, 1992:4–5).

It is thanks to Leila Ahmed, Barbara Stowasser and others that we possess groundbreaking work that has tackled the gargantuan task of 'unearthing and piecing together' (Ahmed, 1992:2) the history of women in Middle-Eastern cultures and the articulation of gender in Muslim societies. These were 'areas of history largely invisible in Middle-Eastern scholarship' (1992:3) as any trawl of the major works of Middle-Eastern history will demonstrate even in recent texts. However, it still remains necessary to provide accurate research that looks at the conditions of women in Mesopotamia, Egypt, Greece and Persia before the arrival of Islam, as well as local conditions in the Hijaz.

This becomes more urgent in the face of the contemporary Islamist argument, which maintains that the establishment of Islam improved the conditions of women. Both defensive apologetics written by men and critiques of male patriarchy in Middle-Eastern societies written by Muslim 'feminists' uncritically affirm the above premise. The past, especially the formative period of Islam, has become the crucial period for defending Islam's position on women. As stated by Ahmed:

> Throughout Islamic history the constructs, institutions, and modes of thought devised by early Muslim societies that form the core discourses of Islam have played a central role in defining women's place in Muslim societies. (Ahmed, 1992:1)

However, the Islamic position describes a situation in pre-Islamic Arabian culture which consisted of corrupt paganism devoid of the values required by God. The existing Middle-Eastern monotheisms had lost their way, corrupted the message of their respective prophets and fallen into decay, ripe for divine renewal. However, this reveals a simplistic view of both pagan and theistic realities, especially with regard to women. The position of women in pre-Islamic Arab culture was probably not as patriarchal as described, neither were women as subservient as the 'emancipated' ideal of the Muslim woman freed by God's revelation would like to think. Ahmed puts the opposite position, arguing that Islam transformed the 'Arabian socio-religious vision and organisation of gender into line with the rest of the Middle-East and Mediterranean regions' (Ahmed, 1992:4). In doing so, it transformed the diverse attitudes to women prevalent in tribal cultures, often venerating female deities, to the dominant norms of the patriarchal family and female subjugation typical of Judaism, Christianity and Zoroastrianism.

Nor is the stereotype of the pagan Arab women liberated from the tyrannical yoke of the godless able to bear close scrutiny. The Qur'an certainly provides images of fearless women who stand their ground against the immorality of their menfolk. But these images of independent women may owe more to the 'pagan' desert tribeswomen than contemporary Muslim polemics would care to admit. Although large numbers of Muslim women are satisfied with the current or historical place of women in Muslim societies, an increasing number of women from within Islam are challenging the overwhelmingly male voice of religious authority, and reassessing the roles of prominent women in early Muslim development, most notably the women of the Prophet's household. Both the Qur'an and the Hadith are under close scrutiny in order to discover what they say about women.

Although the experience of a Muslim woman will be influenced by class and family background, age, rural or urban locality, national identity and her place within the wide variety of religious understandings of Islam, it is to the revelation of the Qur'an and the subsequent rendering into everyday life through the example of Muhammad and his Companions, that her understanding of her place in society is finally made authoritative. Unlike her Christian feminist compatriots, who have recognised serious imperfections in the way women are treated in the religion itself, even in sacred histories and texts, many Muslim women who seek to change their position in society, perceive Islam as the ideal to which their menfolk, both historically and contemporary, have failed to match.

However, the Qur'an's proclamation of equality is in regard to her individual capacity to attain God's rewards and punishments, to follow the revelation of Allah's will. In this respect, the text is clear that men and women are equal.

> Lo! Men who surrender unto Allah, and women who surrender, and men who believe and women who believe, and men who obey and women who obey, and men who speak the truth and women who speak the truth, and men who persevere (in righteousness) and women who persevere, and men who are humble and women who are humble, and men who give alms and women who give alms, and men who fast and women who fast, and men who guard their modesty and women who guard (their modesty), and men who remember Allah much and women who remember – Allah hath prepared for them forgiveness and a vast reward. (Qur'an, Sura 33:35)

However, in other areas equality is not so assured. For example, the testimony of a man is equivalent to that of two women, suggesting that women are less trustworthy. But the Qur'an does provide assertive statements concerning her rights in marriage and divorce, the status of her property and the maintenance of her dignity. She also has a number of Qur'anic models for both right and wrong behaviour. Four women, Asiyah, the wife of Pharoah, Mary, the mother of Jesus, Khadijah, the first wife of Muhammad, and Fatima, his daughter are regarded as perfect role models, but the wives of Lot and Noah provide a warning of wrongdoing.

These women of the Qur'an are archetypes of virtue or vice, but they are, at least in one respect free agents, able to choose to obey both God and God-fearing husbands. On the other hand, they can oppose unrighteousness in their menfolk, striving to bring their men to the right path. Barbara Stowasser writes:

> Many of the Qur'an's women's stories bear the lesson that a woman's faith and righteousness depend on her will and decision, and that neither association with a godly man nor a sinner decides a woman's commitment to God. (Stowasser, 1994:21)

In addition, Muslim women do not have to deal with the stigma placed upon her Christian and Jewish counterparts who are blamed for the fall of 'mankind' through the actions of their primal ancestor.

Both Adam and Eve share the guilt of disobedience equally but neither did their weakness result in a permanent rift between God and
humanity. Human nature remains intact with no lasting defect. Both
Adam and Eve are restored to Allah's mercy and forgiveness and this
is celebrated by all Muslims who attend the annual Hajj in Makkah.
Human beings, regardless of gender, are weak and forgetful but
remain always in the vicinity of God's forgiveness. In addition, Islam
rejects celibacy and monasticism in favour of married life. Sexuality is
celebrated within the confines of marriage and there are Hadith
which proclaim the importance of foreplay and sexual fulfilment for
both men and women.

The formative years of Islam's beginnings provide a number of
high-profile women from amongst Muhammad's wives and descendants. Young Muslim women looking for female role models are
likely to cite Khadijah, the Prophet's first wife or A'isha, his youngest
wife. As economic change in the Muslim world brings more women
into full-time paid employment it challenges the prominent discourse
that curtails women to the domestic sphere. Increasing employment
opportunities bring women into the public domain and some will
achieve leadership roles in professions and government. The Qur'an
has little to say on women in such roles and the Hadith are ambiguous and contradictory. For every individual Hadith that positively
endorses female equality, including even their rights to sexual satisfaction, there will be another that denigrates women as weak and
foolish.

Fatima Mernissi, in an important and controversial book, *Women
and Islam*, looks at the most authoritative Hadith on women and
included in both al-Bukhari's and al-Muslim's collections. It states:
'those who entrust their affairs to a woman will never know prosperity'. The Hadith appears to be a damning indictment of women operating in public life and leadership roles traditionally assigned to men.
Mernissi does not challenge the content but used the traditional
Muslim science of contesting Hadith by analysing its *isnad* (chain of
transmission). She successfully rediscovers the cultural and political
context of the chain's main contributors and seeks out their hidden
motivations for taking up a misogynist position.

Certainly the content of the Hadith could be accused of appearing
to be critical of the Prophet himself who entrusted his affairs to
Khadijah, the older widow with children from two previous marriages, when he was appointed her caravan manager. Khadijah

traded in her own right and even asked Muhammad to become her husband. Yet there is a problem with pushing Khadijah forward as an example of female independence and leadership. Muslims like to believe that the position of women in pre-Islamic Arabia was one of atrocious exploitation and lack of rights only corrected by the implementation of revelation of Allah. Although Khadijah was the first to embrace Islam, her independence and assertiveness was achieved in the pre-Islamic period, suggesting that women were not as badly treated in pagan Arab society as Muslims would ideally like to believe.

After Khadijah's death the Prophet married several women, and certainly the young A'isha and Umm Salama were not passive women restricting themselves to the domestic sphere and blindly obedient to their husbands and menfolk. Mernissi points out that the Qur'an's revelation concerning women's equality with men, cited above, came about after Umm Salama asked the Prophet why the Qur'an did not speak about women as it did about men (Mernissi, 1991:118–119). Certainly this early period of Muslim history provides a number of examples of powerful women, some of whom opposed the Prophet from amongst his enemies in Makkah, once again challenging the Muslim myth of the oppressed 'pagan' woman.

After the Prophet's death, the young A'isha became a public figure of some authority. Known as Muhammad's favourite wife and called the 'Mother of believers', she was immensely respected and even led Muslim armies into battle during the first civil war, when she challenged Ali, the fourth caliph, over his failure to bring the murderers of the third caliph to justice. Yet, once again, A'isha is a double-edged sword as a role model. On the one hand, she provides an example of a woman leading the community but, on the other hand, she could be accused of causing the first division in the Muslim community and thus provides men with a justification to cite the Hadith's message concerning entrusting one's affairs to women.

Mernissi, like Stowasser, agrees that the independent assertive desert Arab woman of the early period gradually disappears as patriarchy reasserts itself into the expanding Muslim world. Mernissi believes that the turning point arrived with the dynastic absolutism of the Umayyad dynasty founded by Mu'awiya, which finally ended the Prophet's experiment in equality and destroyed the democratic tendencies of the desert Arabs. She shows that the women of Makkah who opposed the new religion, offered their own oaths of allegiance

to Muhammad and the new religion, taking part in the negotiations
for the city's future (Mernissi, 1991:191). She states:

> They were not going to accept the new religion without knowing
> exactly how it would improve their situation. The critical spirit
> on the part of these women towards the political leader remained
> alive and well during the first decades of Islam.
>
> (Mernissi, 1991:191)

The colonial period

The situation was to change rapidly in the nineteenth century. Once
again Muslim women were at the forefront of debates arising from
contact with other cultures. But this time the claim that Islam had provided new rights and freedoms to women was to find itself under
threat from the advances made in women's emancipation in Western
Europe. Although it might have been possible to argue that Muslim
societies had provided the impetus for new attitudes towards women
in the formative period of Islam, it now seemed that Western societies
had surpassed anything achieved by the Muslim world. Thus the
West became implicated in contemporary Muslim gender politics.

Muslim nations such as Turkey, Egypt and Iran were heavily
influenced by colonial self-definitions of the backwardness of the
East. Reformers in the Muslim world also insisted that there was a
need to transform their societies in the light of contact with the West,
usually through colonisation. As a part of colonial social reform,
women's rights, and their role within the family and beyond in the
spheres of education and employment, came under close scrutiny.
Often the focus was placed on dress codes and the traditional emphasis of the Muslim world to ascribe to her the domestic realm.
Challenged by the critique of 'backwardness', Muslim societies had to
begin to deal with modernity as defined by the West, where the idea
of 'being modern' became the dominant self-image of the Western
world.

Many Muslims were to respond to the challenge by embracing
Western values. Thus the West was embraced and translated in the
process of 'remaking women' (Abu-Lughod, 1998) leading to a number of Muslim women taking up the cause of emancipation in the
wake of their European sisters. The rediscovery of women's writings
in nations such as Egypt, which felt the full impact of colonisation,

demonstrate the influence of Western education and values. However, it should be noted that these voices of emancipation usually belonged to the literary and the educated and represented the elites of Muslim society. Certainly attitudes towards women began to change in the cultural meeting between Muslims and the West. Anne Roald argues that these placed into an oppositional framework the cultural patterns of the Arab world which were patriarchal and the Western cultural base fixated on equality (Roald, 2001:295). She notes that where Islam and the West closely encounter each other, the Qur'anic notion of *qiwama*, where men are in charge of women, becomes transformed into men having responsibility for women (Roald, 2001:297).

The post-colonial period

With regard to women's redefining of their roles in the Muslim world, the post-colonial period has been most marked by a repudiation of Western values and a reassertion of Islam's superiority. The idea of the 'backwardness of the East' and the advanced civilisation of the 'modern' West has been challenged by the new defenders of Islam. They have provided a critique of both Western values and their own societies which argues that Islam needs to be rediscovered and implemented in its original purity in order to resolve the current world crises and fuel a renaissance of the Muslim world.

In the twentieth century, Muslims have had to deal with the reality of their political decline and the prevailing threat of Western culture and secular consumer values that focus on the material acquisition of possessions as the means to human fulfilment. The more that Muslims have felt their own cultural and religious way of life threatened, the more the onus has been on women to protect and nurture 'authentic' Islamic values and behaviour. Stowasser writes in this context:

> As the images of female spiritual, mental and physical defectiveness were being replaced by those of female nurturing strength and the female's importance for the struggle for cultural survival, old Bible legends ceased to be meaningful. (Stowasser, 1994:23–24)

Although the modern era has resulted in a male-led discourse on the importance of women in maintaining Islamic values, women too have embraced the role, defending it staunchly as their own special domain, but this has led to considerable self-reflection on the rights of women within Islam and the search for truly Muslim role models of womanhood rather than the *isra'iliyyat* (the Jewish women of the biblical period mentioned in the Qur'an).

Thus the theme of women's weakness or women as a threat to men and society began to dominate scriptural-based arguments on gender. These attitudes continue to prevail in traditional Muslim societies which remain highly influenced by medieval interpretation of the Qur'an and Hadith. Thus today it is common for Muslim men to place the onus of maintaining the virtue and honour of the family and wider society on their womenfolk, punishing them sometimes for lapses that bring shame and dishonour. Leila Ahmed argues that the discussion of women in the contemporary period is about far wider issues of identity and power (Ahmed, 1992:2). Abu-Lughod supports this view, stating that 'in the post-colonial world women have become powerful symbols of identity and visions of society and the nation' (Abu-Lughod, 1998:3).

However, she goes on to question a number of preconceptions in contemporary Western feminist critique of the Muslim world. She argues that the opposition of tradition to modernity and the relegation of women's involvement to the domestic sphere in male conservatism is simplistic. She also challenges the common misconception that the emergence of women into the public sector is a recent phenomenon and a radical departure from tradition (Abu-Lughod, 1998:vii). Contemporary attempts by Muslim women to redefine their roles seem to be marked by two overriding concerns. The first is the question of how to be 'modern' but not to become 'Western'. The second is connected to the first, and seeks to find ways of transforming women's lives that are indigenous rather than borrowing from Western feminism. Gisella Webb notes that by this tactic they are able to counter the charge made by conservative elements in the Islamic community which attempt to silence their activities by labelling them as 'followers' of secular Western feminism (Webb, 2000:xiii).

Thus in the latter half of the twentieth century we saw the phenomenon of women moving away from aping the West's struggle for female emancipation to a renewed interest in Islam and the rights that it offered women in the seventh century. The central thrust of the argument was that Islam had liberated women but male patriarchy had refused to let go and grant the privileges given by God in the revelation. Thus contemporary Muslim culture was more the product of ethnic and cultural patterns than it was the manifestation of Islamic principles. Women began the process of textual interpretation providing feminist readings of the *shari'a,* and harnessing personal experience. The product was a renewed religious awareness and the emergence of Islamic feminism. Ziba Mir-Husseini notes that 'one paradoxical outcome of the rise of political Islam in the 1970s was that it helped to create an arena within which Muslim women could reconcile their faith with their new gender awareness' (Mir-Husseini, 1999:6).

One additional factor influencing gender relations was the arrival of significant Muslim communities in North America and Western Europe. The West was to feel the impact of this reverse movement of populations. Muslim women were to have much closer contact with their Western sisters and decide whether they wanted to follow the same road towards emancipation. On the other hand, as commented on by Anne Roald, non-Muslims, both male and female, were to react with hostility to the increasing Islamic presence in Europe (Roald, 2001).

The effect of this was a concentration on the negative aspects of female experience such as female circumcision, polygamy, divorce and child custody, segregation, Islamic female dress, and honour killings. Little attempt was made to distinguish the ethnic or cultural aspects of these from the teachings of the religion. Or to note that many Muslim feminists were also attacking the same practices as not part of Islam but rather various male patriarchal elements brought into Muslim cultures from elsewhere. For example, female circumcision, common throughout sub-Saharan Africa, although almost obligatory for Muslim women from that region is also as widespread amongst Christians or those who follow indigenous tribal religions. Although endorsed by Muslims, its practice is not mentioned in the formative sacred texts nor is it practised in other parts of the Muslim world. It is not in the scope of this chapter to provide detailed analysis of all the above-mentioned features. However, we will explore further both the phenomenon of veiling and female segregation as these seem to have become so closely identified with Islam itself and provide the frontline criticism that posits the 'backward' condition of Muslim women.

The discourse of the veil

There is no doubt that the veiling of women is the *bête noire* of Western feminists. Leila Ahmed argues that the fixation on the veil has come to represent the 'quintessential symbol of Islam' (Ahmed, 1992:14). The Western media will often represent Muslim women as veiled figures and stories of young girls barred from school because they insist upon conservative forms of Muslim dress make the headlines in the national press of Britain. In 2003, the French government banned the wearing of the veil in public institutions such as state schools, to the alarm of its Muslim community who saw it as an obvious act of religious discrimination. The action of the French can be seen as another example of the idea of the backwardness of the East as opposed to the enlightened attitudes of modern secular nations that extended into the twenty-first century from the colonial period.

However, the idea that all Muslim women are forced or pressured to wear the veil by either their fathers or husbands is far from the truth. Although there are some Muslim nations, usually where Islamic governments have been installed, that insist upon the veil in public, in most places it is not obligatory. The surprise is that whereas once Muslim women removed their veils as an indication of their emancipation, since the latter half of the twentieth century, many, especially amongst the young and educated, have adopted the veil as a symbol of resistance and cultural authenticity or as a conscious symbol of their Islamic identity. This process of re-veiling has also extended to older women who may have discarded it in their youth. Ahmed argues that the wearing of the veil may be a conscious rejection of the values of the West and even a conscious resistance to the former European colonial project of de-veiling (Ahmed, 1992:14), now continued in the post-colonial era and extended to Muslim minorities in Europe.

She also makes the point that Western feminists misunderstand the use of the veil and 'devalue local cultures by insisting that their own road to emancipation is the only one' (Ahmed, 1992:14). Certainly Muslim women who have consciously taken to wearing the veil often defend their decision by arguing that it provides freedom, dignity and an assertion that women are not only to be perceived as sexual objects or consumers of fashion. Yet such women should not necessarily be perceived as traditional. It is more than likely that they will be active in challenging their men's understandings of Islam and demanding their full rights as given by Qur'an, Hadith and *fiqh*. On the other hand they can be equally critical of the freedoms gained by their Western sisters, seeing them as exploited by consumer capitalism and reduced to the sexual objects of male lust.

However, the discourse of the veil is complex, and certainly many of the sometimes heated discussions that take place in the Arab world between the defenders of veiling and the secularists who advocate its removal have little to do with the rights of women, but are more concerned with scoring points in contemporary debates about the political futures of Muslim societies as Islamists and secularists oppose each other. In addition, any conception of the use of the veil must take into account Muslim women's own understandings of why they have adopted it or, alternatively, removed it.

In an investigation of the veil undertaken in Cairo, Sherifa Zuhur (1992) noted various reasons for adopting the veil. Whereas some informants spoke of the safeguarding of honour and status and the attitudes of men to unveiled women in public places, others referred to their embracing of their religious practices. Although some older women did defer to parental or male pressure, the younger ones asserted that their families reacted badly to them adopting the veil. For women under thirty the process of taking on the veil was seen as a symbol of change resulting from introspection and involving a personal moral decision. Some, however, were keen to point out the practicalities of wearing the veil in public and how it facilitated being in employment. Of interest to woman's movements was the assertion by most of the young women that the veil gave them feelings of sisterhood and solidarity.

The complexity of reasons for veiling was analysed and categorised by Yvonne Haddad in 1984. After investigating reasons for wearing the veil amongst women in Egypt, Jordan, Oman, Kuwait, and the United States, she classified her informants as follows:

Religious – an act of obedience to the will of God that often resulted from a religious experience that led to them 'reverting' to their faith.
Pyschological – an affirmation of authenticity and a rejection of Western norms which created a sense of peace or well-being.
Political – a sign of dissatisfaction with the existing political regime.
Revolutionary – identification with Islamic revivalist movements who affirm that Islamicisation of Muslim society is essential.
Economic – a sign of affluence.

Cultural – an affirmation of allegiance to chastity and modesty, of not
    being a sex object.
Demographic – a sign of being urbanised.
Practical – a means of reducing the amount spent on clothing.
Domestic – a way of keeping the males of the family contented.
    (Haddad, 1984)

However, most of these categories apply to women who have
returned to the veil, and therefore it is possible to add tradition or
compulsion to the list. Such field studies demonstrate that simplistic
conceptions of the veil by Western commentators on the condition of
Muslim women should be avoided. On the contrary, the veil may be
a symbol of freedom and emancipation to those that wear it.

Segregation of women

Most Muslim societies maintain segregation of males and females in
the public domain. This is also found in the mosque, which remains a
quintessential male domain. Many mosques do not permit women to
enter for public prayer and others provide a segregated space for
them. However, it is true that the majority of Muslim women pray at
home. This has led to a critique that women are denied the religious
equality which is central to the Qur'an's message and are not permitted to participate in the public ritual life of Islam. Some Muslim
women have argued that this was not the case at the time of
Muhammad where both men and women sat before the Prophet
when he preached.

   However, care needs to be taken with this analysis of the participation of women. Not only will it vary from society to society, but there
is also evidence to suggest that where Islamicisation takes place there
is more debate on the rights of women in the religious domain. Far
more fieldwork needs to be carried out in individual Muslim communities by those with sufficient access to discover the reality. In one
such study of Iranian women carried out by Zahra Kamalkhani it was
noted that whilst women continue to maintain the integrity of the
household, they simultaneously took part in wider social activities
and participated in their own religious meetings where men were
denied access (Kamalkhani, 1998).

   Khamalkhani investigated through participant observation the traditional *rowzah*, arranged either in a woman's home or a religiously

endowed building. Here women gather together, either through neighbourhood networks or through kin and friendship circles, to perform elaborate rituals which include night-vigils, and recitals of specific chapters from the Qur'an, to initiate vows for the protection of their families that might include promises to visit a sacred site or sponsor a religious event (Khamalkhani, 1998:14).

The *rowzah* is a merciful and votive act performed for and by women which contributes to the wider religious community and family unity, and reflects the personal piety of the women who attend. Commentary on the Qur'an and courses on the rules of pollution and purity are provided by a network of female preachers and although family affairs dominate the vows, Khamalkhani notes that they are linked to the wider political world of Iran through their performance on evocative public events such as the death of Ali, the martyrdom of Hussain, or on the occasion of the illness of Ayatollah Khomeini. Gatherings of up to a hundred women were common all over Iran in *rowzahs* that took place during the fast of Ramadan (Khamalkhani, 1998:14).

Such studies challenge the classic conception by Western feminists that the home is the sole institution for engagement in religious life by Muslim women. Khamalkhani argues that their studies fail to take into account the 'Islamic core and organisational patterns of the Muslim domestic arena' and suffer from a bias in that they are informed by studies of mosques and theological schools (Khamalkhani, 1998:7). There need to be far more studies carried out in order to achieve an understanding of the involvement of women in Islamic religion and practices in Muslim societies. Khamalkhani concludes that such studies show that women are no less concerned than men with religious performance, piety and duties (Khamalkhani, 1998:7).

Notes of warning for the unwary

Following this condensed overview of the challenges to male and female interpretations of the final revelation, believed by Muslims to have been given by Allah for the benefit of all humanity, it is important to post a warning to anyone interested in the position of Muslim women. The traveller in their domain, whether intellectually or emotionally stimulated, needs to beware the errors of essentialising the Muslim female. We are, I would argue, infiltrated by media stereotypes of Muslim women that need to be recognised, confronted and expunged from our consciousness. For not only is 'woman' problematic but so is the label 'Muslim' itself.

Khan argues that the term 'Muslim' needs to be problematised, in that we need to remind ourselves of 'the power that the term "Muslim" holds in our imaginations' and that we need to recognise both the wide variety that is contained in the term 'Muslim women' and the increasing fluidity of cultural expressions of Muslim belonging (Khan, 1998:465). Faizia Ahmad argues that: 'Historical and contemporary encounters continue to embody Muslim women through cultural and religious frameworks as essentialised oppressed figures of victimhood and despair' (Ahmad, 2003:43).

The danger of essentialising will remain as long as the Western 'gaze' continues to focus on *hijab* and 'arranged marriages' projecting onto Muslim women an image of passivity and powerlessness, thus severely limiting the scope of debate. It may surprise many interested in the subject that neither of these two high visibility issues are high on the agenda of contemporary Muslim female liberation discourse. The reasons for a Muslim female to wear a head covering are varied. It may be tradition, simply the way that it is done and unquestioned; it may be practicality; it may be religious or cultural reasons; or it may be because her family insist upon it. On the other hand, she may have decided to cover herself from her own conscious decision, independent of her family's views and they may even disapprove of her action. If so, she may intensely defend her reasons for doing so as liberating not binding. These arguments need to be seriously assessed as they constitute the attitudes of millions of young Muslim women around the world who are voluntarily taking up Muslim dress codes and contributing in their own unique way to the phenomenon known as 'Islamicisation'.

Arranged marriages are rarely a major issue for unmarried women although forced marriages do constitute a problem in places where they continue to thrive. As long as young women and men are provided the opportunity of refusal or acceptance they generally appear happy with the arrangements by their parents, even in Western minority communities. In fact, they remain critical of the imperfections that they perceive in romantic liaisons as motivation for marriage. Once again cultural differences have to be acknowledged; arranged marriages are far more likely to impact on the Muslims of

South Asia than, for example, the younger generation of Palestinians whose marriages are rarely arranged these days.

The other minefield to be avoided is the trap of setting ourselves up has an elite voice, somehow more knowledgeable or enlightened than Muslim women, who will need our assistance to liberate themselves from the innate patriarchal structures of their religion and culture. This raises wider questions discussed previously concerning who claims ownership of feminism itself. Western feminists need to be careful that they do not place themselves in the position of protectors and liberators of their silent but suffering Muslim sisters. In this regard, the Algerian-born sociologist, Marnia Lazreg argues that the Western feminist emancipatory project has failed as it continues to impose one social standard on to another (Lazreg, 1988:96). She powerfully asserts that it is essential to respect the rights of women to express their lives through their own constructs.

These two cautionary notes are particularly important in Western Europe and North America where migration has created significant Muslim communities contributing to an official ethos of multiculturalism. The term 'Muslim women' is in itself a problem label because of the dangers of essentialising, but the reality of having living Muslim women appear under our gaze can lead to them being categorised as familiar strangers. Familiarity is created by their everyday presence but it then becomes very easy to create categories from the immediate impact of appearance. What is she wearing? What is her skin colour? What language is she speaking? And, after 9/11, is she dangerous? These superficial identity markers can easily lead us towards an essentialised view. It is far more likely, with some rare exceptions, that the Muslim woman will remain a stranger to us. For me, this is certainly true, for although I have extensive contacts with Muslims as valued friends and colleagues, as a man I am segregated from most Muslim women. However, segregation does not equate to discrimination, although it could contribute to it.

Conclusion

For many Muslim women it is not rejection of Islam that leads to their liberation but rather an attempt to restore the rights given to them at Islam's inception, affirmed by the revelation and lived out in practice by the early generation of Muslim women. However, although many Muslims may assert that the Qur'an provided rights for women that were not achieved by Western women until many centuries later, many Western feminists will point out that the newly achieved rights and freedoms of the twentieth century have far surpassed anything that the original Muslims could have conceived. Although it is true that Islam provided rights and duties to women that may have improved their lot in the Middle East, they cannot be compared with the emancipation achieved since the nineteenth century in the West. Many Muslim women may not be satisfied merely with a return to the rights of the Makkan and Madinan period.

There is also an ironical contradiction in the attempt to reclaim the rights and freedoms of the first generation of Muslim women. In doing so, those women who choose to follow their religion seriously, but make the distinction between the Islam practised by the first generation, believed to be unsullied and true to the revelation, and that of those who came after, corrupted by innovation created by contact with other cultures, find themselves allies to various revivalist and reform movements that also believe the same narrative but applied wider than the field of women's rights. Often these are the very same movements who seek to create Islamic states based on complete application of Muslim religious law or even wage *jihad* against the West. Thus these women find their natural allies amongst the men of the twentieth-century revivalist movements who may well champion their right to wear the *hijab* but not necessarily their right to leadership and independence. In addition, the forces of re-Islamicisation often lack tolerance for pluralism and have an intolerance for opposition that could cause problems for the diversity of opinion amongst Muslim women. In Fatima Mernissi's terms, 'the security will never return to the city'. The veil, she asserts, intended to protect them from violence in the street, would need to be displayed everywhere (Mernissi, 1991:191).

As in the West, the future of women's rights will be closely tied to economic fluctuations, education and employment opportunities. In this respect, the traditional Islamic segregation of women can be advantageous as it provides unique employment opportunities for women such as teachers in girl's schools and female doctors and nurses. Here the veil, the symbol of the West's understanding of Islam as repressive to women and restricting her freedoms, where men remain imbedded in traditional values, can come into play as a means to greater mobility.

It has been suggested in this chapter that Islam has not been concerned for the rights of women *per se* but rather has looked out to the women of other cultures or religions that surrounded Muslims, whether pre-Islamic tribal societies, the women of Persia and Byzantine or more recently the emancipated women of the West. If this is true, then the decisions regarding Muslim women have been made for her by men immersed in patriarchal attitudes or safeguarding their own honour and status. A number of authors have argued that the emphasis on women in the twentieth century has more to do with the political environment in colonial and post-colonial periods than with a genuine concern for women themselves. As stated by Leila Ahmed:

> In the modern period, crucial moments in the re-articulation and further elaboration of issues of women and gender in Middle Eastern Muslim societies occurred under the impact of colonialism and in the socio-political turmoil that followed and, indeed, persists to our own day. (Ahmed, 1992:3)

Certainly the renewed interest in Islam and the emergence of Islamic feminism has to be seen in the light of Muslim attitudes towards the West and an attempt to reassert the supremacy of God's revelation over secular values. In such an environment, the earlier attempts by women to liberate themselves by adopting the mores of Western culture become suspect. As stated by Mai Yamani:

> Liberal Westernised attempts at reforms by women are immediately undermined because they are not speaking the language of the nation and are easily suppressed by the authorities. However, those who adopt the newly developed, stricter veil and arm themselves with knowledge of Islamic avenues to power, find themselves better able to confront local obstacles to the advancement of women. (Yamani, 1996:14)

However, it should be noted that Islamic feminism does not show a united face to the world. There are competing variations to be noted. On the other hand, there remain prominent voices who are not convinced of the claim that Islam is liberating. Some question the conventional idea that Islam even improved the status of women in the formative period. Embarking on a study of the literature of the pre-Islamic period, they argue that the Jewish examples found in the

Qur'an were not exceptions but were typical of strong Semitic women before the advent of Islam. The icons of the Islamic feminists, Khadijah and A'isha, were independent not because of a change in attitudes created by the new religion, but because they were permitted to be that way by matriarchal values that pre-existed Islam.

Others have suggested that the Qur'an did little to challenge the prevailing attitudes that women should be under the protection of men. As argued by Ghada Karmi, they were turned into non-adults (Karmi, 1996). Although these women may remain true to the practice of their religion, they demand that the Qur'an should be studied in its historical and social context. More conservative voices amongst women insist that the Qur'an must be liberating as it is from God, and persist in the traditional view that some inequalities between men and women are justified as each contains distinct differences attributed to their respective natures. Even though this is a fact, they argue, women still need to insist upon the spiritual and religious equality given to them by the revelation.

These discussions and differences of opinion are no less than the shades of difference that exist among Western women but we need more study of the actual conditions of Muslim women to demonstrate the variety of experience in the Muslim world and help to overcome the stereotypes existing in the West. In the words of Gisella Webb, 'May Muslim women speak for themselves please?' (Webb, 2000).

GLOSSARY OF TERMS

Abd	A slave or servant of God; one who worships, the ideal of the Muslim.
Adab	Ideal behaviour or customary practice used by Sufis to describe the way in which *murids* model themselves on their *shaikh*. It is also used to describe practices unique to the respective *tariqa*.
Adhan	The call to prayer that takes place five times daily usually from the minaret of the mosque.
Ahl al- Bait (Bayt)	The household of the Prophet; his family members, believed by Shi'a Muslims to have special spiritual status inherited through the bloodline.
Ahl al-Kitab	People of the Book; a term used for communities of God, such as Jews and Christians who also received a written revelation or scriptural tradition.
Ahl al-Suffa	People of the Bench or Porch who sat in the entrance of the first mosque and are regarded by Sufis as their fore-runners.
Ahl al-Tawhid	A title for Islam – the way of unity.
Ahwal	States of being given to the devout Sufi as a gift from Allah.
Alim	Singular of *ulema*, a learned man, usually used for a religious scholar or graduate of a *madrasa*.
Ana'l Haqq	'I am the Truth'. The infamous statement made by Al-Hallaj which led to his martyrdom.
Aqida	Belief or set of doctrines.
Asma al-Rijal	Biographies of the narrators of the Hadith written to establish their reliability.
Awliya	A 'friend of Allah' usually used for a Sufi or deeply spiritual Muslim who has attained mystical proximity to God.
Ayat	Verses of the Qur'an.
Ayatollah	Highly ranked Shi'a clerics who interpret the Qur'an and the Hadith, represent the Hidden Imam and study jurisprudence.
Bab	Historical Shi'a figures believed to be mystical interme-diaries between the people and the Imam.

Bai'at	Oath of allegiance taken on the hand of a *shaikh* when becoming a *murid*.
Baqa	Existence in God.
Baraka	The power to bless given to an *awliya* by Allah. It can be received through physical contact or prayer at a shrine. The tomb or sacred relics may also be endowed with *baraka*.
Bida	An illegal innovation in religion.
Chaddar	The clothes traditionally placed over the tomb of a Sufi in South Asia.
Dar al-Harb	Territory in opposition to Islam; non-Muslim territory.
Dar al-Islam	Territory where Islam is established.
Dawa/Dawah	Proselytising of Islam to both Muslims and non-Muslims.
Dhikr	The remembrance of Allah usually referred to as the continuous and rhythmic repetition of God's names.
Din	Revealed religion that constitutes a comprehensive, all-inclusive way of life.
Din al-Fitra	The religion closest to innate human nature; an appellation for Islam.
Djinn	Creatures made of the element of fire mentioned in the Qur'an. They also have freewill as humans.
Du'a	Prayer of supplication which often uses an intercessor or invokes a blessing. Any prayer which is not *salat*.
Dunya	The world; often used by Muslims to indicate being lost in the world; as opposition to a life where one practises the *din*.
Faiz	The divine light that flows through a living saint and can transform those who come into contact.
Fana	Annihilation or complete loss of self.
Fana fi'l Haqq	Union with the ultimate reality.
(Al-)Fatiha	The opening *sura* of the Qur'an.
Fatwa	Legal opinion concerning an aspect of Islamic law issued by an *alim*.
Fiqh	Jurisprudence; the science of interpreting *shari'a*.
Fitra	Essential human nature or goodness. The natural state of human beings which is in harmony with God's will.
Fuqaha	Shi'a clerics.
Ghayba	The belief of Shi'a Muslims that the last Imam was taken to a place of concealment by God (occultation), from where he will return at the last days.
Hadd	A branch of the *shari'a* concerned with criminal law.
Hadith	Report of the sayings or deeds of the Prophet passed on

	by his Companions. The Hadith collections are second only to the Qur'an as a source of authority.
Hadith al-Qudsi	The most authoritative Hadith believed to have been transmitted directly to Muhammad by Allah.
Hajj	Annual pilgrimage to Makkah that every Muslim should attempt to go on at least once in a life. One of the five pillars of Islam.
Halal	Permitted or allowed by God.
Hanbali	School of Islamic jurisprudence founded by Ahmad Ibn Hanbal (d.150).
Hanifa	School of Islamic jurisprudence founded by Abu Hanafi (d.767).
(al-) Haqq	The Truth, or ultimate reality; one of the names of God.
Haram	Forbidden by God.
Hijab	The covering of the head by Muslim women.
Hijra	The emigration of Muhammad and the first Muslims from Makkah to Medina in 622CE which marks the first year of the Muslim calendar.
Hukm	A divine command.
Ihsan	The perfection of character sought by a devout Muslim.
Ijma	The consensus of the community; a mechanism used in jurisprudence to validate legal decisions.
Ijtahad nabawi	The interpretation of the Qu'ran carried out by Muhammad; the prototype for *ijtihad*.
Ijtihad	Individual scholarly inquiry that goes back to direct interpretation of Qur'an and Sunna rather than *fiqh*.
Ilm al-tasawwuf	The path of self-purification.
Imam	Leader of the community; title given to the founders of the four schools of law; a leader of ritual prayers; an honorific for a religious scholar; used by the Shi'a as a title for the spiritual successors of Ali.
Iman	Faith.
Isa	Jesus, one of the foremost prophets of God.
Islah	Return to the ways of God; the exhortation of the messengers; used by contemporary reformist movements as a term to describe the re-embracing of religion.
Islam	Submission to God.
Isnad	The chain of transmission of the Hadith back to the Prophet.
Istighatha	Seeking assistance or intercession from the Prophet.
Isnad	The part of an Hadith that supplies the chain of narration back to Muhammad.
Isra'iliyyat	The Hebrew figures mentioned in the Qur'an.

Ittihad	Literal oneness with God.
Jahiliya	The time of ignorance first used to describe pre-Islamic Arabia.
Ja'iz	Actions to which Allah is indifferent and is not concerned if they are performed or not.
Jibreel	The angel Gabriel, the messenger of God to the Prophets.
Jihad	Holy war or the struggle to establish Islam. Also used to describe self-purification or the individual effort required to live a righteous or devout life.
Jihad Akbar	The greater *jihad* which refers to the struggle to establish Islam or purify the self.
Jihad Asghar	*Jihad* as holy war.
Ka'aba	The cube-shaped shrine at Makkah and the spatial focus for all Muslims in prayer; variously believed to have been created by Abraham or Adam for the worship of God.
Kalam	Islamic theology.
Karamat	Supernatural power from Allah that enables a Muslim saint to perform miracles.
Khalifa	Arabic term denoting the notion of deputy or successor. Formerly used for the rulers of the Muslim community. During the rapid growth of the community into an empire, the term came to mean imperial sovereignty combining both political and religious authority. It is also used in Sufism to denote authority to teach and initiate conferred on a *murid* by his master. Human beings are also God's *khalifa* or representatives on earth.
La illaha illa'Llah	The first part of the confession of faith meaning that 'there is no god but God' and the most common form of *dhikr*.
Madhhab	The four Muslim schools of law.
Madrasa	A theological college where Muslims study to become members of the *ulema*.
Mahdi	The figure who will lead the Muslims to victory at the endtime. In Shi'a Islam he is the Hidden Imam who will return at that time.
Mahzur	Actions which are prohibited and it is forbidden to indulge in them.
Majalis	Assemblies of mourning; the gatherings of Shi'a Muslims to commemorate the martyrdom of Hussain, grandson of Muhammad.
Makruh	Actions which Allah frowns upon but are not forbidden.

Maliki	One of the four orthodox schools of law in Sunni Islam founded by Malik ibn Annas (d.179).
Mandub	Actions which are recommended and whose performance brings reward but omission is not punished.
Maqamat	The stages or disciplines through which a Sufi is guided by his or her teacher.
Ma'rifat	Gnosis or experiential knowledge of God.
Masjid	A place of ritual prostration; mosque.
Matn	The part of a Hadith which is the content; the saying or deed of the Prophet as opposed to the chain of narration.
Mazar	The tomb of a prophet, saint or Companion of the Prophet.
Mehndi	The traditional South Asian custom to decorate the hands of women at weddings.
Minaret	The towers traditionally placed on a mosque and used to call the faithful to prayer.
Minbar	The raised platform or seat in a mosque used by the *imam* for the sermon delivered at Friday prayers.
Mi'raj	The Night Journey; the mystical elevation of the Prophet to the presence of God which took place after his removal to Jerusalem.
Muharrum	The religious occasion that marks the martyrdom of Hussain, the grandson of the Prophet at Kerbala. It is the major religious event for Shi'a Muslims but is also celebrated by Sunni Muslims in the subcontinent.
Mujaddid	A devout Muslim who comes every century to renew the faith.
Mujahid	Those who participate in *jihad*.
Mujtahid	A qualified Muslim jurist; one able to undertake *ijtihad*.
Murid	The followers of a Sufi spiritual leader.
Musalla	The covered area of the *masjid* (mosque), usually over the *qiblah*.
Nafs	The lower self or ego; the part of the human nature that needs to be purified and brought into submission to God.
Nur	The light of Allah or the light of Muhammad.
Nur-i Muhammad-i	The primordial 'Muhammad' which emanated from Allah's light.
Pir	See *shaikh*. Urdu for a Sufi teacher.
Purdah	The segregation and seclusion of women.
Qibla(h)	The direction to Makkah marked in the mosque by an alcove or niche in the wall. All Muslims will face in this direction in prayer.

Qiyas	The use of analogical reasoning to authenticate re-interpretations of *shari'a*.
Qubbah	See *Mazar*.
Qur'an	The sacred scripture of Muslims. The final and complete revelation of Allah.
Qurban	The ritual sacrifice of goats or sheep.
Qutb	The axis or pole. The title given to the Sufi master at the peak of the spiritual hierarchy of saints.
Qutba	The weekly sermon delivered by the *imam* that takes place at the Friday prayers.
Ramadan	The month-long fast from the hours of sunrise to sunset maintained in the month of the same name; the most sacred period for Muslims when the Qur'an was revealed for the first time to Muhammad; one of the five pillars of Islam.
Razi'a	Pre-Islamic raids on caravans by desert tribes.
Rowzah	An Iranian religious gathering of women.
Safa	Purity.
Sajjada Nashin	Family descendants of a deceased Sufi who often maintain the shrine centre.
Salaf as-Salih	The pious ancestors usually used to refer to the first three generations of Muslims.
Salat	The five times daily ritual prayer; one of the five pillars of Islam.
Shafa'a	Petitionary prayer that calls for the intercession of a saint or prophet.
Shafi'i	One of the four orthodox schools of law in Sunni Islam founded by Muhammad ibn Idris al-Shafi'i (d.216).
Shahada(h)	The confession of faith 'there is no god but God; and Muhammad is His messenger'; the first of the five pillars of Islam and the essential requirement to be a Muslim.
Shahid	A martyr.
Shaikh	The title given to a Sufi teacher.
Shari'a(h)	The principles and application of Muslim law, including religious obligations.
Shi'a	The party of Ali; the second largest group of Muslims. They believe that Ali and his direct descendants are the rightful heirs to Muhammad's religious authority.
Shirk	Idolatry; putting another before God's supremacy.
Silsila(h)	The chain of authority back to Muhammad that supplies authenticity to a *tariqa*.
Sira	Early biographies of Muhammad.
Sufi	One who practises *tasawwuf*.

Sunna	'Custom' as in the traditions of the Prophet and the second source of religious authority for Sunni Muslims.
Sunni	One who follows *Sunna*; also used as a title for the numerically dominant group of Muslims who have accepted the caliphate of Abu Bakr.
Sura	A chapter of the Qur'an.
Tajdid	The process of the renewal of Islam so that it does not lose the initial message of God.
Tamkin	Cessation of self.
Tanzil	The sending down of the Qur'an.
(Al-)Tanzil	One of the names of God that refers to his transcendence or distance.
Taqiya	The permitted practice of Shi'a Muslims to hide their faith in times of persecution.
Taqlid	Blind imitation of the *ulema* without self-reflection.
Taqwa	A state of reverence towards God.
Tariqa (Tarikat)	The various organised or collective disciplines for the practice of *tasawwuf*; Sufi orders.
Tasawwuf	The collective title used both for the schools and the science of purification of the self.
(Al-)Tashbil	One of the names of God that refers to his closeness or immanence.
Tasliya	Prayers that call down blessings on Muhammad and his family.
Tawhid	The central Islamic doctrine of the unity and uniqueness of Allah.
Tawassul	A means to worship or get closer to Allah.
Tazkiyat al-Nafs	Purification of the self.
Ulema	A body of religious scholars or Muslim clerics; plural of *alim*.
Umma(h)	The worldwide community of Muslims.
Urf	Local custom; traditions and practices of non-Muslim peoples that do not contradict the law of Islam.
Urs	The celebration commemorating a Sufi saint, usually held on his or her death-day.
Usul al-Fiqh	The science or study of *fiqh*.
Velayat-i faqih	The government by jurisprudence established in Iran by Ayatollah Khomeini.
Wahdat al-Wujud	The Oneness or unity of Being.
Wajib	Obligatory acts which Allah has commanded and where failure to follow leads to punishment in the afterlife.
Watan	The nation state, fatherland or motherland.
Wataniyyah	Patriotism or loyalty to the homeland.

Wudu (wuzu)	The purificatory rite of washing that precedes prayer.
(Al-)Wujud	The truth of existence; one of the names of God.
Yaqin	Certainty of Allah's existence; the highest state of awareness.
Zakat	One of the five obligatory duties of Muslims to give charity to the poor as a fixed percentage of surplus income.

BIBLIOGRAPHY

Abbasi, Muhammad, *Protestant Islam*. http://www.masud.co.uk/ISLAM/misc/pislam.htm.

Abu-Lughod, Lila (1998), *Remaking Woman: Feminism and Modernity in the Middle-East*. Princeton: Princeton University Press.

Adams, Charles (1983), 'Mawdudi and the Islamic State' in *Voices of Resurgent Islam*, Esposito, John (ed.). New York: Oxford University Press.

Adams, Charles (1985), 'Foreword' in *Approaches to Islam in Religious Studies*, Martin, Richard (ed). Tucson: the University of Arizona Press.

Ahmad, Fauzia (2003), '"Still in Progress?" – Methodological Dilemmas, Tensions and Contradictions in Theorizing South Asian Muslim Women' in *South Asian Women in the Diaspora*, Purwar, Nirmal and Raghuram, Parvati (eds). Oxford: Berg.

Ahmad, Khurshid and Ansari, Zafar (1979), *Islamic Perspectives*. Leicester: The Islamic Foundation.

Ahmed, A. (1992), *Postmodernism and Islam: Predicament and Promise*. London: Routledge.

Ahmed, Ishtiaq (1987), *The Concept of an Islamic State – An Analysis of the Ideological Controversy in Pakistan*. London: Francis Pinter.

Ahmed, Leila (1992), *Women and Gender in Islam*. Newhaven: Yale University Press.

Allen, Christopher (8–10 May 2003), 'Undoing Proximity: the Impact of the Local-Global Nexus on Perceptions of Muslims in Britain'. Paper given at the European Association for the Study of Religions 3rd Congress, *The Globalisation and Localisation of Religion*, Bergen, Norway.

Ansari, Humayun (2004), The *Infidel Within: Muslims in Britain since 1800*. London: Hurst & Co.

Arberry, A. J. (1956), *Sufism*. London: George Allen & Unwin.

Armstrong, Karen (24 December 2001), 'The Roots of Islamic Fundamentalism', *These Times*.

Barker, M. (1981), *The New Racism*. London: Junction Books.

Baruma, Ian (21 May 2002), 'To say that Jihadis are a threat is not Islamophobic', *Guardian*.

Bauman, Z. (1993), 'Modernity' in *The Oxford Companion to the Politics of the World*, Kriegar, Joel (ed.). Oxford: Oxford University Press.

Behrend, T. (2003), *Reading Past the Myth: Public Teachings of Abu Bakar Ba'asyir*. http://www.arts.auckland.ac.nz/asia/tbehrend/radical-islam.htm.

Bodman, H. and Tohidi, Nayereh (eds) (1998), 'Introduction' in *Women in Muslim Societies*. Colorado: Lynne Reinner.

Brown, Daniel (2004), *A New Introduction to Islam*. Oxford: Blackwell.

Caplan, Lionel (1987), *Studies in Religious Fundamentalism*. London: MacMillan.

Cascioni, Dominic (29 September 2001), 'Pledge to Wipe Out Islamophobia', BBC News Online Bulletin.

Chishti, Saadia (2003), 'Fitra: An Islamic Model for Humans and the Environment' in *Islam and Ecology*, Foltz, R., Denny, F. and Baharuddin, Azizan (eds). Massachusetts: Harvard University Press.

Clarke, J. (1997), *Oriental Enlightenment: The Encounter between Asian and Western Thought*. London: Routledge.

Conway, Gordon (November 1997), 'Islamophobia', *Bulletin: the University of Sussex Newsletter*, No.7.

Cragg, Kenneth (1985), *Jesus and the Muslim*. Oxford: Oneworld Publications.

Cragg, Kenneth (1987), *Islam and the Muslim*. Milton Keynes: Open University Press.

Cummins, Will (25 July 2004), 'Muslims are a threat to our way of life', *Sunday Telegraph*.

Dabashi, Hamid (1989), *Authority in Islam*. New Jersey: Transactions Publishers.

Dalrymple, William (14 June 2004), 'Saudi Arabia Created The Monster Now Devouring It', *Guardian*.

Daniel, Norman (1993, 2nd ed.), *Islam and the West: The Making of an Image*. Oxford: Oneworld Publications.

Denny, Frederick, 'Islamic Ritual', in *Approaches to Islam*, Martin, Richard (ed.). Tucson: University of Arizona Press.

Dizaei, Ali (20 August, 2004), 'Force for Change',. *Guardian*.

Dodd, Vikram (9 August 2004), 'Muslims put faith in written word to fight prejudice', *Guardian*.

Doi, Abdur (1984), *Shari'a: The Islamic Law*. London: Ta-Ha Publishers.

Donald, J. and Rattanasi, A. (1992), *Race, Culture and Difference*. London: Sage.

Donohue, John and Esposito, John (eds) (1982), *Islam in Transmission*. Oxford: Oxford University Press.

Doward, Jamie and Hinsliff, Gaby (30 May 2004), 'British Hostility to Muslims could Trigger Riots', *Observer*.

Eade, John and Sallnow, Michael (1991), 'Introduction' in *Contesting the Sacred: The Anthropology of Christian Pilgrimage*. London: Routledge.

Esposito, John (1988), *Islam – The Straight Path*. Oxford: Oxford University Press.

Esposito, John (1999), *The Islamic Threat: Myth or Reality*. Oxford: Oxford University Press.

Esposito, John (2002a), *Unholy War: Terror in the Name of Islam*. Oxford: Oxford University Press.

Esposito, John (2002b), 'Islam and Secularism in the Twenty-First Century' in *Islam and Secularism in the Middle-East*. Esposito, John and Tamimi, Azzam (eds). London: Hurst & Co.

Esposito, John (ed.) (2003a), 'Mosque' in *Oxford Dictionary of Islam, Oxford Reference Online*. Oxford: Oxford University Press.

Esposito, John (ed.) (2003b), 'Shrine' in *Oxford Dictionary of Islam, Oxford Reference Online*. Oxford: Oxford University Press.

Esposito, John (ed.) (2003c), 'Tawhid', *Oxford Dictionary of Islam, Oxford Reference Online*. Oxford: Oxford University Press.

Geaves, Ron (1996), *Sectarian Influences within Islam in Britain*. Community Religions Project Monograph Series. Leeds: University of Leeds.

Geaves, Ron (1999), 'Islam and Conscience' in *Conscience in the World Religions*, Hoose, Jane (ed.). Canterbury: Gracewing.

Geaves, Ron (2000), *The Sufis of Britain*. Cardiff: Cardiff Academic Press.

Gibb, Hamilton (1942), *Modern Trends in Islam*. Chicago: University of Chicago Press.

Gibb, Hamilton (April 1963), 'The Community in Islamic History', *The American Philosophical Society Proceedings*. Vol.107, No.2.

Gimaret, D. (2001), 'Tawhid' in *Encyclopaedia of Islam* CD-Rom Edition v.1.1. Leiden: Koninklijke Brill NV.

Goldziher, I. (1890), *Muhammedanische Studien, Vol. II*. Halle.

Green, Nile (2003), 'Migrant Sufis and Sacred Space in South Asian Islam', *Contemporary South Asia*, 12 (4): 493–509.

Haddad, Yvonne (1983), 'Sayyid Qutb: Idealogue of Islamic Revival' in *Voices of Resurgent Islam*, Esposito, John (ed.). New York: Oxford University Press.

Haddad, Yvonne (1984), 'Islam, Women and Revolution in Twentieth-Century Arab Thought', *The Muslim World*, Vol.74, nos 3–4.

Haddad, Yvonne and Esposito, John (eds) (1998), *Islam, Gender and Social Change*. Oxford: Oxford University Press.

Haddad, Yvonne (2004), 'The Shaping of a Moderate North American Islam: Between "Mufti" Bush and "Ayatollah" Ashcroft' in *Islam and the West Post 9/11*, Geaves, R., Gabriel T., Haddad, Y. and Smith J. (eds). Aldershot: Ashgate.

Hadden, J. K. and Schupe, A. D. (1989), *Secularisation and Fundamentalism Reconsidered*. New York: New Era Books.

Haeri, S. F. (1995), *The Elements of Sufism*. Shaftesbury: Element Books.

Haqq, Nomanhul S. (2003), 'Islam and Ecology: Towards Retrieval and Reconstruction' in *Islam and Ecology*, Foltz, R., Denny, F. and Baharuddin, Azizan (eds). Massachusetts: Harvard University Press.

Harris, Harriet (2001), 'How Helpful is the Term "Fundamentalist"?' in *Fundamentalisms*, Partridge, Christopher (ed.). Carlisle: Paternoster Press.

Heeren, F. (1976), *Women in Islam*. Leicester: The Islamic Foundation.

Herbst, Philip (2003), *Talking Terrorism: A Dictionary of the Loaded Language of Political Violence*. Westport, Connecticut; London: Greenwood Press.

Hitti, Philip (1970), *The History of the Arabs*. London: Macmillan.

Hourani, George (1985), *Reason and Tradition in Islamic Ethics*. Cambridge: Cambridge University Press.

Huband, Mark (1995), *Warriors of the Prophet*. Colorado: Westview Press.

Huntingdon, Samuel (2002), The *Clash of Civilisations and the Remaking of World Order*. London: Free Press.

Hussain, Dilwar (2004), 'The Impact of 9/11 on British Muslim Identity' in *Islam and the West Post 9/11*, Geaves, R., Gabriel T., Haddad, Y. and Smith J. (eds). Aldershot: Ashgate.

Kabbani, Shaykh Muhammad Hisham (1998), *Encyclopedia of Islamic Doctrine, Vols I-VII*. Chicago: Kazi Publications.

Kamalkhani, Zahra (1998), *Women's Islam*. London: Kegan Paul International.

Kandiyoti, Deniz (1992), 'Women, Islam and the State: A Comparative Approach' in *Comparing Muslim Societies: Knowledge and the State in a World Civilization*, Cole, J. (ed.). Ann Arbor: University of Michigan Press.

Karmi, Ghada (1992), 'Women, Islam and Patriarchalism' in Yamani, Mai (ed.). *Feminism and Islam* (1996). Reading: Ithaca.

Kepel, Gilles (2002), *Jihad: The Trail of Political Islam*. Massachusetts: Harvard University Press.

Khalid, Fazlun (2003), 'Islam, Ecology, and Modernity: An Islamic Critique of the Root Causes of Environmental Degradation' in *Islam and Ecology*, Foltz, R., Denny, F. and Baharuddin, Azizan (eds). Massachusetts: Harvard University Press.

Khan, S. (1998), 'Muslim Women; Negotiations in the Third Space', *Signs: Journal of Women and Culture in Society*, 23(2): 463–494.

Lambton, A. K. S. (1989), *Islamic Fundamentalism*. London: Royal Asiatic Society.

Llewellyn, Othman Abd ar-Rahman (2003), 'The Basis for a Discipline of Islamic Environmental Law' in *Islam and Ecology*, Foltz, R., Denny, F. and Baharuddin, Azizan (eds). Massachusetts: Harvard University Press.

Khan, Ibrahim (1978), 'Muhammad as Object and Subject', *Studies in Religion*, 7:4.

Khomeini, Imam (1985), *Islam and Revolution*, tr. Hamid Algar. London: KPI.

King, Richard (1999), *Orientalism and Religion*. London: Routledge.

Lawrence, Bruce (1998), *Shattering the Myth: Islam Beyond Violence*. Princeton: Princeton University Press.

Lazreg, Marnia (Spring 1988), 'Feminism and Difference: The Perils of Writing as a Woman on Women in Algeria', *Feminist Studies*, 14:81–107.

Ling, Martin (1983), *Muhammad: His Life Based on the Earliest Sources*. Cambridge: Islamic Texts Society.

Ling, Martin (1995), *What is Sufism?*. Cambridge: Islamic Texts Society.

Llewellyn, Othman (2003), 'The Basis for a Discipline of Islamic Environmental Law' in *Islam and Ecology*, Foltz, R., Denny, F. and Baharuddin, Azizan (eds). Massachusetts: Harvard University Press.

Majid, Abu (2003), 'Islam in Malaysia's Planning and Development Doctrine' in *Islam and Ecology*, Foltz, R., Denny, F. and Baharuddin, Azizan (eds). Massachusetts: Harvard University Press.

Malek, Mohammed Abdul (2001), 'The Islamic Doctrine of Jihad Does not Advocate Violence' in *Islam (Opposing Viewpoints)*, Hurley, Jennifer (ed.). San Diego, California: Greenhaven Press.

Margoulieth, D. S. (1914), *The Early Development of Muhammedanism*. London.

Marty, Martin (1992), 'The Fundamentals of Fundamentalism' in *Fundamentalism in Comparative Perspective*, Kaplan, Lawrence (ed.). Amherst: University of Massachusetts Press.

Marty, Martin and Appleby, R. Scott (eds) (1994), *Accounting For Fundamentalisms*. Chicago: Chicago University Press.

Marty, Martin and Appleby, R. Scott (eds) (1995), *Fundamentalisms Comprehended*. Chicago: Chicago University Press.

Mawdudi, Maulana (1948), *Towards Understanding Islam*, tr. Ahmad and Murad. Leicester: Islamic Foundation.

Mernissi, Fatima (1991), *Women and Islam*. Oxford: Blackwell.

Mir-Hosseini, Ziba (1999), *Islam and Gender*. Princeton: Princeton University Press.

Mir Mustansir (1987), *Dictionary of Qur'anic Terms and Concepts*. New York and London: Garland Publishing.

Nahdi, Fuad (2004), http://www.q-news.com/special.htm under the title of 'In the embrace of Islam'.

Naseef, Fatima (1999), *Women in Islam*. London: Institute of Muslim Minority Affairs.

Nicholson, R. (1989, 4th ed.), *The Mystics of Islam*. Harmondsworth: Arkana.

Nigosian, S. A. (2004), *Islam: Its History, Teaching and Practices*. Indiana: Indiana University Press.

Nyazee, Imran (1994), *Theories of Islamic Law*. Islamabad: Islamic Research Institute.

O'Neill, Sean (29 July 2004), 'Islamic Colleges in Britain linked to terrorism', *The Times*.

Padwick, Constance (1996, 2nd ed.), *Muslim Devotions*. Oxford: Oneworld Publications.

Panja, Tariq (8 August 2004), 'How fear preys on British Muslims', *Observer*.

Paret, R. (1987), 'Ummah' in *First Encyclopaedia of Islam, Volume VIII*, Houtsma, Wensinck *et al.* (eds). Leiden: Brill.

Partridge, Christopher (ed.) (2001), *Fundamentalisms*. Carlisle: Paternoster Press.

Perspectives, 'A Brief History of the Compilation of the Qur'an', *Perspectives*, Vol.3, No.4. Aug/Sept 1997.

Pipes, Daniel (31 December 2002), 'What is Jihad', *New York Post*.

Pope, Robert (2001), 'Battling for God in a Secular World: Politics and Fundamentalisms', *Fundamentalisms*, Partridge, Christopher (ed.). Carlisle: Paternoster Press.

Rahman, Fazlur (1979, 2nd ed.), *Islam*. Chicago: Chicago University Press.

Roald, Anne Sofie (2001), *Women in Islam: The Western Experience*. London: Routledge.

Rogerson, Barnaby (2003), *The Prophet Muhammad*. London: Little, Brown.

Runnymede Trust (1997), 'Islamophobia: A Challenge for Us All', consultation paper produced by the Commission on British Muslims and Islamophobia. London: The Runnymede Trust.

Ruthwen, Malise (2004), *Fundamentalism*. Oxford: Oxford University Press.

Said, Abdul Aziz and Funk, Nathan (2003), 'Peace in Islam: An Ecology of the Spirit' in *Islam and Ecology*, Foltz, R., Denny, F. and Baharuddin, Azizan (eds). Massachusetts: Harvard University Press.

Said, Edward (1978), *Orientalism*. London: Routledge and Kegan Paul.

Samb, A. (2001), 'Masjid' in *Encyclopaedia of Islam* CD-Rom Edition v.1.1. Leiden: Koninklijke Brill NV.

Schacht, J. (1952), *The Origins of Muhammadan Jurisprudence*. Oxford: Oxford University Press.

Schimmel, Annemarie (1985), *And Muhammad is His Messenger*. Carolina: University of North Carolina Press.

Shepherd, John (2004), 'Self-Critical Children of Abraham? Roots of Violence and Extremism in Judaism, Christianity and Islam' in *Islam and the West Post 9/11*, Geaves, R., Gabriel, T., Haddad, Y. and Smith J. (eds). Aldershot: Ashgate.

Singh, David (2003), *Sainthood and Revelatory Discourse*. Oxford: Regnum International.

Sirriyeh, Elizabeth (1999), *Sufis and Anti-Sufis*. London: Curzon.

Sirozi, Muhammad (2004), 'Perspectives on Radical Islamic Education in Contemporary Indonesia: Major Themes and Characteristics of Abu Bakar Ba'asyir's teachings' in *Islam and the West Post 9/11*, Geaves, R., Gabriel, T., Haddad, Y. and Smith J. (eds). Aldershot: Ashgate.

Sivan, Emmanuel (1985), *Radical Islam: Medieval Theology and Modern Politics*. Newhaven: Yale University Press.

Smart, Ninian (2000), *Worldviews: Crosscultural Explorations of Human Beliefs*. New Jersey: Prentice Hall.

Stowasser, Barbara (1994), *Women in the Qur'an, Traditions, and Interpretation*. Oxford: Oxford University Press.

Vahiduddin, S. (1979), *Studies in Islam*. Indian Institute of Islamic Studies, Vol.XVI, No.2.

Visram, Rozina (2002), *Asians in Britain: 400 Years of History*. London: Pluto Press.

Wansbrough, James (1972), *Quranic Studies: Sources and Methods of Scriptural Interpretation*. Oxford: Oxford University Press.

Wark, Mark (1994), *Virtual Geography: Living with Global Media Events*. Bloomington: Indiana University Press.

Watt, Montgomery (1972), *Muhammad at Medina*. Oxford: Clarendon Press.

Watt, Montgomery (1988) *Islamic Fundamentalism and Modernity*. London: Routledge.

Webb, Gisela (ed.) (2000), *Windows of Faith*. New York: Syracuse University Press.

Werbner, Pnina (2003), *Pilgrims of Love*. London: Hurst & Co.

Westcoat, James (2003), 'From the Gardens of the Qur'an to the Gardens of Lahore' in *Islam and Ecology*, Foltz, R., Denny, F. and Baharuddin, Azizan (eds). Massachusetts: Harvard University Press.

Whinfield, E. H. (tr.) (1979), *Teachings of Rumi*. London: The Octagon Press.

Yamani, Mai (ed.) (1996), *Feminism and Islam*. Reading: Ithaca.

Zaehner, R. (1994), *Hindu and Muslim Mysticism*. Oxford: Oneworld Publications.

Zebiri, Kate (1997), *Muslims and Christians Face to Face*. Oxford: Oneworld Publications.

Zuhur, Sherifa (1992), *Revealing Reveiling*. Albany: State University of New York.

William Boykin quoted in Giles Fraser (10 November 2003), 'The Evangelicals who like to giftwrap Islamophobia', *Guardian*.

Franklin Graham quoted in Giles Fraser (10 November 2003), 'The Evangelicals who like to giftwrap Islamophobia', *Guardian*.

Lorraine Sheridan quoted in Dominic Casciani (29 August 2002), 'UK Islamophobia rises after 11 September', BBC News.

INDEX